D0461534

John Wooden

An American Treasure

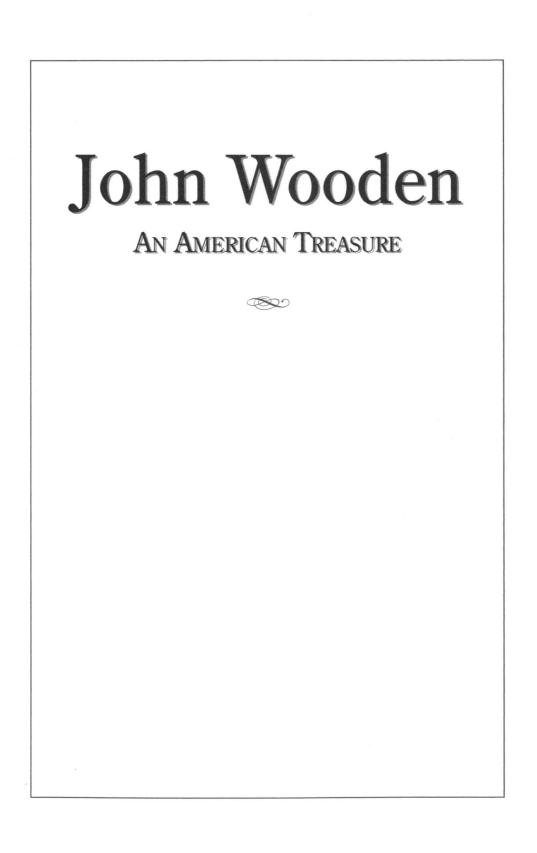

John Wooden

AN AMERICAN TREASURE

Steve Bisheff

CUMBERLAND HOUSE
NASHVILLE, TENNESSEE

Copyright © 2004 by Steve Bisheff

Published by
Cumberland House Publishing, Inc.
431 Harding Industrial Drive
Nashville, TN 37211-3160

All rights reserved. No part of this book may be reproduced or transmitted in any form or by any means, electronic or mechanical, including photocopying and recording, or by any information storage and retrieval system, without permission in writing from the publisher, except for brief quotations in critical reviews and articles.

Cover design: Jim Duncan
Text design: John Mitchell

Library of Congress Cataloging-in-Publication Data

Bisheff, Steve.
  John Wooden : an American treasure / Steve Bisheff.
     p. cm.
  Includes index.
  ISBN 1-58182-407-6 (hardcover : alk. paper)
  1. Wooden, John R. 2. Basketball coaches—United States—Biography. I. Title.
  GV884.W66B57 2004
  796.323'092—dc22

                                        2004018929

Printed in Canada

2 3 4 5 6 7—09 08 07 06 05

For Marsha, Greg, Julie, and Scott,
the loves of my life

Contents

Foreword

I KNOW BETTER, BUT HE KNOWS BEST

Things just seem to be getting better, getting better all the time.

Why would anyone ever listen to a ninety-four-year-old man who hasn't worked in almost thirty years? Why would anybody pay any attention to a walking antique who doesn't have a cell phone, voice mail, fax machine, laptop computer, or Wall Street portfolio, yet stands daily in line at the post office to pay the cost of returning packages to strangers?

Why should we even think twice about a diminutive guard whose missed free throw at the end of a game cost his team the Indiana State High School Championship in 1928? Or, for that matter, the anachronistic, out-of-touch coach at UCLA in the mid-1970s who had never even heard of Jerry Garcia, Bob Dylan, or Neil Young, and whose advice to me as I was about to enter the NBA was, "Now, Bill, when you play against Kareem, don't worry about that skyhook, it's overrated"?

Then again, those seem to be the same elements of the disagreements, distrust, and arguments that defined my relationship with John Wooden that began thirty-six years ago, when I was just fifteen years old. It is nothing short of amazing how little things seem to have changed over the decades. The reality is, though, that *everything* is completely different now—on both sides of the equation.

The most obvious evolution is simply how much smarter Coach Wooden is these days. Not that he watches much television; goes to the movies, malls, or the theater; reads magazines; or that he ever does anything that is generally considered cool or hip—nor that his message of hope, happiness, optimism, and joy has ever really varied much at all. What also has not changed a bit is that Coach Wooden was, and really always will be, a teacher. And like any teacher who is worthy of that lofty role, he is more than ever a student himself first, a student whose thirst for knowledge, truth, equity, and justice is insatiable.

Rising before the dawn on a daily basis, Coach Wooden's life is the embodiment of the lessons he has passed on to generations. The human values and personal characteristics that he tried so persistently to give us pour not so much from his lips as from his soul: enthusiasm, industriousness, friendship, loyalty, and cooperation. Then intentness, alertness, initiative, and self-control, followed by skill development, physical fitness, and commitment to the team. Finally, poise, confidence, and competitive greatness, augmented by faith and patience. And *viola*! There you have it: a changed world—one relationship at a time.

It all sounds so easy—silly, really. That is, until you are there. With so many, talk is cheap, but not with Coach Wooden. Like at his 2003 birthday celebration, when we were all sitting in his living room sharing the laughter and tears of a most wonderful and unique life—ninety-three years young. (I thought he was older than that. If I didn't know better, I'd swear he's taking botox treatments.) But there we were, listening, learning, trying to soak it all up as he started to go into one of those magnificent monologues—much like a timeless rock 'n' roll ballad, or better yet, the eternity of the Grand Canyon.

When he came to the end of this particular soliloquy, there was an awkward pause, as this was really just a simple gathering of friends who had once had a completely different relationship with The Coach. Way back then, that relationship was based on his total and complete power—the power to make or break our dreams and careers. Now, thirty years later, it is a friendship in which we can never get enough of something we once wanted no part of. We thought he was so old then, and always in the way.

As the pause grew ever longer, we all broke the master teacher's overriding principle of always being prepared and in proper balance so that we could quickly get to what's next. I chipped in from across the living room that was now really a home to all of us, "Coach, you don't really believe all that stuff, do you?"

His crystal-clear and radiant eyes twinkled a bit sharper from behind the ever-present glasses, reflecting the pride and passion of the single powder-blue UCLA sweater that he prefers. As he opened his mouth with the gentle love of a confident and self-assured father, the melodious and anticipated response was so John Wooden:

"Bill, I think you already know the answer to that question."

Answers are hard to come by these days in a world that is overrun with greed, selfishness, corruption, fraud, waste, excessive consumerism, and rampant sexism. People are desperately searching for something that is real. It's the same quest that began for me as a Helix High School graduate in suburban San Diego thirty-four years ago. Leaving the perfection and safe haven of a golden childhood, I had no idea that the whole world was not just one glorious day after another. And after the ensuing four years of euphoric bliss in Westwood, why wouldn't I think that?

I didn't know then what I was soon to learn—although I really didn't begin to understand until I left John Wooden and UCLA in 1974. Mostly what I learned was what *not* to do. And that is why I have come back. Back to where it all began. Back to where this little old man—still living in the same small condominium, still driving the same car, still eating at the same restaurant, still telling the same stories, and still wearing those same glasses and blue sweater—is getting stronger, smarter, better, and more relevant with each rhythmic and fortunate beat of his ever-expanding heart.

Along the way I also learned that all I really ever wanted was *more*. More of everything. More of life, more of fun, more of love, more of happiness, more of peace of mind. And now, after all these years, I finally know where to get it.

That is why I am here today. To be back as part of the team. To be in the classroom. To learn how to think and to learn. To get what I want, to be who I want to be. That is why I have come back to learn from the master teacher one more day.

I'm lucky. I know where to find him. Now you do, too.

— BILL WALTON

Acknowledgments

First and foremost, I want to thank John Wooden for his time, his patience, and, most important, his trust. I was honored that he gave his approval to this project. I would like to thank Ron Pitkin, the president of Cumberland House Publishing, for broaching the idea to me and Mitch Light of Athlon Sports Communications for recommending me for the project. John Mitchell, my editor at Cumberland House, was enthusiastic and supportive throughout. He deserves considerable credit, as does Alan Ross, my copy editor, and Jim Perry, a longtime friend and fellow writer who assisted me with some of the interviewing.

Members of the Wooden family were unfailingly cooperative, willing to sit for hours, in some cases, for interviews. The coach's daughter, Nan Wooden Muehlhausen, and son, Jim Wooden, were particularly helpful, as were his grandson, Greg Wooden, and his first great-granddaughter, Cori Nicholson. At UCLA, Marc Dellins's Sports Information Department was a huge help, particularly Bill Bennett, the associate director of sports information in charge of basketball.

The countless players, coaches, writers, and broadcasters who gave their time and insight also have my gratitude. Especially "the Boys of Wooden," as some of the more famous players are referred to in the book, many of whom allowed me into their homes and were only too happy to recount their stories and anecdotes about their favorite coach. I'd also like to thank Andy Hill for allowing me to use a passage from his own book about Wooden, *Be Quick, But Don't Hurry*, as well as providing me with some of his memories when he joined the coach for the presentation of the Presidential Medal of Freedom at the White House.

I'd like to thank Bud Furillo, a great newspaperman and an even better mentor. As sports editor of the old *Los Angeles Herald-Examiner*, he first placed me on the UCLA basketball beat, allowing me the privilege of covering the greatest dynasty in the history of the sport.

Finally, I want to acknowledge my wife, Marsha. Without her love, support, and understanding, it would have been impossible to complete this project.

Introduction

He is so different from all the rest of them, all the rest of the coaches who have won strings of championships and flourished in brief years of glory, only to disappear into the shadows when their time was done.

John Wooden hasn't disappeared. If anything, he has become even more relevant in the twenty-nine years since he last coached a game than he was when his UCLA Bruins were gliding skillfully through the opposition, taking an entire sport's breath away, to establish themselves as the greatest dynasty in the history of college basketball. He is more like a designated sage now, sort of a modern-day Obi-Wan Kenobi, to whom you go for words of wisdom and reassurance. At ninety-four, his is a voice still resonating above the others, still talking not only about the state of basketball, but about the state of our moral fiber. In the tiny den of his condo in Encino, California, the phone rings incessantly with those who want him to speak here or attend there, or those who merely want him to listen. So many of the players he helped make famous now talk about the manner in which he has helped them get through the rest of their lives. He was their coach then. He is their friend now.

In this, the fortieth anniversary of his first national championship season (Wooden and the Beatles both arrived and revolutionized their genres in the same year, 1964), what makes this coach such a wonder is the distance he has traveled and the things he has seen. He has bridged the generation gap of his sport, from the time of the no-center-jump to the era of the non-stop dunks. He has gone from quietly shooting at an iron basketball hoop on a tiny, deserted farm in Indiana to coaching in gleaming domed basketball palaces overflowing with screaming fans in major metropolitan centers. He has played with Stretch Murphy and coached Lew Alcindor. He has listened to "Piggie" Lambert and lectured to Bill Walton. He has matched wits with Pete Newell and competed against Dean Smith. Camp directors who introduce him as an honored guest first mention his playing career, referring to him as "the Michael Jordan of his time." Renowned television announcers describe him as "the greatest coach in the history of sports." And people closest to him wax poetic about this man who seems to exude "goodness and love."

In attempting to write the first biography of John Wooden in more than thirty years, the challenge was to cover all the far-reaching aspects of his life. As great as his coaching feats were, they never came close to meaning as much to him as his dear Nellie, the woman who was his first and only love and life-long soul mate. When she died in 1985, many feared that Wooden would fall into a deep depression. He did for a while, but his faith and the other loves of his life—rooms full of children, grandchildren, and great-grandchildren—gave him the will to carry on. The mini-museum in his Encino den is a happy mix of priceless basketball memorabilia and cuddly pictures of various members of the smiling Wooden clan.

It is his other "family" members, though, "The Boys of Wooden," as described later in this book, who provide the greatest insight into the man. Decades after they played for him, the Abdul-Jabbars and Waltons and Goodriches are still learning from him and still marveling at him. One of them, Swen Nater, writes beautiful poetry about him. Another, Andy Hill, has authored a revealing book entailing how his anger at the coach who rarely played him has been transposed into an awareness of the skills Wooden taught him and how they helped him become a success in business.

In none of the previous books on Wooden, most of them written before his retirement, has he described in detail the events leading up to and follow-ing his decision to walk away from coaching in 1975. The full drama of that memorable weekend at the Final Four in San Diego is recounted, and for the first time, Wooden reveals how he broke the news to his stunned players in the locker room after that semifinal victory in overtime against Louisville. Marques Johnson, one of those players, recalls the reaction among his team-mates and talks about how they vowed not to allow their beloved coach to leave without one more victory in the NCAA Finals, against Kentucky two nights later.

Even after so many years, Wooden's effect on the UCLA program is unde-niable. While the banners still hang from the rafters at Pauley Pavilion, there has been only one national championship in basketball at the school since 1975. Some of the coaches who toiled in his shadow describe how difficult it was. How could it have been anything else after Wooden produced ten NCAA titles in twelve years, including seven in a row? How do you top eighty-eight consecutive regular-season victories, or thirty-eight straight NCAA Tournament wins, or nineteen conference championships in twenty-seven seasons?

The scope of those accomplishments and how they altered other programs and other lives is entailed in fresh assessments of this man from two of his most competitive opposing coaches, two of his more prominent assistants, his pastor, his friend the famous broadcaster, and a sportswriter who has covered him longer than anyone else.

This is in no way an attempt to make the man sound perfect, because he is not. He would be the first to tell you that. For his family's sake, if not for his, he should have gone to UCLA officials and demanded more than the embarrassingly low salary he was receiving right to the end. Yes, his old, mid-western aphorisms can come off corny at times, and every once in a while, there is still a splash of ego you can sense here and there. There are even those still eager to tell of the renegade booster who managed to slink along the fringes of his otherwise immaculate program at UCLA. But one thing was certain about Wooden: Whatever else happened, he never allowed anyone or anything to interfere with the strict, disciplined, classroom atmosphere of his practices. His goal was never money. He is probably the last great American sports figure who *wasn't* in it for the money. What drove him was an insatiable urge to make his players the best they could be, on and off the court. And in the end, his inherent sense of goodness was more than strong enough to over-come any of the outside influences he so disdained.

Once, in the quiet of his condominium, Wooden was asked what made him most proud. He related a story involving Curtis Rowe, the "other" for-ward with Sidney Wicks on two of his national championship teams and a starter on the final Lew Alcindor team. A reporter apparently asked Rowe if

Wooden treated black players any differently than he did white players. Rowe answered, "You don't know our coach, do you? He doesn't see color, he sees ballplayers." Wooden smiled when he told the story. "That," he said, "is what I'm most proud of."

For his staggering achievements and the relevancy he still maintains, Wooden has to be regarded as one of the more extraordinary people of our time, in or out of sports. Our country already has recognized him with its highest civilian honor, the Presidential Medal of Freedom, which only seems appropriate. Because through all these years, John Wooden not only has been America's Coach, he has, in many ways, been America's Teacher.

After reading the following pages, after charting his career from a tiny town in Indiana to a bustling city in California, after hearing from players and coaches, friends and family members, contemporaries and adversaries, the hope is that you will have a much better understanding of why this remarkably insightful, endearing, gentle man has evolved into one of our true national treasures.

PART I

The Early Years

The Friend
Who Changed
Basketball History

Eddie Powell, spry and energetic at age eighty-three, relaxes in his comfortable home in Yorba Linda, California, glancing outside his large family-room window to where a warm spring sun fills his spacious backyard. A miniature street intersection sign is planted in the lush grass a few feet from his dining room. It reads LOAFER'S LANE on one side and RETIREMENT BLVD. on the other. He smiles easily, looking like your typical Southern Californian, happily reaping the benefits of his golden years.

What he doesn't look like is the man who changed college basketball history.

That's what he is, though. Powell did it. He is the one responsible. He is the reason John Wooden came to UCLA and eventually built the greatest college basketball dynasty of all time.

"That's true," Powell says. "If it wasn't for me, John would have been coaching at the University of Minnesota, instead of UCLA."

The year was 1948, and Wooden was leaving South Bend Central High, eager to move into a college coaching position, hopefully in the Big Ten. Frank McCormick, the athletic director at Minnesota, had followed Wooden's career as both a player at Purdue and as a high school coach in

Indiana. He was anxious to offer him the job at Minnesota. At the same time, an old Hoosier friend of Wooden named Bob Kelley, who had moved to the West Coast and become the immensely popular play-by-play announcer for the Los Angeles Rams professional football franchise, had recommended Wooden to UCLA Athletic Director Wilbur Johns.

Both schools made offers to the coach, and Wooden admits his preference at the time was Minnesota. "I was more familiar with the Big Ten and wanted to stay closer to home," he recalls. But there was a problem. Minnesota wanted him to retain Dave McMillan, the man he would be replacing, as his assistant. Wooden wanted to hire his own man, who happened to be Powell.

John always told me, "Never take a job where your predecessor remains on the premises," Powell says. So Wooden told Minnesota he was willing to come, but only if he could bring his own assistant. McCormick, the school's athletic director, said he would have to get approval from the board first. He told Wooden he would get back to him at six o'clock that night. UCLA's Johns was scheduled to call for Wooden's answer an hour later, at seven p.m.

"It just so happened that a huge snowstorm hit Minnesota that day, and Frank McCormick got snowed in and couldn't get to the phone," Wooden remembers. "No call came at six. But UCLA's Johns called promptly at seven. I took the UCLA job." Hours later, McCormick called to tell Wooden the board had agreed to let him bring Powell on. He said everything was all set. "But I had to tell him he was too late," the coach says. "I'd already accepted the UCLA job."

Some fifty-six years later, Powell sits in his home in California and shakes his head at the vagaries of fate. "You hear about phone calls and how they sometimes change history," he says. "Well, I guess that was one of them."

Had it not been for Powell and the close relationship he had developed with Wooden over the years, it might have been Minnesota, not UCLA, that harvested all those national championships in the 1960s and '70s.

"I first met John when I was playing junior high basketball," Powell recalls. "I was from South Bend, and I'd heard of him. He was playing for something called Kautsky's Team in Indianapolis, and I saw him play. I tell you, he was phenomenal. He was very quick, although not very tall. But he could dribble—and I'm not exaggerating—down the floor faster than the rest of the players could run without the ball. One day, he made his 100th free throw in a row—he used to shoot them in the old, Rick Barry underhand style—and the owner of the team stopped the game and gave him a one hundred-dollar bill for doing it. It was the first hundred-dollar bill John ever saw. And let me tell you, back in those days, that was a heckuva lot of money. You know, he was a great baseball player, too. He had a tremendous arm and was a good hitter. And the big thing was, he was always thinking one step ahead of everyone else. He was a fierce competitor. I don't care what he was playing, checkers, table tennis, it didn't matter. He always wanted to beat you.

"I eventually went on to attend South Bend Central High, where he was coaching, and I went out for basketball. He was also my English teacher. You can guess what kind of teacher he was. He was a stickler for good penmanship, and he knew his grammar. He loved Shakespeare and poetry, especially poetry. He was strict in the classroom but fair. He was the same way as a coach.

"My first game at South Central, he told us to meet at the South Central YMCA, because we were taking a bus to go play in a neighboring city. Well, we were all expected to be there at six o'clock. Wooden asks the bus driver what time it is, and the driver tells him it is six. The rest of the players knew the team's two co-captains and two best players weren't there yet. Wooden knew it, too. But he looked at his watch again and told the bus driver to leave.

"The two players scrambled to find their own way to the game, but when they got there, Wooden didn't start them. They both played a total of about two or three minutes. Turns out, the father of one of the kids was the vice principal of the school, and here's Wooden, a new coach. We all figured he was in big trouble. But on the next Monday morning, the vice principal calls Wooden into his office. He says, 'That was the best thing you could have done for my son. You gave him a good lesson. I think we're all going to get along fine.'"

Powell and Wooden didn't always get along fine, though. At least not in the beginning. "I thought I was a pretty good player, and I wasn't starting at South Bend Central," Powell says. "You know how you are at that age. You're angry. I told Coach I intended to quit. He was pretty shook up when I told him, and he said he didn't want me to do that. He said he'd start me in the next game the following night. Later, I heard he told Nell [Wooden's wife] that he was wrong. He shouldn't have told me that and he shouldn't have started me. But he did, and I held the other team's highest scorer to his lowest total of the season. After that, I not only became a regular, I was the team MVP and a captain for two years. John always tells me that my case only proves that even he doesn't always make the right decision. And yes, I still like to kid him about it."

Powell's memory of Wooden as a young coach remains vivid. "He was clean cut, always wore his hair short," Powell says. "He was tough, but you knew that he cared about you. He proved it during the summer months. He'd always be driving by your house, coming to visit you and find out how you were doing. You could tell even then that there was something special about him."

Powell also played baseball with Wooden as his coach, not knowing that it was, and still is, the coach's favorite sport. "He stressed the same things," Powell says. "Fundamentals, fundamentals, fundamentals. If you couldn't bunt, if you couldn't lay down bunts along the first or third base line consistently, he had no room for you. The way he explained it, you move your hand to the bottom of the bat, the other one to the top and you pretend you're going to catch the ball with that top hand. As I began to realize later, he is primarily a teacher. Even through all his coaching, that's what he did best. He was always teaching. He believed that if he taught you well enough, once the game started, he could sit up in the stands and watch. That's how well he wanted to teach his players. And you know what? He was right."

After his playing days were over, Powell was Wooden's assistant at Indiana State. "It was this little teachers college," Powell recalls. "I enrolled there after the war, and two weeks later, I read John Wooden is coming to coach. We had a total enrollment of twenty-two hundred, and I'd say about two hundred or three hundred boys came out for basketball. He knew me, so he asked me to help him cut the squad. Then later, he said, 'Why don't you stay on as my assistant?'"

Powell did. Along the way, he got to see many sides of Wooden, including the coach's rich sense of humor.

"Once, we were in Kansas City with Indiana State," Powell says, "and we realized the men all wore hats in that town. So we were wearing hats, walking down the street one day, when Coach stops a passerby. He asks him how many people live in Kansas City. The guy answers him and walks away. I asked Coach what that was about. So he takes off his hat and there's a pigeon dropping on his head. He says: 'I just wanted to know what my percentage was of having that pigeon choose me.'"

After the famous Minnesota phone incident, Powell was hired as Wooden's assistant at UCLA and served in that capacity for four years. "When we got to UCLA, first thing Coach did was stress conditioning, fundamentals, and team spirit." Powell says. "He told me if I ever become a head coach, what if all my players were in better condition than the other team's players? Wouldn't that be a great advantage? Same thing with fundamentals.

We were playing California or Stanford, I don't remember which, and we were on a fast break. Our man in the middle passed it to a cutter on the side, and he had to reach low for the ball, then when he went to shoot, he hit the basket too low. The next time we practiced, we spent all day running at full speed, then we'd roll the ball out, and he showed us how to handle a ball while going full speed. He told our players if you can pick up a rolling ball at full speed, you can handle any ball that comes to you."

Powell watched Wooden mature as both a coach and a person at UCLA. "When he first came to UCLA, let me tell you, he was lost,"

COURTESY OF EDDIE POWELL

A young Eddie Powell joins his boss and good friend, John Wooden, as they plot strategy in their early years at UCLA. Powell was Wooden's first assistant coach in Westwood.

Powell says. "He was a small-town boy in a big-time atmosphere, and for a while it was difficult for him to adjust. At social functions, he'd stand against a wall and wait for someone to come up to him before speaking. He overcame a great shyness. When he'd give a talk at the beginning, he had a habit of keeping one finger in his mouth, and you could hardly understand what he was saying. I marvel now, when I see him speak, how he's learned and improved. He's a tremendous speaker now."

Basketball wasn't even a major sport at the school when Wooden and Powell arrived in Westwood. "It was considered a minor sport," Powell says. "Shoot, more people would watch a high school game in Indiana than came to see us at UCLA. We even played some of our early games in the afternoon. Nobody seemed to notice."

Soon, however, Wooden's teams began to attract attention, not only on campus but in Los Angeles and other West Coast cities. "He brought the fast break to UCLA," Powell says. "Nobody had seen much of it until that time. Sometimes we not only had two-on-one advantages, we'd have three-on-zero mismatches. Other teams didn't know how to deal with it."

Still, things didn't go exactly as planned at UCLA. The Bruins had to play their games in a tiny on-campus gym affectionately called "B. O. Barn," or they played at the Shrine Auditorium, where the the Academy Award telecasts would be held years later, or at the old Pan-Pacific building, where ice shows were often the main attraction. "At the Pan-Pacific, the lights would melt the ice underneath the playing floor, and we'd have to stop the games and mop up the floor," Powell remembers.

The Bruins' undersized gym sometimes elicited surprising comments from recruits. "I recall when my wife and I went to Indiana on a visit, we heard about this real good basketball player named Johnny Moore," Powell says. "We went to visit, and his mother noticed that UCLA happened to have a black student body president. She told Johnny that's where she wanted him to play. So Johnny enrolls at UCLA, and he's about to play his first game in our gym, which holds less than 2,000. I asked him, 'You excited, Johnny? You'll be playing in front of a packed house and all.' He looks and me and smiles. 'Sir,' he said, 'my last high school game was played at Butler Fieldhouse, and it seats 18,000 people. So no, sir, this crowd won't bother me.'"

Powell grew to know Wooden not only as his boss but as his friend. "My wife and I spent a lot of time with John and Nell," Powell says. "They kind of took us under their wing and taught us the social graces, how to write thank-you cards, and things to do. Nell was great at all that stuff. She was also more fiery than John. I remember one time she got on me. We were playing USC, and Bill Sharman, their great player, was scoring when the referee blew the whistle on us for a foul. Nell taps me on the shoulder during the game and says, 'I thought that Sharman fouled, didn't you, Ed?' I was honest with her. I said no. "Well, where the h—— is your loyalty?' she said. Loyalty had nothing to do with it, of course. But I understood. Nell was just trying to protect her husband."

In Powell's estimation, Wooden could have coached at any level. The Lakers offered him a huge contract at one point, and Powell says he could have been successful in the National Basketball Association. "But I don't think he would have been happy. He was happy at the lowest level. He was really meant to be a high school coach. He was happiest when the kids didn't know anything and they were ready to believe everything."

As the years passed, the world changed, and UCLA students changed with it. Powell watched as his friend learned to adjust to the intricacies involved in coaching kids who had to deal with the advent of drugs, the Vietnam War, and the sexual revolution.

"He changed with the times," Powell says. "He respected other people's wishes, but he had his own wishes. He had a problem with many college basketball players who wanted to use college as a stepping stone to the pros. He didn't like kids who wanted to show off, on the court or off. He could control that, though. If they didn't follow the rules, they wound up on the bench. Even some of the better ones. But it was difficult for him. In the old days, you'd tell kids you want them to jump, and they'd jump. Now, they ask how high, or what for, or 'What's in it for me?'"

It had to be agonizing for Wooden, who was never in the game for the money. "I think they paid him five thousand dollars his first year at UCLA," Powell says. "And I know the most he ever made was thirty-two five. Can you imagine what he might earn if he were coaching today? My God, the figure would be staggering."

When success did come, when he began to win national championships so often that UCLA fans started to think it was automatic, Wooden was happy, but according to most of his friends, not entirely content. "I think he enjoyed it," Powell says. "The circumstances placed him in that position. But I don't think he relished it. He didn't look forward to the fanfare or the accolades. He was always polite to interviewers, but he never sought them out. It is amazing. When John had a birthday party, it was just the Wooden family, his kids, grandchildren and great-grandchildren, and usually my wife and me. That was it."

Although Powell loved working with Wooden, he knew that at some point he would have to move on. "Reporters would call and ask me what Coach Wooden thought about this subject or that one," he says. "I was losing myself, losing my identity, I guess you'd say. About 90 percent of the time, we felt the same way, but there was that other 10 percent where I felt differently. But no one seemed to want to hear it."

So, in 1952, Powell left UCLA and took the head coaching job at Loyola University. "They asked me how much Coach Wooden was making," Powell says. "I told them about seventy-two hundred dollars, and they said they'd match it."

He coached basketball and baseball for one year but became involved with a summer youth camp at the school that proved more financially rewarding. Powell realized he could make more money running the camp for three months than he did coaching for the whole year, which shows just how underpaid Wooden was at the time.

"I enjoyed working with the kids," he says, "but the organization just kept getting bigger and bigger. Soon, I was so busy running things, I didn't have time to work with the kids."

Powell would move on to hold various government positions in cities such as Downey and Irwindale, California. In 1967, he became the city manager of Placentia, located in Orange County, California, a position he held until retiring in 1982. Through it all, he has remained exceedingly close to Wooden, who usually invites Powell to all his family functions.

"Can you imagine how lucky I've been to know this man?" Powell says. "The impact he's had on our lives is amazing. Not many people have been lucky enough to see him with his hair down. He actually has a tremendous sense of humor. He likes playing pranks when you're having dinner. There'll be a little butter cube on your dish, and when you go to reach for it, he'll fix it so you'll end up jabbing your thumb right into the butter. He gets a big kick out of things like that.

"The incredible thing is that he hasn't coached in twenty-nine years, and he's more popular now than ever. Some people stand in line for hours just to spend time with him. It's like being around the pope. But you know, I think it's the aura he has developed. He's deeply religious without flaunting it. You ask him something and he just doesn't come out with an answer right away. He thinks about it and formulates a well-thought out reply to whatever the question was. You go to a restaurant with him, and little kids come up and ask for his autograph. He says, 'You don't even know who I am.' And they smile sheepishly and say, 'It's not for us; it's for our parents.'

"But the more you're around him, the more you realize what a remarkable impact he's had on all kinds of people through the years. And most of it has nothing to do with basketball."

As Placentia city manager for more than sixteen years, Powell made sure to take care of one last detail before he retired. He talked to the officials of nearby Yorba Linda, and today when you travel through a certain part of that well-manicured suburban community, you can still see the famous street signs.

The ones that read WOODEN DRIVE and NELL CIRCLE.

Eddie Powell figures that was the least he could do, considering he's the reason John Wooden accepted the coaching job at UCLA and proceeded to change college basketball history.

John Wooden, Big-League Manager?

John Wooden could have been the manager of the Pittsburgh Pirates.

That's right. The greatest basketball coach of all time actually was given the chance to jump sports and manage a big-league baseball club.

"It happened at a dinner in Los Angeles in the 1960s I attended with Joe Brown Jr., who was the general manager of the Pirates at the time," Wooden says. "He found out I was a big baseball fan, and baseball was all we talked about the entire evening. I guess he was so impressed that, when the dinner was over, he actually approached me and asked if I would be interested in managing the Pirates.

"I said, 'Are you serious?' He said he was, but I told him there was no way I could do it. I never played professional baseball, only two years in high school and two years in college. I would have had no respect from the players. I told Joe, 'They would run you out of town before they did me.'"

Later, a Pittsburgh writer asked Brown if the story was true. Wooden has a worn-out, yellowed news clipping from the old *Los Angeles Herald-Examiner* that quotes Brown this way about UCLA's basketball coach: "Yes. I would have hired him. He can handle any job."

Wooden was an exceptional baseball player who apparently had major-league tools as a youngster. "I did have a great arm," he says. "Not a good arm, a great arm, if I say so myself. I played one summer with a couple of the St. Louis Cardinals, and they told me I had a better arm than some big-league shortstops. But in the summer of my freshman year at college, I had a pitch hit me in the right shoulder, and I could never throw the same again."

The Early Influences

Of all the people in John Wooden's memorable past, the one you wished you could have met was his father, Joshua Hugh Wooden. Hugh, they called him, a tall, lean farmer with a strong mind and a gentle touch. More than anyone else, he shaped the son who would go on to greatness. He provided the solid moral foundation, preaching kindness and consideration for others, teaching a love for the written word, especially Shakespeare and poetry, and demonstrating a powerful will to overcome all obstacles.

At his high school graduation, the son was presented a two dollar bill by his father, one he has kept crumbled in his wallet all these years. On it are the words "The Creed I Live By" as explained by Joshua Hugh Wooden: "Be true to yourself [Polonius to Laertes in *Hamlet*] make each day a masterpiece, help others, drink deeply from good books, make friendship a fine art, and build a shelter against a rainy day."

"I remember my dad as a good person who was strong but gentle," Wooden says. "I always remember something that Lincoln said: 'There is nothing stronger than gentleness.' That described my dad. He just had this way about him. We had two mules on our farm named Jack and Kate, and, like most mules, they could get stubborn. You couldn't get them to move. But Dad would come over and quietly say, 'Just lie down,' and Kate would quickly lie down. The same with dogs. You'd see some who looked vicious and were growling, and Dad would walk over and they'd immediately get quiet and start wagging their tails.

"Once, in town, we came across some horses whose owner was trying to get them to pull out. He was screaming at them and whipping them, and they were frothing at the mouth and wouldn't respond. I saw Dad go over to them, stand between the two of them, quiet them down, pull on their reins, and they would go easily. He just had something about him that people and animals responded to."

Joshua Hugh Wooden was an Indiana farmer in rural Centerton who lost his farm in the depression. He and his wife, Roxie Anna, had four boys and two daughters. One of the girls died at birth, the other at three years of age. "Dad never seemed bitter, though," John says. "He never had much, but never wanted much. And even after we lost the farm, he never complained. We had no electricity, but he would read to us every night. He read the Bible more than anything else. He'd read scriptures, but he'd also read a lot of poetry."

A high school graduate without any formal education, Hugh Wooden loved crossword puzzles and was a whiz at both chess and checkers. "What I remember about him is that he was gentle, but he had very strong hands," says Jim Wooden, John's son and Hugh's grandson. "He had no college education, but he was very bright. I heard he played—and beat—a world-champion checkers player who came through Indiana one year, but typically, he never told me that. Others did.

"Funny what you remember as a young kid about your grandfather. But I remember that he used to take a glass of milk, stuff it with bread and eat it with a spoon. I recall that he was tall and thin, and he never raised his voice. If he didn't have something good to say about someone, he didn't say it. Supposedly, no one heard him complain a day in his life. He never blamed anybody for anything, even on his deathbed."

Eddie Powell, one of John's oldest friends, remembers Hugh Wooden, as well. "I met his father," Powell says. "He was this tall, lanky guy who was very strong willed and very strong of character. He didn't say much, but what he said carried a lot of weight."

John found that out early. He received only one "whipping" from his dad, but it was one he would never forget. "I earned it," he says. "We were work-ing in the barn, and my older brother tossed manure in my face. I went after him and called him some names that weren't very nice. That's when Dad gave me the whipping. I don't think anyone has heard me use profanity since."

Although the family struggled financially, John has fond memories of those days in Indiana, when his father would take his wife and children into Martinsville, the county seat with a population of 5,000, and maybe even splurge for dinner at Riley's Café.

COURTESY OF NAN MUEHLHAUSEN

The Wooden family at home in Indiana (from left): father Joshua Hugh, brothers Daniel and Maurice, John, and mother Roxie. Hugh was among the major early influences in John's life.

"I didn't realize until much later how many hours my dad must have worked to be able to afford that dinner," John recalls. The family lost the farm between John's freshman and sophomore years in high school. His dad decided to raise hogs, and they'd been inoculated for cholera. Except the serum they received was defective, and all the hogs died. "But Dad never complained about it," John says. "That's the way he was. He didn't blame other people when bad things happened."

After the farm was lost, Hugh Wooden found a job at the Homelawn Sanitarium in Martinsville, which was famous for its Artesian wells. "He worked in the bath house and gave massages," John said. "He had very strong hands and his compassion for others, especially those who were sick, made him very good at his job. They used to say people came from all over the area to get one of dad's massages, which must have been true, because he made most of his money from tips."

Nan Muehlhausen, John's daughter and Hugh's granddaughter, remembers making visits to her grandparents home in Martinsville, after they lost the farm. "They lived next door to a fire station, upstairs," says Nan. "I think my grandfather was much like my dad, a very gentle person. I remember he loved to listen to the oldtime radio shows like *Fibber Magee and Molly* and *Amos and Andy*. Funny, the things you recall. I remember whenever he ate, when he was finished, his plate always looked so clean you would have thought he never used it. He always had Wheaties for breakfast in the morning, and that bowl looked like it was licked clean, too. Like Jim, I recall my grandfather putting bread in his milk. Daddy does that, too. I think it's just gross.

"I do remember thinking I felt very loved whenever I visited there. He would take me to the fire station to show me off, and that was always a lot of fun. He showed me where he worked giving massages at the sanitarium. You know, to this day I think that's why Daddy always has been such a generous tipper, because a big part of Granddaddy's income was based on the tips he would get. I think my best time with him, though, was when he would read to me. He loved books."

John learned discipline and self-control from his father. "I remember thinking that I would rather take a whipping than displease him," John says. "In my mind, it was Dad who made each of his sons an honor roll student. All four of us majored or minored in English, and all four became teachers. All of that, I think, was because of the example he set for us and his knack for teaching a love of reading."

John is also thankful that his father was able to see him play basketball, both as an Indiana high school star and an All-American at Purdue. "Oh yes, you could tell he was proud," John says. "But he was always very careful not to give one brother too much credit at the expense of the other. He'd come up to me and say, 'Good game, Johnny. You remind me of Cat [his older brother, Maurice].'"

The elder Wooden came to California once to visit his son while he was coaching at UCLA. "He and my mother drove from Indiana," John recalls. "They liked it here, but they were used to the Midwest. California was a little too fast for them."

Joshua Hugh Wooden died in 1960, four years before his son would win his first national championship in Westwood.

The other great early influence in John Wooden's life, besides his wife, Nell, of course, was his college coach at Purdue, Ward "Piggie" Lambert, who acquired his colorful nickname because of the pigtails he used to wear as a child. A three-sport star at Wabash College in Indiana, Lambert did his graduate work at the University of Minnesota, then coached high school basketball in a state that is usually in a frenzy every Friday night. Lambert became head coach at Purdue in 1916, but his career was interrupted by World War I. He returned to the Boilermakers in 1919 and remained their coach until the 1945–46 season.

A small, frenetic man famous for constantly pacing the sideline, Lambert was one of college basketball's early pioneers. He introduced the fast break, loved big players who could handle the ball, and quick, aggressive perimeter players. Sound familiar? If you're a UCLA fan, it should. Lambert's teams were always noted for their blazing speed. He forged a 371–152 record for a remarkable .710 winning percentage, leading Purdue to eleven conference titles and a Big Ten conference record of 228–105. His 1931-32 team finished 17–1 and was named national champion by the Helms Athletic Foundation.

In a nationwide poll conducted by *Esquire* magazine in 1945, Lambert was named the country's outstanding basketball coach. He was enshrined in the Indiana Hall of Fame and the Helms Foundation Hall of Fame. His published book, *Practical Basketball*, was considered one of the early bibles of the game.

"He was as highly principled a man as you could ever find," says Wooden. "He thought intercollegiate athletics should be played on campus. In 1940, Purdue won the Big Ten Conference title, and Indiana won the NCAA Tournament. Purdue didn't go because the games were held in Madison Square Garden, and he didn't believe in it. Near the end of my sophomore year, Lambert sent for me. He asked if I remembered this doctor I'd met who was a big Purdue fan. I said yes. He said that the doctor wanted to do something for me. He wanted me to quit working at the fraternity waiting on tables, so he was going to make sure I had enough money for books, fees, tuition, everything. He waited for my response.

"'Are you going to take it?' he wondered. I asked him what he meant. 'How are you going to pay him back? I thought you were the kind of person who would want to pay him back.' I left his office and came back a couple of days later. I told him no, I wasn't going to take it. He said, 'That's exactly what I thought you would do. But you do need some clothes. I've seen you without a topcoat out there shivering.' So he told me to go to the local department store and get some clothes. 'It's not a gift,' he said. "Next year, when you are supposed to get three game tickets and an extra ticket, you won't get them.'

"Another time, after I graduated, I had an offer to make some money with a barnstorming team. I really needed the money. Lambert asked me to see him and said, 'What did you come to Purdue for?' I said, 'An education.' He said, 'Then don't throw it away. Use it.' Then he said: 'Always remember, when you play with dirt, you're going to get dirty.'"

Lambert was a stickler for athletes learning to work for their money. Wooden picked up on it early and quickly became semi-famous for his ingenious ways to make an extra buck. John Wooden, the hustler? Well, in a way, at least. First, he spent four years selling football programs at nearby hotels and restaurants where alumni would spend their time.

"I used to do OK," he says, "especially when some of the alumni would

COURTESY OF PURDUE SPORTS INFORMATION DEPARTMENT

Ward "Piggie" Lambert, Wooden's coach at Purdue, was one of the most influential men in his life. Among other things, Wooden learned the fast-break offense and attention to detail from Lambert.

have had too much to drink. Then they might even give me more than the dime I was asking for the programs."

His friend Eddie Powell still talks about how Wooden bought the concession rights on a special train that ran from Lafayette, Indiana, to Chicago. Purdue and Chicago had a famous rivalry fueled by the presence of Amos Alonzo Stagg, who was Chicago's head coach. So the train was always jammed.

"John hired a couple of his frat brothers to work with him," Powell remembers, "and he'd go up and down the aisles selling sandwiches, candy, cigarettes, chewing gum, you name it. It took a lot of work, but he somehow figured out a way to make money from it."

For all the lifestyle philosophy Lambert taught, it was in the technicalities of the game, the theories of coaching and communicating, where he had his greatest influence on Wooden.

"He was very big on conditioning and placed a large emphasis on quickness," says the student who would emulate his teacher when he began to coach. "He taught me that quickness in any sport is the most important thing. I always said I would give up some size to get quickness as a general rule. I was always hoping that three of my players would be quicker than the opponents. You'd like to have all five, but that was asking too much. Yet that was always in the back of my mind.

"He also taught the value of a controlled offense, one that had freelance aspects to it. You build a base from where the offense would start, trying to get movement by design but not necessarily by a precise pattern. There was always somebody moving, in and out, crossing over, and then he would add little changes within that framework. He would try to capitalize on the talent he had available."

Listening to him explain Lambert's theories, you can't help but see many of Wooden's UCLA teams flash before your eyes. "He would utilize the guards more if they were his best players," says Wooden, who had two of the finest guards in the country, Walt Hazzard and Gail Goodrich, the year he captured his first national championship, in 1964. "If he had a good big man, the way he did with Stretch Murphy, who was a senior when I was a sophomore, he'd take advantage of his skills." Wooden, of course, would take great advantage of the skills of his two great big men, Lew Alcindor and Bill Walton, who between them led the Bruins to five national titles.

When Wooden played for Lambert, the coach often used him as an example of a supremely conditioned athlete. The football coach at Purdue must have felt the same way. In his early days at the university, Wooden was convinced to come out for that other, more physical contact sport.

"I actually spent two days practicing with the team during the spring," Wooden recalls. "I played halfback, but in those days, of course, you played both ways. It only lasted until Coach Lambert heard about it. Once he did, he wouldn't let me play football anymore." Still, Lambert stressed almost football-like conditioning for his basketball players, and so did Wooden when he became a coach. Talk to any of Wooden's former players, and they all say they believed they had a huge edge on their opponents when it came to conditioning. And the facts seem to bear it out. No one won more close games in the final minutes, especially in the NCAA Tournament, than Wooden did. Many think it was due to his team remaining fresher and in better shape than the other guys.

"I based my coaching career mainly on Lambert's theories on conditioning," Wooden has said.

The one example he loves to bring up is when he played at Purdue against Indiana, coached by Everett Dean. He often begins by saying, "Coach Lambert told us we would beat Indiana because Dean was too nice." At this point, Wooden's interviewer blinks and usually says something like, "Excuse me?" Wooden will smile. "Coach Lambert said Dean was so nice he wouldn't work his players hard enough. And if we stuck with them for three quarters, we'd wear them down in the fourth. And that's exactly what happened."

The other theory that connected directly with Wooden was Lambert's decision never to be concerned about the opponent. "He felt if we just played our game, we'd win," says Wooden, who became famous for the same philosophy at UCLA. Other coaches were often aghast to learn that Wooden didn't scout future opponents. He didn't think it mattered. If his team followed what it learned at practice and played up to its ability, it wouldn't lose. It was as simple as that, for both Lambert and Wooden.

Then, of course, there was the fast break offense, the one Lambert introduced at Purdue and Wooden helped perfect at UCLA. "He used to say the team that made the most mistakes would win," Wooden says, grinning. "I know that sounds strange, but what he was trying to get across is that the more aggressive team, the one not afraid to make mistakes, usually will get more shots and control the game's tempo."

Lambert was also famous for his attention to detail. The adjective most often used to describe him is *meticulous*, which is interesting, because that's the same adjective used by most of Wooden's players to describe him and his finely tuned practices.

Wooden loves to talk nostalgically of those days at Purdue, when he was known as "the Martinsville Rubberman" and was developing into a Hall of Fame player and the star of a national championship team. But as is usually the case with him, he prefers to discuss other players, such as Stretch Murphy, who was a senior when he was a sophomore.

"I honestly believe Stretch Murphy could have played and excelled in any era," he says. "He was the first really big man who played the game with coordination and skill. I think his presence helped my development as a sophomore and made me a better player. We both wound up making the All-American team that year."

In his senior season, having survived a series of strange mishaps involving screeching trucks and overturned cars, Wooden became the leader and playmaker who was Lambert's extension on the floor.

"We achieved the kind of closeness you hope for between a player and coach, although I don't think I realized it at the time," Wooden says. That national title-winning Purdue team lost just one game, to Illinois, and that came after the coach and player were both involved in an accident on an icy, Midwest road. Wooden cut his right hand deeply on some glass and wasn't at his best that night, and although he'll always wonder if Purdue could have gone undefeated if he hadn't been injured, he has no real regrets.

Those were good years and happy times for John Wooden, the player. It was also an important time of studying and learning for the man who would one day become the greatest basketball coach in the history of the game.

Breakfast at VIPS

John Wooden is nothing if not a creature of habit. He eats breakfast most days at a tiny, old-time coffee shop on Ventura Boulevard in Encino. It's called VIPS, and it is obvious the moment you drive up with him that he is the establishment's most famous and honored customer.

Paul, the smiling owner, bounces out of the restaurant to greet Wooden and help him get out of the car. "Thank you, Paul, thank you," Wooden says, looking slightly embarrassed. When he walks in, the former coach is instantly recognized, and he pauses to greet the customers sitting by the counter.

Some days, Tony Spino, the assistant UCLA trainer who works with him in the morning three times a week, drives him. Other days, Dick Muehlhausen, his daughter Nan's husband, will pick him up. Or maybe former players like Mike Warren or Kenny Washington will drive him. And occasionally, Wooden will climb into his 1994 Taurus and drive himself. "They [the customers] always kid me when I do that," he says. "They say, 'He's driving again. His daughter isn't cracking the whip.'"

Clearly, this is an atmosphere Wooden loves, one with the feel of a small-town community, not unlike Martinsville, where he grew up in Indiana. Even the prices are a throwback to a different time and place. "I always order the No. 2 Special," Wooden says. "It's two eggs, two slices of bacon, toast, and coffee. It's very reasonable at $2.95."

It is the camaraderie he enjoys most, though. "The same people are in here every day," he says. "I know them all, but only by their first names. Ed and Margaret are always in one booth. Millie is in another. At the counter, Lois sits at one end. Barbara is next to her, followed by Gene, Mike, Scotty, and Jerry."

The waiter also knows Wooden and, smiling widely, immediately brings him his hot tea, then pauses to personally pour just the exact amount of honey onto his spoon for him.

On the way out, before stopping at the cash register to pay, one notices five different pictures of Wooden on the wall. In each, he is posing with the owner, who looks as if he's just won the lottery.

You get the idea of his stature in the place when you realize that one of the pictures, the biggest one, almost blocks out another, smaller picture: the one of the owner posing with movie star Harrison Ford.

The Evolution: From Indiana Legend to a New Life in California

H is reputation as a coach has grown so through the years that there is a tendency to forget John Wooden, the player. He was, by all accounts, one of the great high school and college basketball players of all time, a three-time collegiate All-American who was regarded on the same exalted level in his generation as Magic Johnson or Larry Bird were in theirs. The fact that he was the first person voted into the College Basketball Hall of Fame as a player then later as a coach, tells you all you need to know.

Those who saw him play at Purdue say his skill was breathtaking. Always the fastest player on the floor, he could move with the basketball quicker than anyone else without it. The discipline that would make him a great coach later on was evident in his early days as a player, and his outside shooting and foul shooting techniques were exceptional even in that era of low-scoring games. It all began at Martinsville High, where he became a legendary prep player who helped that tiny school ascend the heights of Indiana-crazed basketball.

As the popular movie *Hoosiers* would come to celebrate, nothing was, or still is, bigger in Indiana than the state high school tournament. "It is made up of sixty-four sectionals with sixteen teams each," Wooden says.

"Then there are sixteen regionals and the final round of sixteen, with no rules regarding the size of the schools or the numbers in their class. The smallest school could end up the champion."

Wooden's Martinsville team was in the final championship game of that huge tournament each of his three years on the varsity and won the title in 1927. Even today, Wooden can recall the grueling schedule that could call for a team to play four different games in a twenty-four-hour span. "You can't imagine how big those games were back then," he says.

In today's era, Wooden would have been a nationally known talent widely discussed in recruiting journals and Internet chat sites. Back then, no athletic scholarships were offered. The bait for a college coach attempting to lure a top player was to guarantee the athlete a job on campus, usually waiting tables at a local fraternity house. For Wooden, who was always looking toward the future, Purdue seemed like the logical choice because he wanted to become a civil engineer.

"If I had been given better high school counseling, I would have gone to Indiana University," he says, a revelation that will probably drive old-time Hoosier alums nuts. "Indiana was only seventeen miles from my hometown, only seventeen miles from Nellie [Riley, the future Mrs. Wooden]. Purdue, however, was such an outstanding engineering school, it seemed like the logical choice."

But once again, fate would dribble this man off in another direction. A year later, Wooden discovered he couldn't become an engineer. "It was at the end of my freshman year that they informed me that to stay in engineering school I would have to go to a civil engineering camp every summer," he says. "It was a program that sent you out into the field to work in an engineering project. But you didn't get paid. I couldn't do that. I had to work every summer, because my family needed the money. As much as I wanted to, I couldn't do it. So I changed my major to Liberal Arts. From that point on, I knew I would probably be a teacher. As Lincoln said: 'Things work out best for those who make the best of the way things work out.'"

Wooden certainly made the best of what he had at Purdue. The presence of Ward "Piggie" Lambert, the coach who probably had more influence on his basketball education than anyone in his life, and Stretch Murphy, one of the game's first truly effective big men, helped mold Wooden into a star.

"People today don't know much about Murphy," Wooden says, "but, in my opinion, he was one of the greatest players of all time. He was a great jumper and shooter and a tremendous rebounder. I think his presence on the team when I was a sophomore made a huge difference to me. He and I both made All-American my sophomore year."

Wooden would go on to receive the coveted honor all three of his varsity years at Purdue, and, as a senior, he broke Stretch Murphy's Big Ten scoring record. Although he is too modest to acknowledge it, Wooden's reputation far exceeded Murphy's by the time he was done. To this day, most Indiana basketball purists will tell you the two finest guards to come out of the state are Oscar Robertson and Wooden, which pretty much says it all.

George Keogan, the coach of Notre Dame back when Wooden was playing, once remarked how difficult it was to stop what he considered the greatest player of his time. "I had rigged a perfect defense to keep him away from the basket and thought all my worries were over," Keogan said. "So what did Wooden do but sink eight two-handers from a mile out."

Wooden was as popular in his time as a Wilt Chamberlain or Michael Jordan would come to be generations later. He was the player everybody talked about, the one all the Indiana kids growing up with hoops in their driveway tried to emulate.

A master dribbler and outside shooter, Wooden was also a spectacular free-throw shooter, once sinking 100 in a row with his classic, underhanded style.

"I still believe in the underhanded free-throw style," Wooden says. "If I had coached in high school here [in Los Angeles], I would have had all my players shoot their free throws that way. All my Indiana high school teams did and were very effective. If you start practicing it in high school, it would still work today. I even tried it some when I coached at UCLA later, but the players hadn't had enough practice with it and couldn't make it work."

Wooden's style on the court was that of a tough, hard-nosed kid who would hurl himself on the floor for any loose ball. By all accounts, he wasn't just a good competitor, he was a ferocious competitor. They said he never met a wall he wasn't afraid to run into full bore. Much of that steeliness stemmed from a life forged from hard work, from understanding that you had to fight for everything you could get.

John Wooden, the great Purdue All-American, was anything but a prima donna. He was, in fact, one of the more remarkable student hustlers of his time. Nobody knew how to generate extra money better than Wooden. Nobody better understood how to work the angles. He was as intuitive off the court as he was on it. "You had to be back then," he says.

It began in high school where he worked once a week at the Martinsville Elks Club serving meals, washing dishes, and cleaning up the kitchen. The big money was made when the boys would pass the tray afterwards, asking for tips. On weekends, he'd work as a box boy at the local A&P market or at the Collier Creamery.

"I'd work the mornings, and we'd receive these huge cans of milk from the farmers," he said. "I'd have to unload them. That helped me get stronger, I think. In the afternoon, I'd work helping prepare the ice cream. I got to taste a little, too. I can still remember the strawberry. It was made of real strawberries. Oh my, it was good. I remember wrapping Eskimo Pies, too. Money was always important to me. I worked hard for it and was always careful how I spent it."

When he arrived at Purdue, Wooden put his hustling tactics to even better use. Stretch Murphy allowed him to take over his program concession at basketball games. "I mimeographed the lineups and whatever stats I could find, then I'd get a bunch of high school kids to sell them at the games for a dime. I'd take a nickel and give them a nickel," says Wooden.

Football season usually proved much more profitable. "There was a special train whenever Purdue played Chicago that would travel from Terre Haute to Chicago," Wooden recalls. "We'd get donations from the Elks Club of cartons of apples, maybe cigarettes. I made up a special safety pin with the gold and black colors of Purdue. We'd also get ham sandwiches we made at our house and find programs that were made in advance. We'd sell all those on the train. You'd learn where to go and when on the train. Like, there was one alumni car where the alcohol seemed to be flowing more freely. You'd make sure to go into that car last. After they'd been drinking for a while, they tended to be more generous."

Summers were spent hitchhiking around the area, looking for the best work. "I remember ending up at Kansas University, helping with construction one summer," Wooden says. "I held cement in a barrel and slept at night in the gym on mats. I'd work long, hard hours and have money sent home. But it was more money than you could make staying in Indiana. We'd get paid as high as thirty-five cents an hour, which was a lot back then."

It seems clear that the work ethic Wooden developed as a young man served him well when he ventured out into the real world. Although he played for various barnstorming teams and could have turned pro after he left Purdue, he had no doubt where his future would lie.

"I knew I wanted to teach English," he says. "You hired teachers back then, not coaches." So he soon accepted his first job at Dayton High School in Kentucky, where his annual starting salary was $1,500. "I was informed not long ago that they just named their gymnasium at Dayton High for me," Wooden says.

It was in Dayton, a tough, blue-collar river town with a high school enrollment of barely 300, where John Wooden experienced his one and only losing season. His team went 6–11 that first season, a year that was highlighted by a near-brawl between Wooden, the fiery rookie coach, and Newport High coach Lou Foster, who accused Wooden of coaching "dirty basketball." You have to wonder what Foster would say about Wooden today.

From Dayton, Wooden moved back to his home

Courtesy of Purdue Sports Information Department

John Wooden in his glory days at Purdue, where he was an All-American and the leader of Piggie Lambert's national championship team. Wooden was that era's Magic Johnson.

state two years later to accept a position at South Bend Central High School. Coaching basketball was just one of his duties. He also taught English, coached baseball and tennis, served as athletic director, and was even the school's comptroller. Although he elevated South Central's basketball team to a full-fledged state championship contender, Wooden wasn't the overwhelming success in high school that he would be later coaching in college.

Eddie Powell, who eventually would be his assistant coach at Indiana State and UCLA, played for Wooden at South Bend Central. "We were always rated real high in the state, but we never made it to the finals or won the title," Powell says. "Back then, we used to think Wooden wasn't flexible enough. He wouldn't change his style of coaching in the tougher, more demanding tournament games. He thought he could win just by having the better conditioned teams. I think he learned later on that it took more than that."

Whether he won the state championship or not, Wooden was happy at South Bend Central High, teaching English and poetry to his students and the fundamentals of basketball to his players. He remained there for nine years.

"I couldn't have asked for a much better life," he says. "I was happy, and I'm sure I would have stayed at South Bend Central if it hadn't been for World War II. If I hadn't enlisted in the service, I never would have left. And I think I would have had a happy life. In fact, there's no doubt in my mind about it. There are a lot of things I believe in that people don't believe I believe in. I hope, to this day, I'm a lot more interested in building character than reputation. I could have been very happy living out my life as a high school teacher and coach."

Millions of college basketball fans are grateful it didn't work out that way.

During his three-year tour of duty in the Navy during World War II, Wooden couldn't make his house payments and lost his home. He was offered his old job back, but a position at Indiana State Teachers College intrigued him more, especially since he would be replacing Glenn Curtis, his beloved former high school coach at Martinsville.

"I was ready to move on to college coaching," Wooden says. "I was hoping to eventually wind up coaching in the Big Ten."

It was during the war that fate again intervened in John Wooden's life. He had received orders to serve aboard the aircraft carrier USS *Ben Franklin* in the South Pacific, but just before he was scheduled to leave, he was stricken with appendicitis and had to undergo major surgery. His orders were canceled. The seaman ordered to take his place was Freddie Stalcup, a former fraternity brother of Wooden. A few weeks later, while Wooden was still recovering in Iowa, he heard the news: The *Franklin* had been attacked by a Japanese plane, and one of those killed in the resulting explosion was Stalcup.

Three years at Indiana State were highlighted by equal parts success and controversy. The local folks in Terre Haute didn't take kindly to Wooden's tendency to import players from South Bend. They also required some time to adjust to this coach's newfangled fast-break style, after so many years of Curtis's more traditional, slow-down basketball. Wooden didn't let any of that bother him. He brought in the best players he could find and coached the only way he knew how, eventually convincing the town's fans by winning enough games to qualify for the NAIB Tournament in Kansas City.

It was there that Wooden confronted his first case of racial bias and demonstrated why, even today, many blacks consider him at the forefront of those who helped bring racial equality to the sport. The tournament people didn't want him to bring Clarence Walker, a black sub, on the trip. Although Walker played very little and probably wouldn't have been a factor, Wooden never hesitated. He refused to leave him home and decided his entire team would not go to the tournament. He didn't make a huge issue of it, but there was no questioning his decision. "He didn't even tell me about it at the time," says Powell, his assistant.

Once the news leaked out, however, not everyone in Indiana was pleased. "There were some people upset," Wooden says. "But my players all understood. My dad taught me that no one was better than anyone else. He also said you're just as good as anyone else, too. If they weren't going to allow one of my players to attend, I refused to go. It was that simple."

In 1948, his final season in Indiana, Wooden's team went 27–8 and made it to the NAIB Finals, where it won an exciting semifinal against Hamline University of Minnesota before losing a tough game to Louisville, 82–70, for the championship. Once again, as in high school, there were whispers that John Wooden couldn't win the big one. As strange as that seems years later, it illustrates that even the greatest of all coaches had to suffer and learn and wait for the situation that would provide him the chance to prove everybody wrong.

That opportunity arrived later in 1948, when John and Nell Wooden and their two children left the small town and cozy atmosphere of the heartland to accept the UCLA job, coming to noisy Los Angeles, with its already sprawling suburbs and shopping centers and a population five or ten times the size of what they were used to back in Indiana. "Meet UCLA's new Casaba Coach" read the headline in the UCLA magazine. (Yes, they actually used *casaba* as a synonym for basketball back then.)

"I think Dad and Mom took a while to get used to California," says Wooden's daughter, Nan Muehlhausen, "but it was all very exciting for [brother] Jim and me. We thought it was great."

Wooden wasn't so sure, especially after he checked out UCLA's facilities. Powell, his friend and assistant who would make the trek to Westwood with him, recalls how stunned they were at the difference in basketball interest in Los Angeles compared to Indiana.

"The gyms were all small and the crowds were worse," Powell recalls. "We couldn't believe it. They even played some of their games in the afternoons. And the tiny gym at UCLA, it was smaller than most of the high school facilities we were used to. I don't think John was too impressed."

The lifestyle was foreign, as well. Suddenly, as the head basketball coach, Wooden found himself at banquets and booster clubs, where it was fashionable to drink and join loud conversations. He was the shy midwesterner who wasn't at ease among crowds, and it was a problem in his early years. Powell often had to bridge the gap between his boss and the public, especially at functions where liquor was often too available. "John just wasn't comfortable in those surroundings," Powell says.

UCLA got lucky in one respect. "Purdue had offered me a job before I came to UCLA, but I didn't care for the administration there at the time," Wooden says. "But after my second year at UCLA, the administration changed at Purdue, and they asked me if I was interested. I basically had decided if they offered me the job, I was going. I felt I was more of a midwesterner. The values and all, they fit me better and I felt more comfortable there. I was really set to leave, but then Bill Ackerman and Wilbur Johns reminded me that I had insisted on a three-year contract at UCLA. Well, they got to me and I stayed. But if something had come up in the Midwest after my first three years at UCLA, I would have left."

Fortunately for the future of the sport in Southern California, he didn't. Soon, the image of basketball in the area would change, but it would take time for it to become the No. 1 sport. Red Sanders, a hard-drinking, hard-living, good, ol' boy from the South who was the polar opposite of Wooden in personality and style, was a superb football coach whose classic single-wing teams exuded the crisp discipline and execution Wooden's future basketball teams would feature. Sanders was a media favorite in L.A., where he often could be seen drinking and carousing with sportswriters. When his undefeated team went on to capture UCLA's lone national championship, in 1954, football was never more popular in Westwood—and basketball was still the forgotten stepchild.

Eddie Sheldrake, a longtime friend of Wooden, was a sophomore in his first year on the Bruins varsity the season the coach arrived. "Everything was so different then," Sheldrake says. "I remember his first meeting with us. He said, 'I've never been a loser, and we're not going to start now.' But he wasn't as tough on us that first year as he would be later. A lot of guys on that team had been in the service and been to war. These were guys you couldn't intimidate. They had been shot at, and they liked to smoke and drink beer. So he didn't really come down on them the way he would with players later on.

"I remember thinking that Wooden didn't fit into the usual coaching clique. He didn't like going to parties. He was more of a loner. He had his small group of friends, and they'd meet at Pete's On Pico for lunch, or at the

Westwood Drug Store. They'd go there and sit in the back of the restaurant and eat quietly."

But even in the beginning, even in the formative years at UCLA, Wooden's principles were evident. "You realized right away his fundamentals were precise and strong," Sheldrake says. "Our practices were so well organized. There was no fooling around, no standing around. When you came on that floor, you were either running the whole time or shooting the whole time. We were in shape, I'll tell you that. Coach didn't tell us not to go out at night. He just ran our tails off."

Sheldrake was Wooden's first point guard, although he wasn't identified as such back then. "I was known as his first small guard," Sheldrake says. "George Stanich was the other guard. Oh my, what a great athlete he was. He was probably the third-best all-around athlete in UCLA history behind Jackie Robinson and Rafer Johnson. That's how good he was. He was the star pitcher on the baseball team and an Olympic high jumper, as well. You have to realize, though, we were nobody when it came to basketball. USC was the dominant basketball team in town. At UCLA, football was a much bigger thing. Red Sanders was about to come in and start winning championships. But from where we were when we started, Wooden brought us a long way."

A serious student of the game, Sheldrake was fascinated by Wooden's method of coaching and teaching. "He had four or five basic strengths," Sheldrake says. "He had guys charting practice. He knew who made every bad pass or good shot, and he used that information. He made a lot of decisions based on that information. He didn't play that many people, either. Even when we were way ahead, he didn't substitute much. He wanted us to play together, and he felt the more we played, the more our habits would improve. So he only played about six or seven guys a game.

"The second strength was teamwork. He wanted us to create that. We had no real set plays and only two out-of-bounds plays, I think. But he stressed moving the ball and being unselfish.

"Third, there was his discipline and balance. You'd watch other teams and they'd be all helter-skelter when it came to rebounding, for instance. Not us. We had no choice. There would be five designated spots on the floor, and you'd better get to that one darn spot of yours when you were supposed to. We practiced that so much, getting to the right spot for the rebound. We practiced it hour after hour. He didn't allow any fancy passes, either. He taught you how to pass, taught you the simpler, better way to pass. He tried to get all of us to shoot two-hand, underhand free throws. We didn't, but he always tried."

COURTESY OF UCLA ATHLETIC DEPARTMENT

Eddie Sheldrake shows off the form that made him one of the early stars and the first captain of the John Wooden Era at UCLA. Sheldrake later would become an influential Bruins alum.

Above all, Sheldrake says, Wooden taught people how to compete. "He was probably the toughest competitor I've ever seen. He was vicious. He'd work out with us sometimes, and he was so tenacious you couldn't believe it. But that's the way he thought the game should be played, and he made us understand that's how he wanted us to play the whole time out there.

"Finally, Wooden didn't allow players to fall into bad habits. He felt you were prepared if you practiced properly. So, in timeouts, he never would tell you things to do. In his mind, that would just get in your way. He just wanted you to play the way you practiced. And if you didn't practice properly, he wouldn't put up with it.

"I remember the day he kicked Jerry Norman out of practice. [Norman later became one of Wooden's prized assistants, the year UCLA won its first national championship.] Coach said: 'Norman, see that door? Go out and never come back.' He eventually let him back, of course. But he made his point to the rest of us. We didn't want to screw up and get kicked out of practice."

Soon, everyone could see the results. "We won the Southern Division of the conference all three of my years in school," Sheldrake recalls. "Pretty soon, the gymnasium was full, too. B.O. Barn, everyone called it. It didn't have air conditioning, and people used to say Wooden would turn up the heat to make it tough on opposing teams. It was different, I'll say that."

To give an idea just how different, the tiny, on-campus gym seated only 2,450 people on cramped bleacher seats. Yet there was something about the place; it had a certain aura about it. Unfortunately, fire department officials weren't impressed. By 1955, in Wooden's eighth season, they ordered UCLA to play elsewhere. The Bruins were suddenly home-team vagabonds, playing in a high school gym in Venice one night, or in between ice shows at the Pan-Pacific Auditorium on other evenings. They played in Long Beach, in Santa Monica. Anywhere they could find a place to play, they gave it a try. Wooden, who had been promised a modern, new on-campus facility for years, was getting frustrated. Clearly, it was a major detriment to a basketball program still trying to grow.

"UCLA did not have very good facilities at the time," says Gary Cunningham, the future Wooden assistant who was a young high school player back then trying to decide where to attend college. "When I finally decided to become a Bruin, we played my freshman year at the Pan-Pacific and at Venice High, places like that. The Sports Arena was built in my sophomore year. But the point was, you didn't pick UCLA because of the facilities. You picked it because of the coach. I thought Wooden was a very nice man, but I didn't know how much UCLA had to offer. But I started looking at rosters, and I didn't know how good I was going to be, whether I'd play at somewhere like USC. I thought, I can play more at UCLA. And so, I changed my mind, and that's how I ended up at UCLA."

Bad facilities and all, the Bruins still produced some excellent players in those early years, from Don Bragg to Johnny Moore to Morris Taft to All-American Willie Naulls. It wasn't until the new L.A. Sports Arena was completed in 1959 that UCLA played in a first-rate facility, but still it was fifteen miles from campus and never had the true feel of a home court. Not that it prevented Wooden from finally reaching his goal. He did win two national championships, in 1964 and 1965, playing home games at the Sports Arena. It wasn't until 1966, Lew Alcindor's freshman year, that the gleaming, 12,800-seat basketball palace known as Pauley Pavilion would open.

Eddie Sheldrake, one of only three permanent captains the coach would name in his twenty-seven years at UCLA, has known and observed Wooden more closely than perhaps anyone else from the early years until now. "The one thing you can say about him is that he never changed his lifestyle," Sheldrake says. "As the years went by, I do think he got a little more confident, but that's understandable considering what he accomplished. I don't think anybody in the history of any sport has gone on to develop the talents he has. And the thing about him is that he hasn't gone away. All those other great

COURTESY OF UCLA ATHLETIC DEPARTMENT

John Wooden early in his career as UCLA's head basketball coach.

coaches you used to read about, once they're done coaching you never hear from them. With Wooden, he's remained a great speaker and communicator, a great role model for everybody. It's unbelievable at his age the way he can still communicate, the way he can make a difference."

Sheldrake knows not only the public John Wooden, but the private one, as well. "He came through for me, I'll tell you that," Sheldrake says. "I had four kids, the youngest one still in diapers, when my first wife died of cancer, and he was there every step of the way, helping me and supporting me. He taught me so much when I played for him, too. I think because he never made life easy for me, I learned to scramble the way he wanted me to, to work hard and become a successful businessman."

Today, along with his brother, Sheldrake owns fifteen Kentucky Fried Chicken franchises and fourteen Polly's Pies restaurants in Southern California. When you meet him for breakfast at one of his establishments, the manager rushes over and the waiters and waitresses hover and treat him like royalty. "It hasn't always been like this for me," he will say. "But a lot of this is because of what I learned from John Wooden. I shoot my mouth off a lot when I'm around him, and I think he's probably mad at me most of the time, but he knows what I think of him."

Sheldrake still marvels at the dynasty his favorite coach built. "There will never be another situation like that in history," Sheldrake says. "It was a combination of things. You had J. D. Morgan, an athletic director who was so powerful and bright. You had Ducky Drake, the popular trainer who was Wooden's best friend and so good at keeping kids in line. And you had a great chancellor in Franklin Murphy and a tremendous assistant in Jerry Norman."

Sheldrake has remained a strong booster and donor through the years. He also has remained as outspoken as ever. He misses Norman, the assistant who eventually left the program to go into the stock brokerage business, and he still is angry that his closest friend, the kid he helped recruit to UCLA, Cunningham, the current athletic director at UC Santa Barbara, wasn't offered the same position at UCLA. "They don't always like what I say," says Sheldrake, smiling, "but they always know how I feel."

What everyone knows is how he and nearly all of those UCLA players from the early years feel about Wooden. "He hasn't really changed since I've known him," Sheldrake says. "He's still the same. He still doesn't cuss or have a bad thing to say about anybody. He's unbelievable. I love the guy."

If Wooden's first years in Westwood were admittedly difficult, he soon settled into a lifestyle that he and his family grew to love. Southern California was a wonderful place to be in the late 1940s and 1950s, before the smog rolled in to envelop the area and freeways become too clogged to travel. An avid golfer, Wooden could play all year round in the sunshine, and although he marveled at the way athletes spent so much time at the beach playing volleyball and drinking beer, he soon became acquainted enough with the large talent pool in the area to begin recruiting wisely.

He and Nell might not have known it then, but those first fifteen years, although not as wildly successful as the national championship seasons would be later, were simpler, quieter times. They were seasons when basketball was fun and relatively uncomplicated, when the pressures and expectations of winning weren't so overwhelming, when no one even noticed that the coach's salary was astonishingly low.

John Wooden's rise as a national figure would come soon enough. But along with it would come the assorted problems, pressures, and controversies that follow any program of UCLA's magnitude. He would bask in the spotlight of championship success for a long, remarkable run, but one wonders if he was happier when the only glare he cared about was that from the bright, carefree sunshine of his early days in Southern California.

The Pool Hustler

Marques Johnson swears this is a true story.

It was his sophomore year at UCLA, John Wooden's final year of coaching as it turned out, and as most young college students sometimes do, Johnson was hanging out and missing a couple of classes. He was in the pool hall in UCLA's Student Union, hunkered over a table, cue stick in hand, when he noticed his basketball coach strolling by the door.

"Coach Wooden did a double take, passed by and then came back," Johnson says. "He obviously had just had lunch because he still had a toothpick in his mouth. Without saying hello or anything, he asked, 'Can I see your stick?' I figured he was going to be mad at me for not being in class, and I pictured him banging me on the head with the stick, or something. But he didn't. He calmly bent over, and with that toothpick rolling around in his mouth, proceeded to run five or six balls in a row, never missing a shot.

"Well, the place went completely quiet. I looked up, and everyone was standing there with their mouths open, completely amazed. John Wooden a pool hustler? We couldn't believe it. Well, after he knocks in about the sixth ball in a row, he stands up, hands me back the stick, and with that little smile of his says, 'See you at practice.' And he strolls out the door like nothing happened.

"He told me later that he'd played a lot of pool growing up in Indiana. But it was still an amazing sight and something I don't think I'll ever forget."

04

John and Nell: A Love Story for the Ages

It was the kind of relationship they write poems and love songs about, the kind that seemed to grow and nurture through sixty extraordinary years, from their time in the small, folksy midwestern town of Martinsville, Indiana, to their life in the bustling, traffic-strewn environs of Los Angeles, California. It is a love story that seems almost idyllic, especially for one with such a public face. But what John and Nell Wooden, married partners for fifty-three years, felt for one another was so pure and genuine, it couldn't be hidden. And that is what made it appear even more special, not only to those in the harried world of college basketball but to anyone who came across them in everyday life.

If John Wooden and Nell Riley, both from the same tiny town in the heartland, weren't meant for each other, than no pair ever was. "They were lovebirds," says broadcaster Dick Enberg. "They were a couple of swans. His devotion and love for her was so honest and real, and she was always there to take care of him and help him and protect him."

Wooden never dated another girl, even as a young man in Martinsville. Once he saw Nell, it was over. "She was just so pert and vivacious and had a great personality," Wooden says. The problem was that while "Nellie," as he called her, was outgoing, the farm boy who would become a basketball legend was painfully introverted.

"I was so shy, I didn't know how to act around girls," Wooden says. "Nellie's mother said I was the shyest boyfriend she ever had."

The turning point for him occurred one day when he was plowing a field on his family's farm in Centuron. Nellie and some of her friends drove from Martinsville to see him, parking on a knoll nearby. Although John wanted to go over, he was too shy to do it, and all he could hear was laughter coming from the car.

"I was perspiring and dirty, and I was sure they were laughing at me," he says. But the next day at school, when he expressed that thought to Nellie, she said, "I would never make fun of you." Wooden pauses and smiles when he recounts that story. "Somehow, I knew deep down right then she was the one I wanted to be with for the rest of my life."

Not that it was all smooth and simple after that. It took a while for the two to compromise their differences. Nellie was a fun-loving teenager and loved to dance. Wooden, although a great athlete, always thought of himself as a terrible dancer. Then there was the rule, as ordered by his South Bend Central High coach, Glenn Curtis, that players couldn't date during basketball season. That was tough on Nellie, too. It even got to be a problem, because Nellie's house backed up to the one owned by Curtis. So every time Wooden would be visiting Nellie—"And I was there a lot," he says, smiling—he was always worried that Curtis would notice. All this gave Nellie cause for at least a few doubts.

"She dated others; I never dated anyone else," Wooden says. "Sometimes I wasn't too happy that she was dating other boys. But then, I was fourteen at the time." Not too long after that, Nellie decided she only wanted to date John. "We knew by the end of high school we were going to be married," he says.

But getting married back then was not easy. Their plan for marriage was interrupted when, after saving $909 from barnstorming basketball games in 1932, Wooden ordered a new Plymouth sedan. When he went to the First Bank and Trust Company to withdraw his money for the car, he was hit with the first serious roadblock in his life. The bank was closed, permanently closed. It had gone broke.

"To say we were depressed is understating it," Wooden says. "That money seemed like all we had in the world." Fortunately, the father of one of Nellie's friends loaned Wooden $200, and, with his older brother Cat and his wife, the two couples drove to Indianapolis, where John and Nell were married.

"Afterward, we went to the Bamboo Inn for dinner, then to a theater nearby to hear the Mills Brothers. I guess that's why the Mills Brothers always have been my favorite singing group," he says. That would figure, wouldn't it?

Wooden and the Mills Brothers, they just seem to fit.

From that simple life in Indiana, the Woodens moved around, between the various cities where John was stationed with the Navy during the war. "We lived in Iowa City, and Daddy would have been on the [aircraft carrier] *Ben Franklin*. But he had a ruptured appendix, and the man who replaced him on the ship eventually was killed." says their daughter, Nan Muehlhausen. "We lived in Chapel Hill [North Carolina] and then moved to Williamstown, Massachusetts, where we lived up on the top of a hill, and I remember we learned how to ski. Not many people know it, but we lived next to Cole Porter, although he was never there much. Or if he was, I don't remember him.

COURTESY OF NAN MUEHLHAUSEN

John and Nell smiled a lot when they were young sweethearts in Indiana. When he first saw her, John said he knew Nell was the one for him, and he never dated any other girl.

"Then we moved to St. Simon's Island in Georgia, where we stayed for eighteen months. A hurricane hit while we were there, and for us kids, it felt like a big lark. But the waves were hitting six stories high and were really dangerous, although we kids were too dumb to know it. My mother never liked the ocean much after that."

Eventually, John and Nell went back to South Bend Central, then Indiana State, and, finally, to UCLA, where a new life and new opportunities were waiting. Typically, the Woodens, now with two growing children, faced them together.

"What I remember most is that they had a solid, loving relationship," says Nan. "They were always concerned for the other's needs, always putting each other before themselves. She picked out Daddy's shoes, his socks, his shirts. She washed his hair. It's funny, later when I got married, I asked my husband at the time when he wanted me to wash his hair. He said, 'Wash what?' He thought I was crazy, but that's what I watched growing up, so I thought that was just a wife's duty. In almost every way, Mom was also the perfect complement for Daddy. She was fiery. If she wanted something, she would speak up. I'm very much like that.

"Jim [the Woodens' son, who is two years younger than Nan] is more like Daddy, more quiet and reserved. I can remember once at a game, Daddy was hungry, so he and Mom slipped upstairs to get a hot dog before the game started. A fan approached and said, 'Oh, Coach Wooden, I'm sorry to bother you—' And before the man could finish his sentence, Mom said, 'Then don't.' The poor man apologized and walked away, and I can still remember Daddy chuckling to himself. Another time a reporter once asked Mom what the most memorable thing she'd got from her husband's coaching. Mother turned around and said, 'Colitis.'"

Jim Wooden smiles when he thinks about his mother. "What is it they say, behind every great man? Well, that's what she was," he says. "She was behind him all the way. She was a Riley, 100 percent Irish. And she was his biggest fan. She supported him fully. She was also his protector. She could say something critical about him, but if me or Nan or someone else did—look out. Mom would be all over him. Like Nan said, she did everything for Dad. She laid out his underwear, his shirts, his socks. Whether he needed to or not, I think he felt it was easier to go along with that.

"In all the years, I think I only heard him raise his voice once, and that was about balancing the checkbook. Mom purposely would not enter checks, thinking they would not show up. Dad told me later he always kept $500 extra in the checkbook, just in case. They would talk about that at times, and it's the only time I remember anything close to an argument between them.

"Dad was very easygoing, and Mom was very high strung. It was good, because they complemented each other. Mom was the one who did most of the disciplining. She was pretty strict about things like homework and picking up your clothes. But he backed her on everything."

Those who observe Wooden now would probably be shocked to know he smoked at one time. "Yes," Nan says, "he smoked when we first got here [Los Angeles]. But he always stopped the day practice began. When the season was over, he'd start again. But soon after we came here, he thought it was silly to start again, so he didn't."

The same couldn't be said for Nell. "She never could quit smoking," Nan says. "Dad even took her to a hypnotist near UCLA, but she didn't stop. She wasn't a heavy smoker, but she had emphysema, so she tried to hide it from Daddy. She used to hide two little cases of cigarettes in her closet, then go to a neighbor's house to smoke. She thought she was fooling Daddy, but he knew. They just played this little game between them about it."

The rich laughter they shared, the sparkle that was always in their eyes, and their need to constantly be together served as a model for the many players who observed them through the years both at home and while traveling with UCLA's basketball team.

"John and Nell were completely devoted," says Eddie Sheldrake, the star of Wooden's first teams in Westwood. "I never saw any kind of differences, never saw them argue. She was protective of him, and they were great parents. Both had very high moral standards."

"I wasn't old enough to understand at the time," says Jamaal Wilkes, who was known as Keith Wilkes in his starring days on the Bill Walton–led teams, "but later, I came to realize that most basketball coaches can't wait to get out of town and get away from their wives for a while. Coach [Wooden] was never like that. You couldn't separate him and Nell. Just the fact he would always acknowledge her [with a flick of his rolled up program] before every game was something special. It was a true love affair. They weren't trying to be role models, but it was as real blessing to be a young man still trying to understand life and to see what they had. It sounds corny, but she was part of the program. He loved having her around and involved."

Bill Walton still has warm memories of John and Nell's relationship. "She was tough, really tough," he says. "She was everybody's mom. She was on every road trip and at every game. We'd tease Coach about that signal he'd make to Nell before every game. We'd do it back at him, and he'd get embarrassed and flustered. She was very protective of him, very concerned about people trying to use him or take advantage of him. And they were. He would never say no to anyone."

Sidney Wicks, the dominant player in the post-Alcindor/pre-Walton era, used to marvel at what he thought was a perfect couple. "To me, they were more like twins than husband and wife," Wicks says. "He was yin, she was yang. They were two different people, but it was like they were one person. They were devoted to their family. They put God first, then family. I think it was good for us, as players, to see. It helped us realize this is the way marriage is supposed to be."

One of Wooden's principal competitors when he was coaching at Long Beach State, Jerry Tarkanian would go to basketball conventions and notice the Woodens, who always stood out. "They were inseparable," Tarkanian says. "At the conventions, a lot of guys would go primarily to chase women. A lot of them were mad that Nell was always there, sitting in the lobby and watching. She

COURTESY OF NAN MUEHLHAUSEN

John and Nell were still smiling when they celebrated their fiftieth wedding anniversary in August 1982.

made them feel guilty. They wanted John to leave her at home the way the other coaches left their wives at home. But he never did."

Enberg, who announced UCLA games for nine years, was going through a divorce at one point. "It was the most painful time in my life, and I used to watch John and Nell and wonder why they can they have such a beau-tiful relationship, and others don't work," Enberg says. "I've met a lot of coaches in other sports who have great marriages. But if I had to name one as the most remarkable I've seen, Coach and Nell would be the one."

The only thing that could shake up this lifetime love affair was Nell's fail-ing health. "Her emphysema caused her problems when she had hip surgery in 1982," says Nan, "and her heart stopped during surgery. A close friend, Dr. Jerry Kay, was a heart surgeon, and he revived her. But then she went to her room, and her heart stopped again. She was in a coma, and they had her on a respirator for three months."

The doctors told Wooden to talk to her. "They said in her subconscious she might be able to hear me," he says.

With her husband at her bedside every day, Nell battled back. "Dad was there at the hospital every single day, for sixteen hours a day," says son Jim. "And then, one day, she came out of the coma like she'd never been in it."

Remarkably, Nell suffered no brain damage. "But she needed to have oxy-gen to help her breathe and used a walker to get around," says Nan.

Shortly afterward, Nell was in the hospital again to have her gallbladder removed, and things looked bleak. But once more, she survived. "Our middle daughter, Caryn [Bernstein], went over and took care of her at their house every day," Nan says. "Caryn always called her Momma. That really helped. She had a couple of good years after that."

Although she had to use a wheelchair to get around, Nell traveled with John to one last Final Four, in the spring of 1984. "She enjoyed it," Wooden says. "I think it was one of the last things she was able to enjoy."

It was on Christmas morning that same year, 1984, that they rushed her to the hospital again. This time they found pancreatic cancer. "I was in L.A. playing for the Clippers," says Walton, "and I spent every day with Coach in the hospital. She was in bad shape, but we wouldn't talk about Nell. We just talked about life. We would sit there and laugh and cry. One day I went there, and he wasn't there. I knew what that meant."

Nell Wooden died on March 21, 1985. "She passed away on my birthday," says Nan, who bears a striking resemblance to her late mother. "Daddy wasn't prepared for it. It was devastating for him. He always thought he'd go before her. He was terribly depressed. It was very sad, and we were all worried about him. I think seeing me sometimes is difficult for him, too. I look more and more like Mom all the time. We have the same traits and personalities. He sees so much of her in me. It's also hard because she did so much for him, but I've tried to take care of much of that. I try to sort through the things people want him to do."

Wooden's son, Jim, calls the months immediately after Nell's death the hardest time. "We were very, very concerned about Daddy," he says. "We were very worried about his health and his will to live. He felt like he didn't want to go on."

Even now, Wooden finds it difficult to speak about his grief. "I wasn't a recluse, but I might have bordered on that," he says. "I never, ever contemplated suicide, but I was just sort of existing."

Some nineteen years later, he still goes to the cemetery regularly. "And he still breaks down," says Jim. He still writes Nell letters, placing them gently on the pillow next to where he sleeps every night. "But he sleeps only on top of the bed," Jim says. "It's also why he won't move out of that small condo. He doesn't want to change the way it was when they were together. He doesn't want to leave those memories."

A visitor to the condo can glance in the bedroom and even today find two large pictures of Nell gently placed on one side of the bed, along with other memorabilia.

Many of Wooden's friends and former players were concerned about him after Nell's death. They described him as lonely, despondent, and consumed with thoughts about death. "I was worried about him," Walton says. "She meant so much to him. Boy, he loved her. He still loves her. It's almost like she's still there in some ways."

"It was a tough time," recalls Sheldrake. "He had sat in the hospital all day long with her throughout the whole time she was sick. And when she died, he did say at times that it's not worth being here." Eddie Powell, one of his oldest and closest friends, says he thought Wooden "was going bonkers for a while." He shakes his head. "For years he had her clothes on the bed and wouldn't move them. Finally, he accepted it."

Enberg was another who recognized the concern everyone had about Wooden after Nell's death. "His friends were really worried," he says. "His children, grandchildren, and great-grandchildren gave him a reason to go on. I think he feels he's representing her in that role."

Not surprisingly, Jim Wooden says there were plenty of women who were eager to help his famous father through the rough times. "There were a lot of women after Dad not long after Mom died," Jim says. "He wouldn't say it, but you could see it. He never even entertained those thoughts. He still comes to the cemetery and tells her he will be with her soon. The sad part is, Mom never got to see the great-grandchildren."

Wooden works hard to keep Nell's memory alive. All cards he sends to his family are signed with both their names. "I think that would please Nellie," he says. And although family members and friends have long tried to move him out of his tiny condo in Encino, he refuses. "I won't ever leave, because I see her everywhere," he says. "I miss her as much today as I ever have. It never gets easier."

Rick Reilly, the award-winning columnist for *Sports Illustrated*, once posed an idea for a book he wanted to do on love, much of it centered around John and Nell and the remarkable relationship they had over the years. "I finally got Coach Wooden to agree to do it," Reilly says. "I flew out to California on a date we'd agreed upon and drove to his home to begin the interviews. I buzzed downstairs to get in, but there was no answer. So then I buzzed again. Finally, after several minutes, he came out and tears were streaming down his face. He said, 'It's too soon. I can't do it. It's just too soon.'" Reilly pauses for a moment and then adds, "It was seventeen years after Nell had died."

Wooden talks about death and even admits that he once had some fear of it. "But not anymore," he says. "I won't hurry it along, but when it comes, I will be ready. I won't be afraid. Because I know I will be joining her. I will be back with Nellie."

The legendary coach looks up and offers a warm, tender smile when he says this, and you realize that, even now, nothing has changed. As much as he loves life, he always has and always will love his Nellie more.

Bruin Buddies

They are two of the most esteemed figures in UCLA athletics history, so it shouldn't come as any great surprise that they became fast friends.

John Wooden and trainer Elvin "Ducky" Drake worked together on the UCLA basketball team for twenty-seven years. "He became my closest friend," Wooden says. When he arrived from Indiana for his interview in Westwood in 1948, Wooden stayed at the home of Ducky and his first wife, Ethelyne. "I remember they had these huge chimes," Wooden says. "I was waiting for Nellie to call me back, and when that call came, I hit those chimes when I got up. I used to kid him about that a lot."

Drake was both the Bruins' track coach and trainer when Wooden arrived. "J. D. (Morgan, the athletic director) made him give up one or the other," explains the coach. "He was a very good track coach. He coached Rafer Johnson."

Wooden and Drake got along because they were similar. They were both home bodies who didn't drink or hang out in bars. "Our temperaments were the same," Wooden says. "On the road, Nellie and I spent a lot of time together with Ducky. He was so much help on our trips. Ducky had a unique way of bedchecking the players. He'd knock on their door, and if they weren't there, the player would return and find Ducky in his bed. He'd usually sit up in lobbies or just patrol the hallways. A player would see him in the hallway as he was trying to leave and say, 'Don't worry, Ducky, I'm just going down to get a paper.' Athletes considered him tough, but he cared for them."

Wooden got another bonus hanging out with Drake. "He was the best barber in Westwood," the coach says. "He cut my hair more than anyone else. The price was right, too."

Drake had "a very dry sense of humor," according to Wooden, who should know. He could be described the same way. "After games, the three of us—me, Nellie, and Ducky—might be in a coffee shop or something like that, just talking about what happened that night, going over the game, discussing what to do next. He was a great sounding board."

In a move befitting the man's contributions, the track and field stadium on the UCLA campus officially was renamed Drake Stadium in 1973.

Ducky Drake died on Dec. 23, 1988. He was eighty-five years old.

PART II

Building a Dynasty

The Championship
Years: Great Success
but New Problems

THE FIRST ONE

I t was before *SportsCenter*, before Dick Vitale and his "Diaper Dandies," before Al Maguire's colorful monologues and Billy Packer's humorless dialogues. College basketball hadn't yet nudged itself into the national consciousness some forty years ago, in 1964, when even the NCAA Finals weren't televised in prime time, let alone all the regional match-ups leading to it. There were no million-dollar sneaker deals, no high school prodigies threatening to bolt for the pros, no national recruiting lists that identified every hotshot prep player from New York to California.

This was a kinder, gentler time for a sport that was still trying to assimilate the idea that a group of five African-Americans from Texas Western could beat up on Adolph Rupp's good-ol'-boy team from Kentucky. It was in the midst of this relatively subdued, low-profile atmosphere that the first seeds of John Wooden's national championship hopes were planted.

It all started with Walt Hazzard, a flashy guard from Wilt Chamberlain's old haunt at Overbook High in Philadelphia, who somehow decided he wanted to bring his stylish, East Coast game to California. "I didn't recruit Walt Hazzard," Wooden says. "Walt Hazzard recruited UCLA."

Hazzard actually wrote the Bruins' coach a letter, expressing his desire to come west. There was a problem with his grades, but Hazzard even consented to attending Santa Monica City College first to qualify academically. When he finally arrived in Westwood and began to practice, the reaction was unanimous. This guy was part revelation and part freak. No one on the West Coast had ever seen someone play the way he did: threading passes through arms and legs, bouncing a ball perfectly to a streaking outlet man, looking one way and passing another.

"Walt was a little hot dog-ish," Wooden says, "but I knew I could correct that."

For a long time, it was Hazzard's teammates who had to make the biggest adjustments. Basketballs were hitting them in the head, bouncing off their chests and shoulders, flying into them from angles none of them had ever seen before.

"After a while in practice," says Steve Aranoff, who was the team manager at the time, "Coach Wooden told Hazzard to just keep hitting them in the head. Eventually, they'll figure it out." And eventually, they did. Still, there was a fine line to be walked between flashy point guard and fundamentally sound coach.

"Hazzard would play to the oohs and ahhs of the crowd," Aranoff says. "Coach didn't go for that." Maybe not, but the audience sure did. "All that stuff Walt did," says Keith Erickson, who joined the playmaker on the varsity in Hazzard's senior year, "he was the first one who brought Showtime to L.A. Behind-the-back dribbles, no-look passes, passing the ball through an opponent's legs, he did all that stuff before anybody else."

But there was substance behind all that style, too. Hazzard was, above all, a great point guard who might have set collegiate assist records had they kept them back then. He was UCLA's unquestioned floor leader, even as a sophomore. And because he was so gifted, and maybe more important, so unselfish, the older players immediately respected him. He was not a great shooter. His best offensive move was a kind of modified runner of a jump shot. But he could handle the ball superbly, and he scored plenty of points on drives, collecting more than his share of foul shots. Best of all, he always found his teammates when they were open.

In 1961–62, Hazzard's sophomore season, he turned a frail looking, less-than-physical team into the kind of fast-break machine Wooden loved. "Hazzard may not throw the ball where someone can catch it, but he throws it beautifully," Wooden joked at the time.

Most of the time, someone could catch it. Players such as Pete Blackman, Fred Slaughter, Johnny Green, and Gary Cunningham learned, although it took a while. They started out 4–7, but by the time the season passed the halfway mark, they had adjusted to the point guard some called "East Coast." With Cunningham and Green shooting spectacularly off feeds from Hazzard, UCLA won fourteen of sixteen games, capping its streak with NCAA regional victories over Utah State and Oregon State to send the team fast-breaking its way to Louisville and Wooden's first Final Four appearance against a powerful, intimidating University of Cincinnati team that was overwhelmingly favored to win.

It was that night, in a remarkable, yet frustrating NCAA semifinal game, when people could see the first hints of what the future would hold for UCLA. The Bruins pushed the eventual national champions as far as anyone could, finally losing when a defensive-minded guard named Tom Thacker, who had gone 0-for-6 from the field the rest of the night, hit a twenty-five-foot

COURTESY OF UCLA ATHLETIC DEPARTMENT

Walt Hazzard demonstrates his passing wizardry. Hazzard's flashy, East Coast style took time to assimilate, but once his teammates adjusted, UCLA's offense, especially its fast break, was impossible to stop.

jumper from the corner with three seconds left to win it for Cincinnati, 72–70.

Wooden's team didn't make it to the Final Four the next year, Hazzard's junior season, losing in the regionals to Arizona State. But even then, the coach thought he saw signs of encouragement. "I knew before 1963 that we had a chance to be real good," Wooden says. "I thought we had the makeup, and we were improving. I remember I even wrote a poem to Pete Blackman saying we could be champs in '64."

The Bruins turned out to be more than champs. They turned out to be the most exciting college basketball team many of us have seen, before or since. Slaughter, the athletic senior center, was the biggest man on the team at six feet five, but that didn't matter. UCLA was quicker, smarter, and more explosive than any other team in the country. And happily for Wooden, the Bruins also had a young, intense assistant who proved how true his head coach's old adage could be. "Never hire a 'yes man' as an assistant," Wooden always said.

Jerry Norman, a star forward on Wooden's teams in the early 1950s, was anything but a yes man. It was Norman who convinced Wooden to utilize the full-court press that would come to define the 1964 team and revolutionize the college game that season. It wasn't anything new to Wooden, who had used the press extensively at South Bend Central High School and at Indiana State. But he wasn't sure it could work against more polished, better ball-handling college guards. Norman convinced him otherwise.

"I don't know why I didn't use the press sooner at UCLA," Wooden said later. "I've always second-guessed myself a little for that, because I had success with it in high school and at Indiana State. But somehow I felt, maybe, that I was up another notch and it wouldn't work as well. I think I was wrong."

It is a measure of the flexibility of this coach that he allowed an assistant to change his mind. Lots of great coaches would be too stubborn or too egocentric to admit it. Wooden wasn't. Happily, the result was some of the most fascinating basketball the college game has witnessed. To this day, Wooden will tell you the 1964 team is his favorite. "Your first championship team always is your favorite," he'll say. But it is more than that. This team not only overcame huge odds because it was so undersized, its pieces meshed better than any of the great UCLA teams Wooden would produce later, even the ones dominated by a superstar center.

With Hazzard still its centerpiece, the '64 team also featured a skinny junior named Gail Goodrich, who was the perfect, good-shooting complement to America's finest point guard. Nobody moved without the ball better than Goodrich, who proved to be the team's most consistent scorer, whether he was corkscrewing his tiny body into the air on a jump shot or weaving his way through traffic to field a pretty Hazzard pass for an easy lay-up. He was also a tremendous defensive player and a great point man in the press. Slaughter, at center, was a good rebounder and a far better athlete than most people suspected.

"He was the quickest guy on the team," Goodrich says. "If you raced everybody from one end of the court to the other, he would win."

The forwards were Keith Erickson, a terrific high school baseball and volleyball player Wooden still describes as "the finest athlete I had at UCLA," and Jack Hirsch, a bony, competitive, six-foot-three former high school center who was one of the best "garbage" players of his time. Huge bodies would be colliding under the basket, and suddenly, out of the crowd would come the spidery Hirsch, the leanest guy in the group, grabbing the rebound and somehow putting it back up and in. Time and again he would do that.

"Jack was amazing," Goodrich says. "I thought he was the best forward in the country."

Off the bench, Wooden had Kenny Washington, a springy sophomore who played his best in the postseason, and Doug McIntosh, a solid wide-body who could come in and crash the boards.

What the coach loved, though, was the way the team fit defensively, the way it was so ideally suited for the press. "Erickson was a tremendous No. 5 man, or safety, in the press," Wooden says. "He blocked and altered more shots than anybody. Everybody else was good at their spots, too, especially Goodrich at the No. 1 [defending the in-bounds pass]."

The result had to be seen to be believed. Games would be close, then the Bruins would create a half-dozen turnovers off the press, and in a three- or four-minute span, they'd go off on a 14–2 explosion and the game would be over.

"It happened so fast, other teams couldn't even call a timeout," Erickson says. "We'd just give you the rat a tat and you couldn't breathe." Slaughter says the secret was their quickness and speed. "Our full-court press killed teams," he says. "It was one of the greatest things John Wooden did. We would run people to death. There I was, waving my arms, and Keith was back there picking off passes, and Gail was sneaking in there and stealing balls, and we just killed them."

What the press also did was create a faster tempo, spreading the court and forcing opponents to play to the more athletic Bruins' strengths. The early lesson would be one that frustrated teams would learn the hard way later on: Whatever you do, don't try to run with these guys.

In the Holiday Tournament in Los Angeles early that season, UCLA went up against No. 1-rated Michigan, led by quick Cazzie Russell and Bill Buntin and Oliver Darden, a couple of heavyweights who were part of what was called the "Anvil Chorus." The muscular, highly regarded Wolverines never had a chance. The Bruins went into that blur of a full-court press, and the nation's top-ranked team crumbled before the eyes of a stunned crowd at the L.A. Sports Arena.

"In all my years at UCLA, there were two halves I remember when we played as perfect a game as you could hope for," Wooden says. "One was the first half against Houston in our rematch in the NCAA semifinals after they beat us in the Astrodome. The other was that first half against Michigan in the Holiday Tournament the year we won the national championship for the first time. Our press was as good as it could possibly be that night."

It was pretty good most nights, although no one ever would have known it from the players' interaction off the court. "They were not close off the floor, not close at all," Wooden says. "I equated them to those great Oakland A's teams Charlie Finley used to have, with Reggie Jackson and Joe Rudi and Rollie Fingers. They say they didn't really get along very well, either. With our team, it was a hodgepodge of people. Their personalities were entirely different."

Hirsch might have been the most unique. He was free-spirited and outspoken, sort of the UCLA precursor to Bill Walton. Already married, Hirsch had been bequeathed a chain of bowling alleys by his father, who died a month before the season.

"Jack Hirsch would say all kinds of things you'd think would really cause problems," Wooden says. "He'd say to a teammate, 'You're the tightest guy I've ever known; you never spend a nickel.' He was always abrasive and he might be to me. He may be one of the few I ever had as a player who'd call me John. Well, I never asked the players to call me Coach or Mr. Wooden, but he's the only one who ever called me by my first name."

One time at training table, Hirsch suddenly screamed out, "I'm not going to eat this slop." Wooden said, "Get out, Hirsch." The forward answered, "I'm going to." Wooden said, "Well, get going. Get out and don't come back." Hirsch said, "I can go have a steak." At that point, Wooden just looked at him. "I know, Jack," he said, "you've got a lot of money. You can buy a nicer car than I can. You can live in a nicer home. You can have steak every day. The rest of us think the food here is pretty good, though."

Ten days later, Wooden said Hirsch came to his office and said, "I'm sorry." The coach smiled and said OK, but the team didn't let Hirsch forget the incident. "From then on," says Wooden, "they were always asking him, 'How's the food, Jack?'"

When he looks back now, Wooden is still amazed at how well this group of players could work together on the floor. "They all went their own way," he says. "I don't think there was a lot of friction. Just because you don't like each other doesn't mean you have to have friction. Many of them didn't like each other. Everyone liked the two sophomores [Washington and McIntosh], but I don't think that was true of a single other member of the starting five. But they played so well together. I've had other teams that were very compatible off the floor that didn't play that well together. This one did."

The team remained unbeaten through the regular season and the NCAA Tournament regionals. But the culmination came at the Final Four in Kansas City, where, typically for that era, a modest crowd of 10,000 at tiny Municipal Auditorium was allowed to watch the official start of what would become college basketball's greatest dynasty. There were no 70,000 people stuffed into a giant dome, no weeklong media circus, no over-analysis by a bunch of smirking cable-TV anchors. Only a relatively small audience and a bunch of still-disbelieving basketball coaches from across America, many of whom remained convinced UCLA's luck had to run out against teams like Kansas State and Duke.

It almost did. The Bruins didn't play their best game in the semifinals, and with seven minutes to go, they trailed Kansas State, 75–70. It was at that point UCLA threw its first press-ignited "two-minute explosion" at a national audience. From five points down, the Bruins needed just 120 seconds to go on an 11–0 run and take a commanding 81–75 lead, ultimately prevailing, 90–84. Meanwhile, in the other semifinal, Duke, led by All-American Jeff Mullins, was throttling Michigan, 91–80, and reaffirming its status as the championship favorite.

"Maybe people thought we were underdogs, but I didn't," Wooden says. "I remember sitting in the Hotel Muehlebach in Kansas City the morning of the Finals. A lot of coaches were coming up and saying, 'You got a fine little team, but Duke is so big.' But then this European coach came by, and he said, 'UCLA win. UCLA win. UCLA is team. UCLA is real team.' I remember thinking that was a pretty good compliment." It also proved to be a pretty good prediction.

Duke coach Vic Bubbas was one of those who remained unimpressed with the Bruins' press. "I think we can beat it," he was quoted before the game, "and I'm not so sure we can't run with them."

Early on, at least, it appeared he might be right. The Blue Devils were slashing through UCLA's defense so well that Wooden was forced to replace Slaughter with McIntosh and brought the energized Washington off the bench, as well. A stolen pass here, a converted mistake there, and soon the Bruins were in control the way they'd been all season. Wooden's coaching, as usual, had something to do with it. He ordered his center to go out even higher in his high-post offense, drawing seven-footers Jay Buckley and Hack Tison out and clearing the middle for Hazzard and Goodrich to work their magic on drives. Goodrich scored twenty-seven points, his first high-production effort of the tournament.

But the real star of the Finals was Washington, the smiling sophomore who had traveled 2,400 miles in the back seat of a Greyhound bus from Beaufort,

COURTESY OF UCLA ATHLETIC DEPARTMENT

Walt Hazzard (42) shoots, while his backcourt partner Gail Goodrich (25) arrives to help. Goodrich and Hazzard were the guards who led Wooden's Bruins to their first national title.

South Carolina, to Westwood just to play for Wooden. Painfully shy, Washington struggled as a freshman to feel comfortable both on and off the court. He had rare physical tools, especially his ability to leap and the kind of quick hands Wooden liked, but his technique needed work.

"I shot funny, kind of from behind my head," Washington says. "Coach Wooden changed that." Washington worked on his shot the entire summer prior to his sophomore year, and all that practice paid off.

Nobody played better against Duke than he did. He made eleven of sixteen shot attempts, scoring twenty-six points, and also grabbed twelve rebounds. It was Washington's performance and the Bruins' press that forced Duke into an uncharacteristic twenty-nine turnovers, that proved to be the difference in a convincing 98–83 victory to cap a perfect 30–0 season. Wooden's post-game speech that night has become the stuff of legend, the words that tell you so much about this man on the night of his first major success.

"I am immensely proud of you," he told his players. "You're really the best. You've proved it. Now, don't let it change you. You are champions and you must act like champions. You met some people going up to the top. You will meet the same people going down."

Hazzard, who kick-started the whole thing, later reflected on his accomplishment. "It started the beginning of an era," he said. "It set a precedent for UCLA basketball and established a style of play. And that's a great deal to do."

Outside the UCLA locker room that night, Wooden made his way through the crowd of boosters and well-wishers to find the only person with whom he wanted to share this personal moment. He hugged and kissed his wife, Nellie, whispered something softly in her ear, and they both smiled. Daughter Nan, celebrating her thirtieth birthday with the best present imaginable, was seen glowing nearby.

They had come a long way, from Martinsville to Westwood to Kansas City, and now they had a right to enjoy these precious moments together. They'd captured the coveted national championship they had dreamed about for so long. Little could they have known, in the giddy, celebrating hours of that happy night, that this would only be the start.

THE REPEAT

There was no real reason to believe UCLA could repeat as national champions in 1964–65. Not with Walt Hazzard, Fred Slaughter, and Jack Hirsch gone from the team that had been undefeated the previous season. Only Gail Goodrich and Keith Erickson remained from the starting lineup.

"I didn't think we'd be as good," Wooden says, "but I knew we'd be a good team. We had the two important ingredients in Erickson and Goodrich, probably our two best players on the press. We had a talented sophomore in Edgar Lacey coming in, a new, good-shooting guard in Freddie Goss, and then Kenny Washington and Doug McIntosh had played so well in the tournament. I thought we'd at least be contenders."

The coach and his assistant also thought this press had to be tinkered with some to make best use of the team's personnel. "We went from a 2–2–1 to more of a 1–2–1–1 alignment," Wooden recalls.

"After the first pass," Goodrich says, "it was pretty much the same press, but it gave us a different look."

The real difference in this team is that Goodrich became the leader. "I basically took Walt's position," he says. "Offensively, I had the ball a lot more."

It was a good place for the ball to be. Goodrich had large hands, and he was "long," as basketball coaches like to say these days. That means he had a huge arm span for someone barely six feet one. "Stumpy," is what they called him later during his celebrated NBA career with the Lakers, but on this UCLA team, he played more like the tallest tree in the forest.

Erickson was the other force, a senior who loved to spend his spare time playing volleyball on L.A.'s sun-drenched beaches. Eventually, he made the

Basketball's most enthusiastic ambassador, Dick Vitale, pauses to chat with Wooden before a game at Pauley Pavilion. Like everyone else in the sport, Vitale is awed by Wooden's record.

U.S. Olympic Volleyball Team, and the timing he developed in that sport helped him in basketball. In many ways, he was like a miniature Bill Russell for UCLA, laying back as the safety valve on the press, taking on 2-on-1s and batting basketballs back into the crowd. They didn't keep blocks on the stat sheets in those years, but Erickson had a ton. "He played that position as well as it could be played," Wooden says.

Still, this was not the smooth, cohesive bunch of the previous year, and the 1965 Bruins did not go undefeated. In fact, they were jolted in the opener at Illinois, suffering an embarrassing 110–83 beating. Seven weeks later, making more turnovers than they were accustomed to, they endured an 87–82 loss at Iowa. Some coaches would have been inconsolable. Wooden would only say, "Sometimes, it can actually help a team to lose a game, especially early in the season." It was his way of saying that some teams require a wake-up call, and if that's what happened, this one certainly woke up.

"After that loss to Iowa, we just kept getting better," Goodrich says. The Bruins won their final eleven games of the regular season, then blew past Brigham Young and the University of San Francisco in the NCAA regionals. Suddenly, they were back in the Final Four at Portland, preparing to play Wichita State in the semifinals and, more than likely, No. 1-rated Michigan in the championship game. As popular as UCLA had become the previous year, it was not the crowd favorite. That privilege went to Princeton, the Ivy League school led by its charismatic All-American, Bill Bradley, the future Senator.

But Michigan overwhelmed Bradley and Princeton in the semifinals, and UCLA had little trouble disposing of Wichita State, 108–89, behind fifty-two points from Goodrich and Lacey. That set up the game everybody wanted to see: the rematch of that Holiday Tournament rout the Bruins had completed the year before. Again, it was Cazzie Russell, the flashy Wolverine junior, facing up against Goodrich, the senior All-American who had become one of the most accomplished scorers in the country.

Again, Washington, UCLA's super sub, proved to be a catalyst, coming off the bench to hit two quick baskets and revitalize the press early. Before Michigan knew what had happened, the Bruins were off on an 11–2 blitz to take a 24–22 lead. Michigan battled back, but then the press ignited another 13–4 run and it was 47–34 at halftime, with the Wolverines never able to draw closer than twelve points.

After that, the night became Goodrich's showcase. Twisting his body like a corkscrew in mid-air, he was unstoppable, making jump shots from everywhere on the floor and driving through the thick Michigan bodies to score on acrobatic lay-ups. He finished the game with a school-record forty-two points, the most ever scored in an NCAA Finals at that time. "Even now, when I look back forty years later," Goodrich says, "it is still a highlight of my career."

Remarkably, and probably unfairly, it was not enough to earn the UCLA guard the tournament's Most Valuable Player award. Princeton's Bradley scored fifty-eight points in the consolation game—they still had them then—against Wichita State, and although it didn't produce a championship, it did produce enough votes from a press corps that seemed decidedly biased toward East Coast players.

"I would have thought," Wooden still says today, "that scoring forty-two points to lead your team to the national championship might have been a bit more significant."

Not that the snub took anything away from UCLA's accomplishment. Back to back championships had put the Bruins in rarefied company, right there with the great Bill Russell teams of USF a few years earlier, and although Goodrich and Erickson would be departing, it was clear Wooden was building a major program in Westwood, a program good enough to attract great basketball players not only from Southern California but from across the country.

Any doubts people had about that were officially laid to rest when, a couple of months later, the tallest and most famous high school player of his generation announced at a New York press conference that he had made his college decision. Lew Alcindor was coming to UCLA to play for John Wooden.

Wooden's Main L.A. Adversary

Throughout the glory years in Los Angeles, John Wooden's main adversary was a tall, basketball-lifer named Bob Boyd at Southern California. Before Boyd arrived, Wooden's UCLA teams used to beat USC like a cardinal-and-gold drum. But once the former Seattle University coach, who had grown up in nearby Alhambra, California, strolled onto the scene, the whole tenor of things changed.

Boyd was a terrific coach in his own right, and although he didn't draw the consistent flow of talent Wooden attracted in Westwood, he always kept things interesting. In 1969, faced with the indomitable task of trying to beat UCLA with Lew Alcindor, Boyd devised a brilliant slowdown game and not only defeated the Bruins, he did it at Pauley Pavilion, marking UCLA's first at home since its new basketball facility opened in 1966. The tactics created a huge controversy around the nation, but particularly in Los Angeles, where Wooden said the ploy was "bad for basketball." Boyd vigorously defended his stance.

"That's one thing that still irks me," Boyd would say years later. "Not long after that, Pete Carril's Princeton team beat UCLA [not coached by Wooden] in a slowdown game, and everybody said what a great coaching job it was. But when we beat UCLA using that style, people screamed we were ruining the game. They said it was bad for basketball. It wasn't bad for basketball."

What was bad for Boyd was the presence of Wooden and UCLA, not only in the same town but in the same conference. Back then, only the champion from each conference, was allowed into the NCAA Tournament. In 1971, Boyd had probably the finest team in USC history, led by Paul Westphal and Ron Riley. That team went 24–0 against everyone else and 0–2 against UCLA and Wooden. Rated No. 1 in the country for much of the season, USC lost that second game to UCLA in the regular-season finale, and with a 24–2 record, the Trojans had to sit home while Wooden's Bruins went on to capture another NCAA title.

The frustration of coaching against the overpowering program across town simmered in Boyd for many years. But as time healed some of the pain, he had no problem putting Wooden's achievements into proper perspective.

"We had some great duels through the years," Boyd says. "The accolades and recognition he received are well-deserved. All that is predicated on winning. And no one was ever more successful than Coach Wooden."

The Alcindor Era

If the Walt Hazzard-Gail Goodrich undersized teams had to overcome big odds, the arrival of Ferdinand Lewis Alcindor Jr. at UCLA meant that the Bruins would have to meet even bigger expectations. Hazzard and Goodrich helped change the image of UCLA basketball under John Wooden. But Alcindor changed the scope.

The little underdogs suddenly had morphed into what everyone expected to be college basketball's dominant force, and along with the added glare of the national spotlight would come increased pressure to win.

The year was 1965, and while President Lyndon Johnson was beginning to struggle with the problem in Vietnam that would eventually divide the country, the mood had grown ugly in Los Angeles, where that summer flames flickered in the sky, gunshots rang in the night, and riots broke out in Watts. Some of us, fresh out of college, were members of the California National Guard, armed with loaded weapons we hadn't yet been taught how to fire. It was a scary time to be young and trying to survive in the heart of an angry city.

A few miles away, in the more tranquil environs of Westwood, the gleaming new facility Wooden had been promised for so many years finally was near completion at UCLA. Pauley Pavilion, a $5 million, state-of-the-art basketball arena complete with comfortable theater-type seats splashed with blue and gold colors, would be ready just in time for the debut of the most heralded college freshman since Wilt Chamberlain went from Philadelphia's Overbook High to the University of Kansas.

"When Lewis [he always has called him Lewis] was a junior in high school, he and his coach watched us win the national championship on television," Wooden says. "They were apparently impressed by the way we played team basketball. So when Lewis decided to make a recruiting visit to UCLA, the first thing I did was take him to see Pauley Pavilion being built. It was going to be one of the nicest arenas on the West Coast, and I told him, 'You are going to dedicate this. This is going to be ready by the time you arrive to go to college, and you can be the one who will be remembered for dedicating this building.'"

It helped that UCLA had an advocate in Willie Naulls, the respected NBA star who had played in Westwood for Wooden and had strongly recommended the school to Alcindor, who had sought out Naulls for advice in New York. It also didn't hurt that Wooden and Jerry Norman, his assistant in charge of recruiting, flew across the country and spent a long evening in conversation with Alcindor's parents. "I don't know how many hours we were there," Norman says. "I just remember when we left, it was very early in the morning."

If it all seemed to work out beautifully, especially after Alcindor committed to Wooden and the Bruins, there was only one problem. Freshmen weren't eligible to play for the varsity back then, so the debuts of both Alcindor and Pauley came in the annual varsity-freshman game. It was an evening that would portend much about UCLA's future, both for the coming season and the following three years when the precocious young man with the breathtaking ability would begin his varsity career.

The new facility, sparkling like the nearby lights of Hollywood, was filled to capacity with fans who could hardly wait for their first glimpse of the seven-foot-one wonder they'd read so much about. Alcindor didn't disappoint them. It was astonishing to see a big man who was so quick and agile at a time when centers were large and lumbering. His agility and mobility were jaw-dropping. Sitting there that night, observers sensed they were watching the beginning of a new and special era in basketball. They also sensed a UCLA varsity that was demoralized before its season even started.

Alcindor scored thirty-one points, grabbed twenty-one rebounds, and blocked shots all over the floor in helping the freshmen beat up on the defending NCAA champions, 75–60. It wasn't enough that Goodrich and Keith Erickson, the team's two best players from the previous season, were gone and Freddie Goss, the top returning guard, was diagnosed with osteomyelitis in his lower back. Now the returnees such as Kenny Washington, Mike Lynn, and Doug McIntosh had to deal with the embarrassment of having their noses rubbed in the dirt by a bunch of freshmen.

Of course, these weren't just any freshmen. It was a spectacular freshmen class, topped by Alcindor but also led by three other prep All-Americans—Lucius Allen, a wonderfully skilled guard; Lynn Shackelford, a brilliant shooter with a soft, unorthodox-looking rainbow jumper; and Kenny Heitz, whose skinny frame didn't prevent him from being a hard-nosed competitor, especially on defense.

Burdened by injuries for much of the year, the 1965-66 Bruins varsity never did play up to its potential, finishing with an 18–8 record (8–4 in the conference) and failing to advance to the Western Regionals, which were held, ironically enough, in Pauley Pavilion that season. Some said it was just a matter of bad luck. Others felt this team never really

COURTESY OF UCLA ATHLETIC DEPARTMENT

Lew Alcindor soared above the rest of college basketball at UCLA. The Bruins went 88–2 during his three years in Westwood and won three national titles. Alcindor was MVP of all three NCAA Tournaments.

got over the shock of that loss to Alcindor and the freshmen on opening night. Either way, UCLA fans were less concerned with the outcome of the current season as they were enthused about the prospects for the next three.

"My expectation," says Wooden, "after seeing Lewis as a freshman was that we would have our foot in the door [for a national title] for the next three years. We just had to make sure no one slammed it on us."

The only one doing the slamming was Alcindor, who was so proficient at it that the NCAA eventually outlawed the dunk for a few years. Still, Wooden was nervous. He always preferred teams that could overachieve. This one, with the bar already set so high, almost had to win the NCAAs every year or it would be a disappointment.

"I remembered those great Ohio State teams with [Jerry] Lucas and [John] Havlicek," the coach says. "They were going to win all those championships, and they didn't. The only thing I felt good about is that I had as smart a basketball player as I've ever had coming in to lead that team. As great as Alcindor was, if I hadn't had Mike Warren, I don't think we could have done it."

Warren was, and still is, one of Wooden's all-time favorite players. It wasn't just that he came from South Bend Central High, where Wooden had coached in Indiana. It was the style the smooth five-foot-eleven point guard exuded. He was always under control, always understated but effective, always in charge on the court. He was the veteran who allowed the fabulous freshmen around him to grow and mature. Not that Alcindor had to do much more growing or maturing.

In his first varsity game, against USC at Pauley, Alcindor was unleashed in all his fury. Bob Boyd's free-wheeling Trojans chose to play him straight up, man-to-man, and the big fella proceeded to score a school-record fifty-six points in a 105–90 rout of the crosstown rivals. Afterward, both the crowd and the coaches seemed stunned by what they had just witnessed. "I can promise you we won't play him that way again in the next three years," Boyd said after the game. "He looked like a man among boys out there. He's even better than advertised."

Wooden, almost sheepish in the post-game interviews, said this wasn't the way Alcindor would play the rest of the season. Alcindor agreed, explaining he was more comfortable passing the ball to open teammates. But what this game had demonstrated is that the kid from Power Memorial Academy in New York was so gifted, he could have broken every scoring record in college basketball history if Wooden had been so inclined. But that wasn't the agreement between coach and player.

"I asked him very early, 'Do you want to break scoring records or do you want to win?'" Wooden says. Alcindor's reply was: "I want to win." No coach could have asked for a better answer. "To be honest, I knew what he was going to say," says Wooden, smiling, "or I wouldn't have asked the question."

If it seemed like an easy three-year championship cruise after that, it wasn't. Along with Alcindor came an assortment of new challenges for Wooden. First, he had to change his style of offense.

"In forty years of teaching, I spent thirty-four of those years playing a high-post offense," he says. "There were six years when I didn't. The six years I had Alcindor and [Bill] Walton. They were both such gifted players inside, I had to feature a low-post offense that would take full advantage of their skills."

He made it work, of course, but the coach was never comfortable playing it, primarily because it called for one man to get most of the touches and, usually, most of the points. Wooden was always about the team, not the individual. But when you had two of the most talented individuals in the history of the sport, even he knew he had no other choice.

Then there was the matter of Alcindor's adjustment to life as a seven-footer 3,000 miles away from home. "I had so much to deal with at that time in my life," says Kareem Abdul-Jabbar, who was known as Lew Alcindor before he accepted the Muslim faith and changed his name. "It was not an easy time for me."

Extraordinarily bright, well-read, and articulate, Alcindor didn't get much of a chance to interact with the Los Angeles media, because Athletic Director J. D. Morgan, Wooden, and the school's sports information department were intent on protecting his privacy. That's too bad, because no one got to know the real Alcindor. In the end, the young man with the fertile mind who could be fascinating in a one-on-one conversation was generally painted as a loner who was difficult and uncommunicative most of his years at UCLA. That reputation carried over into his NBA career and probably has hurt him even today, as he searches to find work as a professional coach. Someday, when the historians look back, Alcindor might be remembered as one of the most misunderstood athletes of his time.

The one thing no one ever misunderstood, though, was his ability. Alcindor and his talented teammates were so good that UCLA games became more like boring Xerox copies for most of that first year. They breezed through a 30–0 perfect season, with the only blip coming against USC when Boyd, a creative coach who was determined to do something different against Alcindor, went into a stall that almost cost the Bruins their spotless record. The Trojans worked their coach's strategy beautifully, and only a near-miss by their best player, Bill Hewitt, at the buzzer and a couple of big plays by Bruins sub Bill Sweek and Warren in overtime saved a 40–35 victory for UCLA.

Wooden, somewhat taken aback by Boyd's ploy, admitted it was a good strategy afterward but added that he thought "it was bad for the game." Opposing coaches across America must have laughed when they read that. How about getting beat 122–57 or 120–82, as a couple of Bruins foes had been earlier? Could that be bad for the game, too? In the NCAA Tournament, the only game that caused a stir was the semifinal against Houston, when Elvin Hayes, far from intimidated by Alcindor, outscored him, 25–19, and out-rebounded him, 24–20. But remaining unflustered and unconcerned about his stats, Alcindor quietly led UCLA to victory, 73–58. While the Bruins went on to flatten Dayton in the Finals to win Wooden's third NCAA crown, it was the Houston game that created much of the post-tournament conversation and set up the much-hyped event the following season that would change the face of college basketball forever.

First, though, Alcindor and his teammates had to deal with a new problem—complacency. When you go 30–0 as sophomores, as four of these starters did, when you pound almost everyone into submission and run away to win by thirty, forty, even fifty points, something strange and different filters into the locker room.

"The one drawback after our sophomore year was that everyone was expecting us to win every game." Abdul-Jabbar says. "It started to repeat itself. It felt like if we didn't win three national championships, we would be looked at as failures."

Maybe the first sense the team was beginning to feel that way came in the opener at Purdue, where the Bruins barely escaped with a harrowing 73–71 victory over Rick Mount and the Boilermakers. After that, the old overpow-ering style kicked in and the games started to look like mismatches again, Until, of course, Alcindor was poked in the eye and injured against California, a week before UCLA was scheduled to fly to Houston for the monumental game on January 20, 1968, in the cavernous Astrodome.

"The thing was, I never really wanted to play that game in the Astrodome," Wooden says. "J. D. [Morgan] scheduled it and then asked me later if I wanted to play it. J. D. would do that. He'd ask me things he'd already decided. I felt the game would be a farce in a building like that, and I didn't want to make a farce out of the game I loved. J. D. disagreed. He said it would be a great thing, probably the most televised event of the time. We were also going to get quite a bit more money. And you know what? He was right. It was good for basket-ball. I think I was right, too, though. It was a farce as far as a place to play. I told my players before the game, 'If you have to go to the bathroom, go now, or you'll have to walk a quarter-mile to go later.'"

Still, the attraction was enticing. Houston was rated right up there with the Bruins, and Hayes was enjoying a magnificent season. "The crowd was 53,000," remembers Dick Enberg, who broadcast this first prime-time college game, "and a huge TV audience. It was probably the most people ever to watch one college basketball game."

Alcindor had suffered all week with a scratched eyeball that had been serious enough for his admittance to the Jules Stein Eye Clinic at UCLA, where he was confined to a darkened room, wearing an eye patch, while undergoing treatment. The doctors were unsure when he would be able to play, although few, if any, doubted he'd somehow be there for the Houston game.

In Texas, where two years earlier the University of Houston had played before 2,500 fans in a high school gym, the excitement was the greatest ever seen for a sport other than football. The Astrodome was sold out ten days before the event, and when UCLA arrived with a subdued and still-injured Alcindor, fans gawked and followed his every move from the airport to the hotel to practices.

"They seemed surprised to find out," wrote Houston sports columnist Mickey Herskowitz, "that he had two arms, two legs, and lived out of the water."

UCLA was riding the crest of a forty-seven-game winning streak and probably went into the game a slight favorite, despite Alcindor being at less than full strength. But Houston had not only the multi-talented Hayes, it featured a great defensive guard in Don Chaney and a solid center in Ken Spain. As it turned out, the event itself was something less than an artistic success, except for Hayes, who played the game of his life. He rained jump shots from everywhere on that strange, isolated floor, scoring twenty-nine points by half-time. But still, the Cougars were only able to cling to a 46–43 lead.

The suspense continued in the second half, even though Alcindor was clearly not himself, looking passive and anything but overpowering. Lucius Allen, switched to forward, picked up the slack and actually tied the game at 69 on a pretty lay-up, as the explosion from 50,000 people cascaded around the 'Dome. Then Hayes was fouled and sank the two free throws that would be the winning margin when Chaney and guard George Reynolds forced Allen to throw the ball away in the waning seconds. Houston prevailed, 71–69, and UCLA wouldn't go undefeated for Alcindor's three years. The pro-Texas crowd went nuts. But those in the media who knew the real Bruins, with Alcindor healthy and playing his best, realized that if and when these two teams met in a rematch during the NCAA Tournament, UCLA would win convincingly.

In the end, the real winner on this night was college basketball. Sports fans across the country could talk of nothing else for the next couple of weeks, and a game that always had been overshadowed by major league baseball, pro foot-ball, and professional basketball had taken its first significant step to a new level of notoriety.

"I don't think I realized the scope of the event at the time," Abdul-Jabbar says today. "One subtle thing I came to understand, though, was that after that game, all athletic directors in the South realized they had to go after home-grown black talent. Hayes and Chaney were both from the South. I think that game was graphic proof of the failure of the whole segregation thing in sports. Those attitudes died right there."

Meanwhile, in Los Angeles, Wooden was being second-guessed, as if he'd lost the NCAA title instead of his first game in two years. People wondered why he didn't play Edgar Lacey enough and why he stayed with Alcindor for the full twenty minutes of the second half. The coach handled the criticism with his customary class, but those who knew him well could see that he was rankled by the reaction after he'd won the previous forty-seven games in a row.

Eventually, Wooden and his players shook it off and won the remainder of their games leading up to the rematch everyone in college basketball wanted to see. It would come, fittingly enough, at the Los Angeles Sports Arena, in the semifinals of the NCAA Tournament. Houston against UCLA again. Hayes against Alcindor. The Sports Arena was sold out, and the game, not televised in Los Angeles, was shown on six closed-circuit locations throughout Southern California. This undoubtedly would be another game for the ages, right? Uh, not exactly.

In a game the Bruins' coach geared up for probably more than any other in his career, UCLA played the finest first half of the Wooden Era at UCLA, executing in textbook style, frustrating Hayes with a diamond-and-one defense, intimidating the Cougars with its press, causing turnover after turnover, and forcing Houston coach Guy Lewis to practically swallow the polka-dot towel on which he was always chewing. The lead bloated to forty-four points in the second half, and the final score was 101–69.

"I certainly think we enjoyed that game more than any we ever played," Abdul-Jabbar says. "It points out a lot of Coach Wooden's success. The way he got five guys to react instantly to a big-game situation."

All these years later, even Wooden gloats about that game. "I knew we were going to whip them," he says. "It's not an ego thing. I just had no doubt with Lewis healthy, I thought we'd beat them. I didn't think it would be like that, but I knew we'd win. If Lewis was healthy, we'd have beaten them not just nine of ten games, but ten of ten." Few people even remember that UCLA drubbed North Carolina, 78–55, in the Finals to wrap up Wooden's fourth national championship.

If Alcindor's junior season was about redemption, his senior year was about fulfillment. With the clever Warren at guard, the 1968 team was probably the best of the Alcindor Era. But the 1969 team was not too bad, either.

"I think the '68 team was better than the '67 team," Wooden says, "but the '69 team was pretty good. We had some very good players who never got enough recognition. Take Kenny Heitz. He was a forward as a sophomore, a sixth man as a junior, and then a starting guard as a senior. Then we had Curtis Rowe starting as a sophomore and Sidney Wicks, who was very talented but was still learning how to play, coming off the bench."

What they didn't have was a backcourt player who could be a leader. With Lucius Allen gone, the Bruins had to use a point guard by committee, and that made some games more tenuous than others.

Again, the most controversial moments in Alcindor's senior season involved USC. As a coach almost obsessed with beating the Bruins, Bob Boyd again ordered his team into stall tactics and almost won the first of the two-game weekend set before losing, 61–55, in double overtime at the Sports Arena. The next night, amid the boos reverberating back at the Bruins' homecourt at Pauley, the Trojans played it the same way, and this time an unflappable senior named Ernie Powell hit a last-second shot to win the game, 46–44. It was UCLA's first loss at Pauley Pavilion, its first defeat in forty-one games dating back to the first Houston game the previous year. It was also Boyd's first victory over Wooden. Again, the ethics of playing "Stall Ball" crept into the newspaper headlines the following week, but when a team has to face someone like Alcindor, what else is a coach to do?

Wooden reiterated that the slowdown style was bad for the game. Years later, however, he would smile and admit, "I have always felt Bob was a fine basketball coach, and I probably would have tried something similar under the same circumstances."

Once the debate from that game faded, UCLA resumed its winning ways, and slowly the pressure began to build for Alcindor and this team that would still be deemed a disappointment unless it finished its task and captured its third straight NCAA title. Making it to the tournament was a foregone conclusion. Most of the speculation was that Purdue, with its great All-America shooter Rick Mount, would provide the only real competition. But in the semifinals, an amazingly quick upstart team from Drake almost spoiled the whole party.

"Quick teams gave us the most trouble that year," Wooden says, "and Drake was very quick. They gave us a good scare."

You could even say Drake gave UCLA the "Willies," considering that the Bulldogs' two best players were Willie McCarter and Willie Wise. John Vallely, a blond guard from Orange County who could have passed for a beach life-guard, was UCLA's finest outside shooter, and he poured in twenty-nine points that game to go with Alcindor's twenty-five and the Bruins somehow survived, 85–82.

That set up the final and another of those rematches. Purdue had almost upset UCLA in the season opener, and now the Boilermakers were back, led by Mount, one of the finest pure shooters in the history of college basketball. When Mount hit a shot, the ball didn't just float through the hoop, it *whooshed* through, which is probably why they called him "Rick the Rocket." But as excited as the Purdue rooters were, they failed to realize that this was the cul-mination for Alcindor. This was an evening when all his pent-up emotions, all the pressures he'd overcome, would be released in a torrent of brilliant basket-ball. He scored more points in other games and rebounded better in some, but never in his three wondrous years as a collegian was he as animated as he was on this night. A young beat writer for the *Los Angeles Herald-Examiner* named Bisheff wrote it this way in his game story:

> LOUISVILLE—The elderly gentleman broke into a big grin as he moved into his seat in the middle of the UCLA band and proudly began playing first trombone.
>
> He looked a little out of place at first, but forty minutes later, you could hardly blame Ferdinand Lewis Alcindor Sr. for blowing his own horn a little.
>
> He had just finished watching his son make col-lege basketball history by culminating a fabulous career with what may have been his greatest all-around performance yet.
>
> Lew Alcindor, the young man who had dominated the game like no one ever before, scored 37 points, snapped up 20 rebounds and played splendid defense, to swallow up Rick Mount and Purdue, 92-72, in the finals of the NCAA Tournament Saturday.
>
> And while Alcindor was scoring 20 points in the first 15 minutes, Kenny Heitz was completely shut-ting off Rick Mount, Purdue's super shooter.
>
> Rick the Rocket popped in his first two jumpers,

```
but then something went wrong at mission control.
The rockets began missing their targets. With Heitz
tracking him closer than one of those ABM missiles
and Lew sagging off his man to help out, Mount pro-
ceeded to miss his next 14 shots, and the
Boilermakers were dead.
```

So it was that the Alcindor Era would finish with an 88–2 record, with the only two losses coming by a total of three points, one of them on a night when the great center was nowhere near his physical best. "Lewis," as Wooden called him, not only is the lone center to lead his team to three consecutive NCAA crowns, he was the MVP of all three postseason tournaments in a career most basketball people think qualifies him as the greatest player in college history. Thirty-five years later, it is still difficult to argue with that assessment.

THE POST-LEW YEARS

The true measure of John Wooden's ability as a coach isn't so much what he achieved with the Alcindors and Waltons as it is what he achieved without them. After five national championships in a startling six-year run, UCLA's reign was expected to end with the departure of Alcindor, who became the No. 1 overall pick in the NBA draft by the Milwaukee Bucks.

"No way they can win again without the big guy," coaches sneered.

But Wooden found a way. As much as he savored his success as the new dominant coach in the sport, what he really loved was surprising people with teams that weren't expected to win. It wasn't that UCLA figured to be bad. It's just that nobody thought the Bruins could win again without an overpowering force in the middle.

"I always call that team the team without," Wooden said. "People say, 'Without what?' And I say, 'No, without *whom*.'" The coach smiles and reiterates that the 1970 team was one of his three favorites, along with the 1964 first-time champs and the 1975 final-year champions.

"I remember I had to discipline Sidney Wicks for something before the season actually began, and he finally came to my office later and said he was sorry. I said, 'That's OK, Sidney, just go out tomorrow and be good.' Sidney gave me that big smile of his and said, 'You bet, Coach. We're going to show them we can play without the big guy.'"

They did show them, too. Wicks, Curtis Rowe, and an underrated center named Steve Patterson formed a terrific, well-balanced front line. Wicks was the most spectacular of the group, a devastating talent who needed to harness his game that first year on campus. "But once he did," says Wooden, "he became the finest forward in college basketball his last two years."

Rowe wasn't far behind. Not as flashy, he was more polished and steady—the kind of fundamentally sound player Wooden loved. Patterson, at six feet nine, was not Alcindor, but he was a banger inside who had enough of an outside touch to allow Wooden to return to the high-post offense he preferred. His new backcourt featured the returning Vallely and Henry Bibby, the current head coach at USC, who arrived from North Carolina to develop into an extraordinary two-way player.

The motivation for this group was simple. As much as they might have tried to deny it previously, they had been overshadowed by Alcindor. The three previous national titles were his. He received all the credit, along with Wooden. And while everyone acknowledged the big guy's ability, they ached to prove they could play—and win—without him. They might not go undefeated, they figured, but they wouldn't lose nearly as many games as basketball people were projecting.

At the end of the season, a remarkable 29–2 record demonstrated they were right. Just in case there were still doubters, Wicks and the Bruins settled the issue once and for all by crushing a much more touted Jacksonville team, with "the new Alcindor," Artis Gilmore, at center, in the NCAA Finals. Wicks, about five inches smaller than Gilmore, asked to play him early in the game, then proceeded to block five of the towering center's shots, single-handedly taking over the game and leading the Bruins to their fourth consecutive national championship and their sixth in seven years. "We had a great year that season," Wooden says, "and winning four in a row was very satisfying."

At UCLA, of course, even four in a row isn't enough. So the Bruins went for five in 1971. "That was the year Steve Patterson really took over as a great high-post player for us," Wooden says. "By the time he was finished, he probably was the second-best high-post player I'd ever had. Willie Naulls, back in the 1950s, was the best. Patterson always wanted to play the low post, but I said no, no. You've got to get the ball to them before they get the shots. That proved to be one of our better balanced teams. Bibby had become a great outside shooter and very good defensively, probably one of the finest defenders I ever had."

Although that team didn't have an overpowering post presence, it rattled off fourteen victories in a row before Notre Dame's Austin Carr scored forty-six points to beat the Bruins, 89–82, in South Bend. If some on the team were inconsolable after the dream of another perfect season had been shattered, Wooden was not. A loss, particularly a non-conference loss, in the early or mid-part of a schedule rarely bothered him. When none of his players happened to be close by, the coach would even confide that a defeat sometimes could help a team. It could jar it a bit and, in the case of a group trying to maintain an unbeaten streak, maybe take some pressure off.

Most of the pressure that season manifested close to home, where USC had meshed into the finest team of the Bob Boyd era. For much of the year, the Bruins and the undefeated Trojans were ranked 1–2 in the national polls. Since only one team from each conference could go to the NCAA Tournament in 1971, the pressure slowly built to tremendous proportions as the season progressed.

COURTESY OF UCLA ATHLETIC DEPARTMENT

Steve Patterson was UCLA's forgotten center. Wedged between the Alcindor and Walton years, Patterson nonetheless was a pivotal player in two different national championship runs for the Bruins.

Ask Wooden which, of all the players he recruited through the years, he was most sorry to lose to another school, and he never hesitates. "Paul Westphal," he says. A big fan of the fluid guard who grew up in Southern California, just ten or fifteen miles from the UCLA campus, Wooden had worked hard to recruit him and thought he'd won the battle. "He told me on a Saturday he was coming to UCLA," Wooden says. "I was just elated. Then he called back on Monday to say he was going to USC."

Westphal arrived in downtown Los Angeles at the right time. Boyd had an All-America center in Ron Riley and another outstanding guard in Mo Layton. The Trojans had blitzed everybody on their schedule but UCLA, losing to the Bruins, 64–61, in their first conference meeting, setting up a climactic battle for the conference title and the NCAA Tournament bid in the final game of the regular season.

For much of that game, USC looked like the superior team, especially when it sprinted ahead, 59–50, with nine minutes to play. Boyd, who'd waited his whole career to beat a Wooden team in a high-stakes game, looked flushed, and his assistant coaches, especially spindly Jim Heffner, were as emotional as they'd ever been during the rivalry. This was their moment. This was their time, they thought.

But what made Wooden's UCLA teams so extraordinary through those prime years was not only their physical ability, but their mental flexibility. Under pressure, they always seemed to play better than their opponent, and this proved to be a disheartening example of that for USC. Whatever flow and momentum Boyd's team had built dissipated in the heat of those excruciating final minutes. The Trojans failed to score a field goal and squeezed out only one more point in the final nine and a half minutes as UCLA, with Wicks flashing not only his muscles but that intimidating glare of his, came back to win, 73–62.

"I was very sorry to lose Paul Westphal," Wooden would say years later. "But he never did beat us, so I guess it turned out all right."

The NCAA Tournament that year also turned out all right, as UCLA, relying on what now seemed like inexorable fate, barely escaped Jerry Tarkanian's gritty Long Beach State team, 57–55, in the regionals at Salt Lake City.

"I still don't know how we lost that game," Tarkanian said, only recently. "I swear I thought we had it won, but somehow Wooden's teams always found a way."

The Bruins found a way again in the Final Four, first defeating Kansas, 68–60, then beating Villanova, 68–62, in Patterson's finest hour. The center who had played in the shadows of the two great players before him scored twenty-nine points to lead UCLA to its biggest victory of yet another memorable championship season. The title count now reached five in a row and seven out of eight. Like the Yankees and the Celtics in the midst of their great championship runs, the Bruins now had their enemies, some jealous and others just tired of their dominance. "Come on, it has to end sometime soon," the detractors were muttering not long after that victory over Villanova. "It has to. Doesn't it?"

It certainly seemed that way, until somebody mentioned a young, red-headed sophomore-to-be named Bill Walton.

J. D. Morgan's Reign of Power, Success, and Controversy

Some considerate it UCLA's great fortune that John Wooden and J. D. Morgan were working partners, forming a confluence of skill and power perhaps unmatched in collegiate athletics before or since. Wooden, the great coach, and Morgan, the commandingly effective athletic director, oversaw the dynasty that would become Bruins basketball with a relationship that was both unique and often controversial.

If Wooden was more professorial, Morgan was more fiery. A stout, combative man who conducted business the way he must have played football, basketball, and tennis growing up in Oklahoma, Morgan was a four-year letterman in tennis at UCLA before taking over as head coach of the Bruins' tennis team and leading it to seven national championships. In 1963, not coincidentally a year before Wooden's first national championship season, he was named the university's new athletic director. Perhaps more than any other athletic department head in recent memory, J. D. had an almost seething desire to win. His florid features would turn beet red in the heat of a big UCLA game, and his voice—booming and pontifical—could often be heard barking at an official, even above the raucous crowds.

Morgan was a shrewd, if somewhat tyrannical businessman who could work a back room at NCAA Conventions better than most politicians at a Democratic or Republican convention.

"J. D. was a remarkable guy," says Pete Newell, who was athletic director at the University of California in Morgan's early years. "He was a real operator. He's the best athletic director the school ever had, but he could break every darn rule in the book. He was able to get more for UCLA than any athletic director in the history of any school.

"I remember back then that we used to exchange scholarship lists, and one day I'm looking at UCLA's and I realize (Lew) Alcindor isn't on the list. Well, I call J. D. and I ask him, 'Where's Alcindor on this list, J. D.?' He tells me, in that unmistakable voice of his, 'Well, Pete, Alcindor was able to get a summer job that paid him much more than he received for his scholarship. So we didn't have to put him on the list.' I couldn't believe it. Later on, someone told me what his great summer job really was. Supposedly, he carried a big can of film to New York and back. I'm telling you, J. D. was a piece of work.

"You had to admire what he got done, though. Look at all the regionals he got for UCLA. They didn't just play them there by accident. J. D. somehow convinced the powers-that-be to do it. No one really knew how he did it, but he did. I don't know how J. D. would have operated at, say, Yale, or some place like that. But I'll tell you this much: He was sure a smart guy."

Morgan loved controversies. He would jump into them with both of his ruddy cheeks puffed and attack them full force. The more controversial an issue, the more he seemed to like it. Once, while covering the team for the *Los Angeles Herald-Examiner*, I wrote a story noting how strong of a home court advantage UCLA had at Pauley Pavilion, describing it as one of college basketball's new "pits," as far as opposing teams were concerned. Certainly, the facts seemed to back up my theory, considering it had been a couple of years and the Bruins hadn't lost a game there yet.

At the weekly Los Angeles Basketball Writers luncheon, a few days after my story appeared, Morgan walked into the room with huge roles of architectural schematics of every arena in UCLA's conference. He rolled out his proof on a table, called me over and carefully pointed out how much closer the fans sat at other arenas compared to their distance from the floor at Pauley. He didn't have any precise figures concerning noise levels, and as strongly as he argued, he failed to convince me that my story was wrong. But even then, you had to admire his effort. The man would have made a great lawyer.

"J. D. recognized what Coach Wooden wanted to do and let him do it," says Steve Aranoff, who closely observed the machinations of the program as a team manager in the early 1960s. "If there was any controversy, J. D. got involved in it, trying to take the pressure off Wooden. Of course, sometimes he did overstep his bounds.

"I remember once when Coach benched a couple of his stars for disciplinary reasons, J. D. was livid. He thought the people who paid to get into the games came to see the stars, and when Coach didn't put the players in the game in the first half, he was angry. He went to Denny Crum [the assistant coach] at halftime and told him, 'You get in there [the locker room] and tell him what the people came here for. Tell him to get those players in there now.' Having overheard the conversation, I waited until after the game and went over to Denny, asking him what he told Coach Wooden. 'Are you kidding?' he said. 'I didn't tell him a thing.'"

This is not to say that Morgan didn't get his way on other occasions. The reason UCLA played Houston in the Astrodome in 1968 was because of his conviction that it would be good both for the Bruins' program and the sport of college basketball. Wooden didn't think so and actually argued the case with J. D. But as he looks back on it now, he realizes he was wrong. "We made a lot of money for the university, and the sport got more exposure than I could have imagined from the telecast," Wooden says.

As a member of the NCAA Basketball Tournament Committee, Morgan helped negotiate a lasting commitment from NBC. He also helped a company known as Television Sports Network, or TVS, get started.

Morgan was more aggressive than his predecessor, Wilbur Johns. He fought for the athletes, trying to give them the best conditions possible. Wooden often talks about how J. D. somehow convinced university officials to allow his team to fly first class and how much that helped recruiting.

"He was very good at what he did," says Wooden, who admired Morgan's ability to stay in touch with all athletes and programs at UCLA. "We never had any problems."

Well, almost never. In the midst of the basketball dynasty, Morgan made every road trip and, early on, sat on the team bench next to Wooden at all games. No one ever accused J. D. of not having an ego, and his critics thought he loved the idea of being coupled publicly with the greatest coach of the modern era. Wooden wasn't enamored with the ploy, although he never would admit it, even to this day. But if you knew him and could read his body language, it wasn't too difficult to figure out. What coach would like to have his athletic director breathing hard next to him in the pressure of big games?

J. D. didn't just sit there, either. He would let his opinions be known, especially toward officials, with whom he rarely agreed. Coaches on other teams began to get angry over the situation, and after a couple of seasons, they gathered at a league meeting with university presidents and began the process that removed athletic directors from the bench during games.

As legend has it, immediately after the final vote was taken at a hotel, a couple of coaches were in the men's room, discussing it. "J. D. is going to s—— when he hears what we've done," one said to the other. Just then, a loud flushing noise was heard from one of the nearby cubicles, followed by the unmistakable tones of that familiar booming voice. "Gentlemen," J. D. reportedly said, "that's precisely what I'm doing now."

Morgan and Wooden didn't always agree on scheduling, either. The coach liked to play his share of difficult games before the conference season started, helping his team to get accustomed to strong competition.

Morgan preferred home games against weaker teams to: a) fatten UCLA's win-loss record, and b) rake in the cash, since games at Pauley Pavilion were sold out in that era, regardless of the competition. In the end, Morgan won more often, which explains why the list of opponents traveling to Westwood during that time included Tulsa, San Jose State, The Citadel, and West Virginia, among others.

Then, there was the infamous Sam Gilbert situation, detailed at length in another section of this book. Suffice to say, the coach and the athletic director were not on the same wavelength when it came to the program's most influential and controversial booster.

But for any disagreements they might have had through the years, Wooden and Morgan always maintained a relationship of genuine respect, each knowing that the other was only trying to help in the overall scheme of UCLA athletics. Would they have been close friends or associates if they hadn't landed together in the university athletic department? Probably not. But with each compromising in his own way, the two forged what proved to be one of the most unforgettable partnerships in the history of the sport.

When Wooden retired in 1975, it was generally felt that he wanted his top assistant, Crum, who would later go on to become a Hall of Fame coach at Louisville, to succeed him at UCLA. But not everyone close to Wooden agreed, especially because Crum had recently undergone a divorce. Besides, all the power now belonged to Morgan, and he was determined to handpick his own man for the job.

So, against the feelings of most Bruin alums and boosters, J. D. selected Gene Bartow, the low-profile coach from Illinois by way of Memphis State, who actually posted a more than creditable 52–9 record with a pair of conference titles during two brief seasons in Westwood before leaving amid complaints that the pressure to succeed Wooden was too over-whelming. If failing to select Crum was a mistake, J. D. never would admit it. He clasped his strong hands around the throat of the program at that point, and he was going to run it his way.

It remained that way for five more years, or until Morgan, who had undergone heart surgery two years earlier, retired June 30, 1980.

He died December 16, 1980, at the age of sixty-one.

The Walton Gang

The year was 1971, and a bunch of writers were sitting around the sports department of the now-defunct *Los Angeles Herald-Examiner*, a beloved, old newspaper many of us will always miss. A couple of my colleagues who were not exactly UCLA admirers were talking about the basketball program and how tired they were of watching the Bruins win every year. "At least this will be it," one of them, a strong USC supporter, said. "Yeah, after [Sidney] Wicks and [Curtis] Rowe leave, that dang dynasty of theirs finally will be over," said another.

As it happened, I had just covered a game the previous night that was preceded by a match featuring the UCLA freshmen. "I don't know how to break it to you guys," I said, "but I just saw this kid Walton play for the Bruin freshmen last night. And you're wrong, it's not over. In some ways, this guy Walton might be even more talented than Alcindor was."

The guffaws that statement generated from my sportswriting friends could be heard all the way into the *Herald* City Room. "Come on, nobody could be better than Alcindor was," one buddy said. "Besides," said the other, "I hear this Walton kid is just some skinny redhead. How good could he really be?"

They and everyone else found out a year later. In style, Walton was almost the polar opposite of Alcindor. Lew operated in an emotional shell, rarely demonstrating any of his feelings, coldly putting opponents away, sort of like a tall, skinny hit man for the Mafia. Bill played the game with an unrestrained joy, often smiling and laughing as he led his teammates to one overpowering performance after another, similar to an oversized kid having the time of his life on a playground. But if their personalities were different, their skill levels were eerily similar. If Walton didn't have the breathtaking agility of Big Lew, he certainly moved well enough. He was also a better natural rebounder, a superior passer, and a more effective shot blocker. Nobody will ever be as devastating an offensive force as Alcindor. But even he wasn't as gifted all around as Walton.

"I knew as soon as I saw Walton as a freshman that he would be a superstar," John Wooden says. "He loved the game so much."

What Wooden couldn't know at the time is that with the new superstar would come a new era and, yes, new problems. While Walton was whetting the never-satiated appetites of Bruin alums and boosters, young men his age were beginning to die at an alarming rate in Southeast Asia. Crowds were forming in the biggest cities in America, holding anti-war signs and shouting for the government to get out of Vietnam. Watergate wouldn't creep into the picture until later in Walton's career, but the seeds of turmoil were sprouting everywhere, and young, bright kids like the tall, skinny, redhead at UCLA were not only taking notice, they were actively participating.

"Bill was very much anti-establishment," Wooden says. "He was always protesting something. He took over an administration building, stopped classes, even laid down on Wilshire Boulevard and got arrested once. Every year I told my players that I didn't care about their political feelings or religion. When you believe in something, you should stand up for it. But I said that I did ask one thing of them: Always stay open-minded and listen to the other person."

Little did Wooden realize at the time that the one who would have to be the most open-minded during Bill Walton's three years on the varsity was the head coach. The bespectacled little man with old-fashioned midwestern roots would have to bend and be flexible enough to understand the anger and confusion espoused by a new generation that was watching teenagers get drafted and then killed fighting a war most of them didn't believe in.

Happily for Walton, he was as passionate about basketball as he was about protesting or listening to Grateful Dead records. The freshman class that became sophomores in 1972 included Keith Wilkes, a quiet, studious minister's son from Santa Barbara, California, who was as smooth as he was thin and a brilliant, if somewhat unorthodox, jump shooter. The point guard was Greg Lee, a good-looking honor student who had come with glowing press clippings from nearby Reseda High in the San Fernando Valley. He was as slick as he was cocky, and he quickly became Walton's closest friend on the team, which proved to be both good and bad at times.

The other newcomer was Tommy Curtis, still another rail-thin, quick-moving guard with an infectious smile who was the first black basketball player at his high school in Tallahassee, Florida. They were joined by junior Larry Hollyfield, a prep legend of sorts at Compton High before pausing at Compton College to improve his grades en route to UCLA. Hollyfield had "game," the kids all said. He was the

COURTESY OF UCLA ATHLETIC DEPARTMENT

The leader of the Walton Gang goes up for a rebound. Bill Walton quickly became a star whose UCLA teams raced to two undefeated seasons in his first two years on the varsity.

kind of flashy, one-on-one player who usually didn't fit into the Wooden system, but he had so much ability, even the Bruins couldn't turn him down.

Another junior, Swen Nater was also on this team, a six-foot-eleven late-bloomer who probably could have started at center for almost any other team in the country. Nater made the United States Olympic Team in 1972, but he never could crack UCLA's starting lineup, not with Walton in front of him.

What this young team needed most was an on-court leader, and it had one in Henry Bibby, the senior who already had started on two national championship teams. Now the head coach at UCLA's fiercest rival, USC, Bibby was as tenacious then as he is today, specializing in intimidating defense, besides being the owner of one of the more accurate jump shots in the Wooden Era. Bibby was the veteran the kids on this team relied on, the one who was always there to show them the way.

But even that year, even when the tall, curly-haired redhead was just a sophomore, it was his team. Soon enough, it was labeled as such. "The Walton Gang," they called it, and for two brilliant seasons, this dominant center and his buddies might have played the purest, most impressive basketball ever witnessed at UCLA. It started in 1972, when they scored 100 points in their first seven games and never looked back.

"I can't tell you how much fun it was to play that kind of basketball," Walton says.

It was the kind he'd watched as a high school prospect in San Diego. It was beautifully selfless basketball, with the sophomore who was already the best player in the country operating from the high post, waiting for defenders to crowd around him before finding his open teammates. A ferocious rebounder, Walton's blur-like outlet passes allowed UCLA to return to the fast break Wooden originally made famous in Westwood, with sleek athletes like Wilkes, Hollyfield, and another good-looking sub, Larry Farmer, racing the floor to make spectacular finishes. Lee and Walton, the two inseparable friends, could be an unstoppable combination on the floor. Lee was an expert at the lob pass, often setting up Walton for easy, high-percentage baskets. The big redhead would, in turn, prove adept at executing the give-and-go pass, allowing Lee to get his share of lay-ups.

The victories started to mount, from ten in a row, to twenty, and eventually to thirty, a perfect 30–0 season, with only one team ever creeping as close as six points at the end of a game. It wasn't until the NCAA title game against Florida State—the closest Final in the Wooden Era—that the Bruins had to sweat. They uncharacteristically turned the ball over and played generally sloppily, with Walton in foul trouble. But in the end, their poise and experience carried them to a 81–76 victory and a sixth consecutive national championship for their coach.

Afterward, Walton and a couple of his teammates appeared testy and unhappy in the interview sessions, as if it weren't enough to capture the NCAA title. At that point, at UCLA, you not only had to win it, you had to come away as a dominating presence. Wooden and Bibby tried to intervene and smooth over some of Walton's remarks, but the media and public reaction was beginning to build against both the controversial young center and this team that seemingly couldn't be beat.

Since everybody except Bibby was back, the beat went on the following season, aided by some new additions. Dave Meyers was an aggressive power forward off the bench, while Ralph Drollinger, another tall center from San Diego, arrived to make the Bruins three deep in the post. Hollyfield and Farmer both took on bigger roles, but it was still the foursome who came up together—Walton, Wilkes, Lee and Curtis—who did most of the damage.

"When we were at our peak that year," Wooden says, "I think we were playing as well as any of my teams."

The winning streak no one had noticed for a while was now growing to epic proportions. It reached sixty consecutive games when the Bruins defeated Loyola of Chicago, 87–53, to tie the NCAA record set by Bill Russell's USF teams. But that mark was soon left in the blue and gold dust, with the Walton Gang kicking it into yet a higher gear. They won twenty-three of twenty-six regular-season games by ten points or more, and before one 30–0 season officially begat another, Walton topped it off with the signature game of his UCLA career, making twenty-one of twenty-two shots and scoring forty-four points in the NCAA championship final against Memphis State. It was a performance that is still regarded as the finest in the tradition-rich history of the NCAA Tournament, where the Jordans, Birds, Chamberlains, and Magic Johnsons all have played.

Considering that Walton was the subject of season-long rumors concerning the possibility he might take a multi-million dollar offer from the NBA or the fledgling ABA, it was not surprising that Wooden approached him after his spectacular display against Memphis State. He wanted to know if Walton was staying at UCLA.

Walton recalls asking the coach, "Are *you* coming back?" To which Wooden responded, "Why, yes, Bill. I promised all of you that I'd be there for the completion of your college careers."

Walton said that was good enough for him. "If you're back, I'm back, too," he said.

Typically, Wooden felt it would only be right to inform the representatives from the NBA and ABA who were at the NCAA Finals about Walton's decision. "I wasn't too thrilled with that idea, but I went along," Walton says.

They all met in the suite Walton was given after he'd complained to Athletic Director J. D. Morgan that his hotel room was too small and noisy. After the NBA and ABA people presented their offers, waving more money than most people would see in their lifetimes, Walton, who had already made up his mind to remain in college, smiled and waved his arms at his unusual sumptuous surroundings. "How could you possibly make my life any better than what UCLA does for me?" he asked.

Life is indeed good when you've helped your school reach a record seventy-five consecutive basketball victories (the total includes fifteen wins posted before Walton and company joined the varsity), which is where things stood after two seasons.

"You know what was funny?" says Lee. "We were blissfully ignorant about how many consecutive games we had won."

If the players were blissful, the public and the media were not. "What John Wooden has done to college basketball is wreck it," wrote Georg Meyers of the *Seattle Times* in 1973. "What used to be a tingling spectacle has become when the Bruins are in town—any town—like feeding time at the zoo. You don't really expect the boar to bite back at the lion, but there is a certain fascination in watching him crick it with his jaws." Glenn Dickey of the *San Francisco Chronicle* wrote: "It's a sad thing what has happened to college basketball. UCLA makes everybody else play for second place." L. H. Gregory of the *Portland Oregonian* put it this way: "Gets rather monotonous, doesn't it? UCLA week after week, month after month, season after season, winning every basketball game it plays."

Not everyone was angry. There were some basketball purists who were awed by what was happening. "They are like Muhammad Ali with a sparring partner," said George Raveling, who was Washington State's coach at the time. "They are probably the best college basketball team ever to play the game. UCLA is like an IBM computer. You just punch out W-I-N, and that's what they do."

Many opponents sounded defeated before they started. "Having to play UCLA," said Abe Lemons, the quick-witted Oklahoma State coach, "is like having to think about buying a cemetery plot." Washington coach Marv Harshman, who had to play the Bruins at least twice every season, said, "It's like watching a hanging. You don't really want to see it, but it's so intriguing."

It was into this increasingly antagonistic atmosphere that the Walton Gang moved into its final season. The winning streak had reached seventy-five games heading into that 1973-74 schedule, and not surprisingly, some of the players began to feel they couldn't lose. "I think we'd begun to believe in our own invincibility," says Wilkes.

That's not all they began to believe. This was the early 1970s, when Haight-Asbury was overflowing with flower children, when college kids everywhere were into new drugs and free love.

"We had a lot of the guys on the team experimenting," says Wilkes, who wasn't one of them. "We had guys into vegetarianism and transcendentalism. Bill was into all the political stuff, and he always pushed the envelope. Because he was so out front, there were a lot of people in his ear. Looking back now, I marvel at how Wooden, this little guy from Martinsville, dealt with all of it."

The pressure had begun to build to such epic proportions that it was affecting

COURTESY OF UCLA ATHLETIC DEPARTMENT

Bill Walton goes into the stratosphere to block a shot. Wooden still describes Walton as the best all-around basketball player he ever coached. One reason was his timing on defense.

everyone, even Wooden. To friends and some writers, the coach quietly confided, as he had during the Alcindor era, that it had reached a point where he felt less like he was trying to win and more like he was trying not to lose. He was proud of the streak, but you almost had the sense that he wouldn't mind losing somewhere along the way, just to take some of the heat off him and his players.

He didn't have to wait long. On a cold January day in South Bend, Indiana, in front of what might have been the loudest, most raucous crowd in Notre Dame basketball history, the streak that had reached a mind-blowing eighty-eight consecutive victories was finally snapped in a pulsating 71–70 upset by the Irish. "We had an eleven-point lead at one point in that game and still lost," says Wooden.

But that wasn't the most devastating loss of the '74 season. That would come later, in the NCAA semifinals against David Thompson and North Carolina State, in a game Wooden still calls the most painful of his UCLA career.

"Perhaps we got a little overconfident that year," he says. "I blame myself for part of it. We began thinking that no matter how far behind we got, we could come back. Against North Carolina State, we had a nine-point lead at one point in the second half and a seven-point lead late in the first overtime." Still, the Bruins lost, 80–77 in double overtime.

"March 23, 1974, the darkest day of my life," Walton says. "It was horrible. We never should have lost to that team."

Later, in reflecting on the game, Walton, who finished with twenty-nine points and eighteen rebounds, said the turning point came in the second half. "Everything changed when they went to a slowdown offense," he says. "It was good strategy at the time. Obviously, Coach [Norm] Sloan had done his homework on our team, knowing we didn't play well in a slowdown game or with the lead. We lost interest. We lost momentum. It just . . . the fun wasn't there. Even though we were playing for the championship. When State slowed the ball down, we said, 'What is going on here?' But to take nothing away from David Thompson and State's fine team, we beat ourselves that day. I have unbelievable memories of little short shots I had over the top of Tommy Burleson that just rolled off the rim. I tell you, I would love to be able to take those shots one more time."

He wasn't the only one having trouble making baskets. Several of the Bruins, including Lee, took outside shots when UCLA was still leading, shots that would come back to haunt them through the years. "Yeah, I think we'd all like to play that one over," Lee says. Wooden, too, has confided many times that he would "do some things differently" if he could play that game again.

"Our locker room was very somber afterwards," Walton says. "There were some tears from some of the young guys, but Coach Wooden would have none of that. He would tell us, 'No excessive celebration or jubilation with victory and no excessive depression with defeat.' He had created an atmosphere in which, from the day you got there, you expected to win the title. You expected to go undefeated, to be king at the end, and this was the first time we had lost in the playoffs in my years at UCLA. It was very, very bitter. It still is to this day."

When Wooden talks about it, you can still see the frustration on his face. "I've always said my last high school game and that [North Carolina State] game are never out of my mind," he says. "In high school, we lost the state championship by one point. We were ahead in the final seconds, and the other team tried to take a timeout and didn't have one. They got a technical foul, and we tried to refuse to keep possession. I shot the free throw and missed it. Here I was, supposed to be the best free-throw shooter in the state, too. Well, then we had a center jump, and their center got the ball and threw up a half-court shot that went right through, and we lost by one point. That's why those two games are never out of my mind."

The only sad part is that the Walton Era had to end on such a disappointing note. Alcindor had won three national titles, and Walton wound up with only two. But in many ways, Walton's career was every bit as impressive. He averaged 20.3 points, 15.7 rebounds and shot 65 percent overall. He was a three-time winner of the Naismith Player of the Year award and certainly still ranks among the greatest collegiate centers to play the game. He and Wilkes, both of whom went on to greater heights as professionals, might have been the two finest players Wooden has had on one team, certainly for three years.

And for all the problems Walton might have caused with his political fervor and his strong beliefs off the court, his speech after winning the Naismith the third time tells a lot about the man and how he felt about his coach and his years in Westwood.

"I'm extremely proud and privileged to be a three-time winner," Walton said. "But when you honor an individual in a team sport, it's the team's success that most deserves special recognition. Thanks to Coach John Wooden, our UCLA teams played a beautiful style of basketball that was appealing to watch, not just because we won but because of the way we played. My three Naismith trophies bring back my happiest memories of my days at UCLA."

The Sam Gilbert Debate

The one blot on the otherwise pristine résumé of John Wooden always has revolved around the late Sam Gilbert, a Los Angeles contractor and controversial UCLA booster with tentacles that reached far beyond the borders of the coach's office.

Some say Gilbert was an evil that Wooden quietly lived with, trying his best to look the other way. The other view is that Gilbert was forced upon the coach by Athletic Director J. D. Morgan and other members of the athletic department who prevented Wooden from cutting the cord between the omnipresent booster and the players.

Either way, Gilbert was the polar opposite of Wooden. Picture a short, stocky, bald man, a slightly taller Danny DeVito. Gilbert was big city. Wooden was small town. He was wealthy. Wooden's salaries at UCLA were embarrassingly small. Gilbert was worldly. Wooden was the archetypal midwesterner, who thought a big night out was treating the family to ice cream after the game. Talk to former Bruins players now, even the most prominent former players, and they admit that "Sam" took good care of them. "Pappa Sam" is how they addressed him, and he invited players to his home on a regular basis. Sunday morning breakfasts with Sam were wildly popular with most of the players at the time.

In many ways, Gilbert was well-received by the players because, emotionally, he provided them what Wooden couldn't. The coach was the authoritarian, the parent, the disciplinarian. Gilbert, who wasn't there every day, was the relative to whom they could vent, someone who would listen as they aired their complaints. The problem was, he didn't stop there. He gave them gifts, often lavish, expensive gifts, in obvious violation of NCAA rules.

"It was pretty obvious most of the time," says Greg Lee, who played with Bill Walton. "When you'd get on the bus for a road trip and three different players would get on wearing the same expensive coat, it wasn't too hard to figure out where they got them." Some said Gilbert paid for abortions of players' girlfriends. Others hinted he even paid for cars.

It was well known that Gilbert negotiated Lew Alcindor's $1.4 million contract, a huge deal at the time, when he entered the NBA, reportedly without asking for any kind of fee. He reportedly did likewise for Sidney Wicks, Lucius Allen, Curtis Rowe, and Steve Patterson, among others. He was like the rich uncle they all seemed to enjoy being around, whether he was opening his wallet or his heart, or in many cases, both. Even today, most of the players speak well of him.

"Sam, God rest his soul, was very loyal and raised huge amounts for the school," says Walton. "I have not a bad word to say about Sam Gilbert. I went to Sam's house on Sunday mornings or on Thanksgiving, but Coach Wooden never had any part of that. Wooden never talked about Gilbert. I don't think he was involved with him in any way."

Eddie Sheldrake, who starred on Wooden's first team at UCLA, has remained close to the program ever since. He, like most everyone around the team, knew about Gilbert.

"To the best of my knowledge, Sam Gilbert didn't recruit anybody," Sheldrake says. "I know when Jerry Norman was there [as an assistant coach], he tried to keep him away. But when some of the kids grew famous, it became harder to do."

Wicks, who played in the years when Gilbert seemed most prominent, talks about him openly. "Sam was a great guy," Wicks says. "He had only the players in his heart. He didn't do anything for any other reason. Everything he did, he did to help the players. As far as I'm concerned, he did nothing illegal. I went to his house a couple of times, yeah." Most of the prominent players went more than a couple of times.

Quietly, Gilbert was known as something of a nuisance to many involved with the UCLA basketball program. They said he often would "interfere," pestering players on the road and calling them on the telephone at the wrong time. Others insisted Sam provided something Wooden couldn't or wouldn't. A great coach can't be a player's friend. "That's one thing Coach Wooden never was," says Lee. "He was never your friend."

He didn't want to be. Wooden felt he couldn't be as effective a teacher if he got too close to his players. So, that vacuum often was filled by Gilbert, who wanted desperately to be the players' friend and needed the players to always remind him how much they appreciated it. He would help them find places to live and advise them on their love life. He would be the second father that Wooden couldn't be. Unfortunately, his alliance with the players often became too public, and it shed an ugly light on a program that was widely considered the most successful in the country.

There were, and still are, Sam Gilberts involved in collegiate athletic programs across America. There are probably more than you can count associated with big-time football schools, especially in the South. Most of the time, they get away with what they do. But the fact that this one man was associated with a coach who espoused everything that was good and clean about college sports made many in the industry uncomfortable and some even whisper the ugly word *hypocrite*.

"Come on," says Jerry Tarkanian, the coach who has been under more NCAA scrutiny than anybody else, "everybody knew about Sam. It was a joke, an absolute joke. No question that was all wrong. But Coach Wooden always said he wished Gilbert would stay away. What he did at the time was what any coach would have done. He never spoke to him [Gilbert], and he told him to stay away from the players. It was J. D. [Morgan] who turned his back."

Morgan was a man of far-ranging strength and ego, and on issues away from the actual games, he often overpowered Wooden. "J.D. would ask you your opinion," Wooden says, "but he usually already had his mind made up." Apparently, Morgan's mind was made up about Gilbert. The booster was a huge donor and he made the athletes happy, so Morgan apparently let it go.

Either way, Gilbert was a dark splotch on UCLA's otherwise clean record. In 1987, four days after his death, a Florida grand jury, unaware that he had just died, indicted Gilbert in a drug-money laundering scheme. Even now, there is debate as to how much Wooden could or couldn't do in regard to Gilbert's "affiliation" with the university.

"I never invited Gilbert into the program, never sent him a recruit or a player," Wooden says. "I think Sam meant well. I think he felt what he was doing was right, even if it was against the rules. But I soon realized I could only coach the players. I couldn't baby-sit them."

The Los Angeles Times eventually did a series of stories focusing on Gilbert's involvement with the program. "The man who seems to be the object of the [Times'] allegations was never involved in recruiting in all the time I was there," Wooden reiterates. "The NCAA looked and found nothing significant. I never would have wanted a player who wanted money, and people know that."

Opinions still vary about Gilbert's role, especially among those in the coaching profession who were, and still are, jealous of Wooden's success. It is almost as if they would like to find something, anything, that could take away from his extraordinary achievements. I can only report that I have known and covered John Wooden for some thirty-nine years, and when you've spent as much time as I have around him, it is impossible to think that this man with morals as strong as steel girders would have chosen to have a Sam Gilbert around.

Gilbert's "relationship" with players was never something Wooden requested, but because of the powers above him, it was something the coach had to accept. Could he have threatened to leave if Gilbert wasn't dispatched? Maybe, but Wooden was too loyal and true to UCLA to do that. And whatever else you think, believe this: John Wooden would have been a great basketball coach and won just as many NCAA titles with or without Sam Gilbert.

The Final Season

I t was a season of surprise, a season of shock, but more than anything, John Wooden's final season of coaching began as a huge empty canvas that eventually would be painted with everything he taught and preached and practiced, all coming to life in living, vivid colors.

"Oftentimes," Wooden says, "it is a year when you weren't expected to succeed that gives you the greatest pleasure."

This was one of those years. There was no Alcindor. There was no Walton. There was no Wicks. This was, in many ways, a *Back to the Future* kind of season for Wooden but one that provided the kind of challenge he relished. He never would say it publicly for fear of demeaning the accomplishments of some of his greatest players, but Wooden was always most comfortable as an underdog.

The pressures were gone and so were many of the fetishes that clung to the Walton teams. The tall redhead was such a radical, and many of his teammates were into different eating and meditating habits. This 1974-75 team had none of that. And it had none of the expectations the coach hated. That's why he still describes his first national championship team, the one with no player over six feet five, as his favorite, and why he also includes the 1974-75 group, the one with a solid corps but no dominant star, among the three teams he cherishes most in his twenty-seven years at UCLA.

"We had lost Walton and [Keith] Wilkes, two superstars who had enjoyed great careers at UCLA," Wooden says. "We also lost Greg Lee and Tommy Curtis, two of our better guards. We only had one returning starter, although he was a good one. David Meyers was one of the better players and leaders I had at UCLA." It wasn't like this team lacked talent, though. There was plenty.

Meyers was a ferocious competitor and a fine all-around player. "I appointed three permanent captains in my twenty-seven years at UCLA," Wooden says. "One was Eddie Sheldrake. The second was Mike Warren. Meyers was the third. In each case, it was the only returning starter from the previous team. But that was not enough. Each had to set a good example for the team. Meyers set a wonderful example."

Marques Johnson would go on to become national Player of the Year and be the first recipient of the John R. Wooden Award as a senior. But as a sophomore coming off a major illness, he wasn't yet the confident, overpowering player he would become later in his career. Richard Washington, a senior center, was a solid college player who unfortunately suffered from comparisons to some of the great Bruin big men before him. Andre McCarter and Pete Trgovich arrived in Westwood as two guards with hotshot reputations. Their skills were obvious, and at many schools, each could have been a flashy star in his own right. But at UCLA, they had to tone down their games and learn to play Wooden's more controlled, unselfish kind of basketball. Heading into their senior seasons, neither seemed to have fully grasped that idea, so the struggle continued.

"The big thing I remember," Johnson says, "is that we never had any inkling, none at all, that this would be Coach's last season. He had never given us any hint that he was thinking about retiring. Personally, that season was tough on me, because a couple of days before practice was scheduled to start, I contracted hepatitis. I became violently ill and lost twenty pounds in five days. It was mentally and physically challenging to try to battle my way back from that, and I didn't start for the first few games of the season, because I still wasn't 100 percent healthy. We had a real good group of guys on that team, though, and we were anxious to show we could still win in the Post-Walton Era. Coach never showed that much emotion, but you could tell he was excited by the challenge of trying to win without a dominant player."

Wooden was back to his roots, back to teaching and prodding and shaping kids into winners. McCarter, who came from Walt Hazzard's old school, Overbrook High in Philadelphia, was by all accounts his most difficult student. "Andre, he was a hot dog," Johnson says. "He used the basketball court as a way to express his creativity. Oh, man, Coach would get on Andre so hard, I felt sorry for him. Andre would go between his legs with the ball to complete a pass, and Coach would stop practice and scream, 'Goodness gracious sakes alive, if you do that again you'll never play a minute here.' Coach kept telling him that he was trying to get the street game out of him. The thing was, Coach knew Andre wouldn't quit. He always knew how far he could push you."

Trgovich was another whose game had to be restructured. With his mop-like hair, he bore a physical resemblance to Pete Maravich, and he played a little like the Hall of Fame scorer, as well. He averaged 23.4 points on the freshman team, pumping in forty-seven points in one game. He wanted to shoot first and worry about everything else later. Wooden, of course, didn't let Alcindor or Walton or Wicks play that way, let alone a skinny, six-foot-four guard out of East Chicago, Indiana.

"Pete and I were kind of cool to each other," Johnson says. "I had taken his job as a freshman, so there was

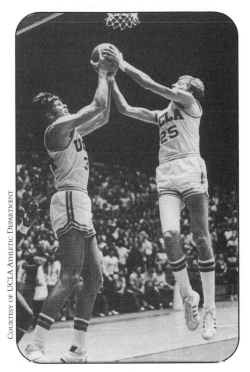

COURTESY OF UCLA ATHLETIC DEPARTMENT

David Meyers (left) and Pete Trgovich, both reaching for this rebound, were major contributors on Wooden's final national championship team that won the title in 1975.

some history there. But what helped Trgovich and McCarter is that they were both really good defensive players. Andre was tall for a guard, especially back then, and Pete was long. They helped make our press effective."

Wooden agrees with much of that analysis. "McCarter and Trgovich, in my opinion, were the best pair of defensive guards I had at UCLA," the coach says. "They were not as great individually, but both were very quick, and Trgovich had long arms. They could make it very tough on opposing guards."

Johnson says that he could see the team improving as the season progressed. "After three years of being constantly berated, it all kind of came together for McCarter. And Richard Washington's maturation was a big key to our improvement, I think. Coach Wooden was the master in knowing when to lean on us and when not to.

"One time early in the year, when I was frustrated because I was still recovering and not starting, I came down on a two-on-one in practice on Ralph Drollinger, and I went up and threw down a dunk on him. Not long after that, Gavin Smith, another player on the team, dunked on him, and Coach got on Gavin real good. But he didn't get on me. It was like he knew what I was going through, how frustrated I was, so he just let me vent. That was the thing with Coach. He knew how to handle each player."

Although this team rattled off twelve victories in a row to open the season, no one thought it was good enough to run the table. There were flaws here, and eventually they would be exposed. It happened first in a road game at Stanford, then in another at Notre Dame, where Wooden and the Bruins already had a history with Digger Phelps and the Irish. Finally, there was another road loss to Washington in late February. After that, though, Wooden got into his late-season mode, and UCLA closed out with three consecutive victories heading into the NCAA Tournament. It was there, in the Western Regionals in Pullman, Washington, that it received its first major scare.

Michigan, another old nemesis, took the Bruins into overtime before losing, 103–91, when Wooden's kids responded the way all his teams always did when under pressure. After Montana was dispatched in another close game in the regional finals, it was on to San Diego and a semifinal game against Louisville that reeked with old blue and gold feelings. Denny Crum, who played for Wooden before serving him as a faithful assistant for many years, was head coach of the sleek, fast-breaking Cardinals, who looked much like the UCLA teams of earlier years.

"Was I concerned about that game? Oh, yeah," Johnson says. "Playing Louisville was like playing a mirror image of ourselves."

It was Crum, trying to coach his way to his first national championship, against Wooden, who was seeking his tenth. Little did anyone realize that, as dramatic as this game looked to be, it would be overshadowed by what immediately followed. The game itself proved to be one of the more nerve-racking of the Wooden Era. Louisville wouldn't go away.

"I recall Junior Bridgeman catching a couple of lobs and scoring easily," Johnson says. "Remember, dunks were illegal back then. But they had some great athletes, and Allen Murphy was a terrific scorer."

The game went into overtime, and in the final moments, it appeared the Cardinals and Crum would prevail. Louisville led by one point with twenty seconds to play, and UCLA's Jim Spillane fouled Terry Howard, who had made twenty-eight of twenty-eight free throws during the season. "That isn't who we wanted to foul," Wooden would admit later.

Eerily, almost as if fate had intervened, Howard failed to convert the front end for his only miss of the year, and the Bruins' Washington made a turn-around jump shot to win the emotional game, 75–74.

But if emotions were running high then, they were about to be spiked even more over the course of the next hour.

"For the first time, after that game, I just didn't feel like going to the room to greet the media," Wooden recalls. "I'd never had a problem with that before, but suddenly I didn't want to go. Right then, I realized that if I feel that way, it was time to get out of this. I decided right then, without anyone else knowing it, that I was going to announce my retirement."

Some of this had to be in the back of his mind before this day. He'd suffered some heart problems the previous season, and his wife, Nellie, who also wasn't well, was whispering in his ear, telling him he should think about leaving. An NCAA Tournament official also had made a disparaging remark about Wooden not allowing reporters into his dressing room, a quote that found its way into all the newspapers, that irked the coach and possibly influenced his decision. Still, to this day, Wooden insists that he didn't make up his mind about retiring until several minutes later in the corridors of the San Diego Sports Arena.

For the first time, this is Wooden's official account of what transpired next:

"I went into our locker room to talk to the players. I told them, 'I congratulate you on a fine game, one of the best games both teams played all year. I'm proud of you. I don't know how you're going to do against Kentucky [in the Finals two nights later], but I think you'll do fine. Whatever happens, no team has ever given my any more pleasure. And that's a nice thing to say about the last team you'll ever coach.'"

Wooden said the locker room went into shocked silence. "Ducky [Drake, the trainer] almost fainted," he says. "Denny [Crum] almost fainted. Frank Arnold [Wooden's assistant] almost fainted. The players immediately looked at each other and were obviously surprised."

Marques Johnson was one of those players. "We were all in the dressing room after the game hugging and celebrating, and then he steps up and drops the bombshell," Johnson recalls. "He said the game Monday would be his last. Obviously, we were disappointed. But the way he put it to us, we realized it was his life and his time to move on if he wanted.

"I remember sitting next to Andre McCarter, and he said, 'Man, no way we let Coach Wooden lose his last game.' I think Coach had us so well trained mentally that—and I know it sounds crazy—but we felt like it was just another game. We walked through some Kentucky plays on Sunday, something we never did. That felt a little odd. But we were so well trained, it was almost as if we knew how to react. We didn't have to think. We all thought alike."

Meyers was as impressed by Wooden's words as he was shocked by the news. "He's the greatest coach college basketball has ever seen," he told reporters, "and he just wanted us to know no matter what happened in the championship game he was very proud of us. Everyone was very silent after he told us."

On Monday night, against a Kentucky team that was bigger and stronger than UCLA, Wooden's Bruins, perhaps inspired as never before, played a game that looked as if it had just sprung to life from the pages of one of the coach's textbooks. Few of Wooden's teams have executed as well as this one did. McCarter, the kid who was never under control, suddenly was the steadiest player on the floor. Trgovich, who was obsessed with scoring early in his career, concentrated on defense and shut down Kentucky's hot-shooting Jimmy Dan Conner. Richard Washington was a force in the post, and from off the bench came little-used Ralph Drollinger.

"I think Ralph played the best eleven or twelve minutes he ever played for us that night," Wooden says. "He was a terror out there."

Johnson still chuckles when he talks about Drollinger's appearance. "He came in for me, and I figured he'd come in and screw up. But to my amazement and consternation, he played the game of his life," Johnson says.

It's a good thing, too. UCLA only utilized six players in the game. "To my knowledge," Wooden says, "that's the only time I ever did that in my entire career."

Kentucky played hard, but with UCLA's players on an emotional mission, it never had a chance. With eight minutes to play, the Wildcats cut UCLA's lead from 74–67 to 76–75, but then Kevin Grevey, who was their best player on the night with thirty-four points, missed the front end of a one-and-one and a technical foul shot, and it was never really close again. Washington had twenty-eight points and twelve rebounds. McCarter finished with fourteen assists, and Drollinger, in sixteen and a half minutes, grabbed thirteen rebounds and scored ten points against the Wildcats' Rick Robey-led frontline that averaged six feet ten. The Bruins won, 92–85, and Johnson took the basketball and flung it into the arena's rafters.

"I remember being embraced by Marques," Wooden says, "then getting a long, warm handshake from Meyers and a hug from a female fan."

Later, he would remember something else. Something that has stuck with him through all these years. A longtime Bruin booster walked up to Wooden and said, "Great victory, John. It makes up for your letting us down last year."

This dunce accused Wooden of "letting us down" because he had failed to win one national championship after capturing nine of the previous ten. That was the sort of pressure he'd been under, the kind of outlandish expectations some people had placed on the program.

Away from the frenzy on the court, the mood in the UCLA locker room afterward was mixed. "We wanted to win it bad for The Man," Trgovich told reporters. "We're not a team that jumps and screams before games. But I could look at each of the guys tonight and just tell. We were all ready in our own way."

Johnson and Washington were sitting in the hotel coffee shop having breakfast the next morning when Wooden sat down next to them. "He started talking about what this team meant to him," Johnson recalls, "and how that booster came up to him afterward and said he had made up for last year. He told us the way the booster's remarks kind of reinforced in his own mind that it was time to get out of the game. We said, 'Coach, go ahead. Have a good life.' We truly loved him."

Every once in a while, as a sportswriter, an event comes along that intimidates you. It is so big and so meaningful, you don't feel you can do it justice in print. This was one of those events. But if nothing else, I was lucky. Unlike most of the writers from other areas of the country covering the game that night, I wasn't on a tight deadline. I worked for the now-defunct afternoon newspaper in San Diego, the *San Diego Evening Tribune*, and I had all night to write my column, if I wanted. This was one night when I wanted.

I don't know what time it was when I finally left the office, where I had gone to write after Wooden's final game. But it was closer to dawn than it was midnight. I wanted to capture not just what happened in the game, but to try to let the readers grasp the entire scope of Wooden's career, especially since I'd been fortunate enough to witness much of it. Exactly how close I came I'm not sure. But this was the column I filed for the following afternoon's newspaper:

> SAN DIEGO—None of them ever went out this way. Not Rockne. Not McGraw, not Rupp, not Lombardi. None of them ever went out with such a storybook finish, with such a skillful demonstration, such a textbook performance. None of them ever went out with his style and his class.
>
> None of them ever dominated a sport like he has, either. Not with players coming and going every year, not with a nation full of hungry, competitive schools clawing at his heels. Not with the pressures and the turmoil and the distractions. None of them ever did it.
>
> Only John Wooden.

John Wooden

* * * * *

He sat there last night, arms folded, the ever-present program clenched tightly in his hand, chomping hard on stick after stick of gum as his UCLA team fought off those muscle-bound kids from Kentucky, showing its poise, maintaining its character, winning that precious tenth national championship, 92-85.

And for a while, the whole boisterous scene at the San Diego Sports Arena took on a surrealistic tone. The shots and the rebounds and the players meshed with other years and other teams, and it was as if the entire Wooden Era was slowly making its way past center court.

It's like the people who saw Ruth or Grange or Mikan in their prime. each has his own special moments, his own personal link to a great man's past.

* * * * *

When Wooden started, Pauley Pavilion was just another clod of earth on the campus in Westwood. His Bruins teams performed at the old Pan-Pacific or at Venice High, or, best of all, in the school gym, better known to UCLA students as B.O. Barn.

It was in that small, crowded gym where the odor would come wafting up into the grandstand that John Wooden first previewed the dynasty to come.

The year was 1962, and the two most important players on the floor were newcomers, a flashy dribbling sophomore from Overbook High in Philadelphia, and a skinny, undersized freshman from L.A. who looked about 15 years old.

Walt Hazzard and Gail Goodrich. More than anyone else, they were the two who turned it around. They were the two Wooden recruits who started the long string of success in Westwood.

And that night, in a varsity-freshman scrimmage, the first hints were there.

Hazzard, directing and passing with flawless skill, and Goodrich, corkscrewing his slight body into the clear to sink jump shot after jump shot.

Sitting in the stands that night watching, it was impressive. But no one really knew what it meant. No one. Not even Wooden.

* * * * *

The writers sitting in front of the wire-service machine nudged each other with elbows as the story began with a bell or two and the message that this would be a "BULLETIN."

Everyone knew what the story was about. Then they read it and winked knowingly to one another.

Lew Alcindor, it said, had made his choice. He was coming to UCLA.

And the second part of the Wooden dynasty had begun. He won twice, first with Hazzard and Goodrich and his famous zone press. Then with Goodrich and Keith Erickson as the only returning starters.

The predictions the third year were just as bright. But injuries knocked him out of it early, although some insist that isn't really what did it.

Some say it was that night at Pauley, that unforgettable night when a freshman named Alcindor destroyed the varsity in the annual preview game. The club that had a chance to make it three straight national titles never did have much confidence after that.

But oh, how they looked forward to the next year, when Alcindor would be eligible to play varsity ball.

*****

It wasn't easy, though, even with Lew.

Wooden would never admit it, but the Alcindor Years were not his happiest at UCLA. They weren't even close, despite the fact he won NCAA titles in each of Alcindor's three seasons.

He liked coaching smaller, hustling, more aggressive-type teams, teams that fast break and play that disciplined high-post offense.

Well, he had to change all that for Alcindor. He had to change a lot of things.

He had the most celebrated college player in America, and he inherited all the problems that went with him.

Attitudes and lifestyles were changing, and college kids were changing with them. Wooden's stern midwestern upbringing created something of a barrier between kids like Alcindor and Lucius Allen.

But he always tried to communicate, to put his team ahead of any individual, to maintain the balance that was always the trademark of UCLA basketball.

And now the media was on his back, too. A media

that no longer was satisfied with simple game stories and clichéd explanations.

*****

It was at a basketball writers luncheon in L.A.
when he was challenged, when the order that none of
his players could talk to reporters after games was
seriously questioned.

A young writer, much too young to be doubting the
best college coach in America, stood up and suggested maybe Wooden was wrong. He said he shouldn't
hide his players, and that the country had a right
to hear what they had to say, especially since they
were No. 1.

For one of the few times in public, Wooden lashed
out. He started talking calmly, then began yelling at
the writer. The rest of the room went silent, and when
he was finished, there was a long, uncomfortable pause.
Someone finally changed the subject, and the meeting
soon was adjourned. Later that same day, Wooden happened across the writer and motioned him aside.

And the UCLA basketball coach, maybe the greatest
basketball coach of all time, apologized to the impetu-
ous, headstrong kid who was young enough to be his son.

It was John Wooden's way, and the writer would
never forget it.

*****

After Alcindor, it was Sidney Wicks and Curtis
Rowe and two more NCAA championships. But some
thought that would be it. That would finally be the
end, at least for a while.

Then they saw Bill Walton. And they knew.

It started all over again, even though it didn't
end very happily. Titles eight and nine were
recorded in Walton's sophomore and junior seasons,
but it seems clear now that last year, Walton's senior year, left a bad taste in the coach's mouth.

He stood in front of a microphone in San Diego
just four days ago, the day before the start of the
tournament, and talked about this present team and
how much he enjoyed it.

"It has so much togetherness," he said. "It does
everything together. We're even eating together again.
There is none of this vegetarian over here and meditating over there. Everything we do, we do together."

*****

So there they were last night, together, trying to win the last one, the biggest one, for the coach who had announced this would be his parting shot.

And they were so good, so determined, so intense, so polished.

It was as if Wooden's whole career, everything he preached and worked for, was reflected in this team and this game.

Maybe more than any of the others, the performances of his guards showcased what John Wooden is really about. Andre McCarter and Pete Trgovich both came to UCLA with glittering high school reputations, both were the stars, the main men. McCarter from Hazzard's old school in Philly and Trgovich out of East Chicago, Ind., near Wooden's hometown.

Both were wild, uninhibited kids who were out of control when they arrived at UCLA. But Wooden was patient with them. He molded them, made them fit into his style and framework.

"I'm glad I came here," said McCarter last night. "I needed someone to discipline me. Otherwise, I would have gone somewhere and been the star and done whatever I had wanted. I would have never known it could be like this."

The two ex-scorers, the two former big guns, did their own special things to help deep-fry Kentucky. McCarter quarterbacked and dictated the feverish tempo, never allowing the Bruins to lose control. Trgovich popgunned 14 points in the first half and played relentless defense for 40 minutes, shutting off the Wildcats' good-shooting Jimmy Dan Conner.

*****

And then, after it ended, they all sat there in that stuffy dressing room and smiled at one another and talked about how good it felt and how nice it was to be able to have won such a historic game, a game that meant so much to their coach.

"The first championship," said Athletic Director J. D. Morgan, "that was for him and his team. The other eight were for him, his team and UCLA.

"But this one—this one was for him."

For John Wooden. And posterity.

101

The Salary Disgrace

Maybe the most amazing fact of all those associated with the John Wooden Era is the salary he made in his final year as UCLA coach.

It was $32,500. No, there are no zeroes missing. That's the actual number.

How could it have been that low, even in 1975? How could he not have been earning well into six figures long before that? How is it possible that the greatest basketball coach of all time was also the most underpaid?

"All I can tell you is that Mom [Nell Wooden] especially was really angry about that," says Nan Muehlhausen, the Woodens' daughter. "She would argue with Daddy about it, but Daddy would always say, 'I'll never ask.' Our question is, why wouldn't UCLA have done something about it?"

Actually, the story gets worse. When Wooden originally accepted the job for the princely sum of $6,000 in 1948, he didn't know that his checks were being signed by the president of the student association. The Associated Students weren't paying into a retirement fund, so as a result, Wooden earned no retirement benefits from his first twelve years on the job.

"If I had known that, I never would have come to UCLA," Wooden would say later. "But I took the job, so I wanted to honor my contract."

Wooden's middle-American principles cost him untold money over the years. If anyone would have had the leverage to go to then-Athletic Director J. D. Morgan and demand a new contract, it was this coach who was racking up national championships faster than anybody could count. But that wasn't Wooden's way. He was a man of pride, not a man of greed. He did make a little more money with radio and off-season camp appearances. In later years, after his retirement, boosters offered to build him a new home, but he refused, because he was too emotionally attached to the Encino condo he shared with his late wife, Nell.

Morgan and the athletic department helped the program out in innumerable ways through the Wooden Era, but they'll never explain how they allowed a Hall of Fame coach to be paid less than a bottom-rung assistant at many major universities.

In the midst of all of UCLA's glowing basketball success, the Wooden salary issue remains a lingering disgrace.

Wooden's Real Secret: It's All in the Details

For years, basketball junkies have studied tapes and searched through books and sat through clinics hoping to find the answer. There must be a secret, they surmised, some hidden reason John Wooden won all those games at UCLA. It didn't happen by accident, they all agreed. Certainly, once the dynasty got rolling, he never lacked for talent. But there was more to it than that. There had to be.

What made his Bruins teams so smooth, so poised, so relatively mistake free? Why did they always seem to make other teams create the errors that would turn games around? Most of all, how did they win so many close games at the end? What magic potion did this man have that allowed his team to play so skillfully and under control in pressure situations? Other coaches look at his thirty-eight consecutive NCAA Tournament victories and simply shake their heads. It's not possible, they say. It just can't happen. Yet it did. There has to be a reason. There has to be some version of Wooden's Holy Grail hidden somewhere.

Basketball archaeologists may be disappointed to hear, after talking to countless players and coaches who worked and performed for him, as well as any number of opponents who were forced to play against him, the consensus is that Wooden's real secret was simple. He was merely more precise than everyone else. He concentrated on the tiny details of basketball and drilled his team on them ad nauseum. He ran repetitions on fundamentals until his players could execute them without a second thought. What Wooden did in basketball is what NFL people say Vince Lombardi did in football. His basic plays weren't any different than those of other teams. It's just that his team ran them better. Wooden's classroom on the court revolved around the four basic laws of learning: demonstration, explanation, correction, and repetition.

"The level of detail in his coaching was amazing," says Gail Goodrich, who starred on Wooden's first two national championship teams. "We would go twenty minutes running the offense in practice without taking a shot. He wanted you to know what to do on the weak side when the ball was on the strong side. He'd talk about on-ball defense and spacing. He'd show you the crouch position with your legs a certain amount apart. He wanted one hand pointed at the ball and one hand pointed at the man. He'd make a little circle with his hands and move his feet. When he was demonstrating, it was so funny to watch. Here's this fifty-two-year-old man doing this. We used to chuckle and call it a 1920s defense. But he was so right."

Greg Lee, the point guard on the great Bill Walton teams, learned early not to laugh about the coach's theories. "You never for one instant thought he's just winging it," Lee says. "Everything he did had a focus and an emphasis. In games, you didn't have to think. You knew what to do from hours of repetition."

From his college coach, "Piggie" Lambert, the man he says was his greatest influence, Wooden learned that preparation was paramount. "Coach Lambert had a fetish for details," Wooden says. So did Lambert's protégé. "One of my strengths, if I had a strength, was in my practice organization," Wooden says. "We ran everything to the minute. I had little three-by-five cards I kept, and my assistants had cards, too. At 3:30 we'd start. From 3:30 to 3:35 we'd have weakside defense drill. Then I'd whistle for the next drill, which might be a three-on-two conditioning segment for ten minutes, followed by a fifteen-minute drill on something, then another ten-minute drill on something else. I never wanted my drills to last too long. I also made it a point before I started a new drill to always explain it fully. I never did anything to kill time. I felt the players responded better if they understood the purpose of the drills we were running."

Even some of the great players who were difficult to deal with early quickly got with the program. "All the drills were done to perfection," says Sidney Wicks, who had to rank near the top in that difficult category. "The intensity in practice was so high. He didn't just want you to do the drills. He wanted you doing them perfectly. That was his whole shtick. Get everybody to play so well, so you were basically mistake free. It was all about mistakes. He didn't just want you to do your defensive sliding. He wanted you to do it right."

Gary Cunningham, former player and assistant coach for Wooden who eventually became the second coach to succeed him at UCLA, probably studied the man's methods more closely than anyone else.

"Everything he did was precise," Cunningham says. "Everything was fundamentals, and that's the way everybody did it. People often said that UCLA teams were kind of robotic in a lot of ways—and they were. I mean, you had your individualism that you could do within the context of the offense, but all of the footwork and all of the pivots and all of the jump shots—everything was the same. Everybody had their hands up on rebounds. *Everybody* had them up. Everybody had to have their shirts tucked in their shorts. You left your locker clean after practice. He used to give us a carton of orange juice, and you had to throw it in a trash can. If you didn't get in the trash can, nobody gets orange juice tomorrow. You had to have your shirt in your shorts. Why? All of this he felt was his theory of discipline, and everything that he did had a purpose.

"He didn't believe in scrimmaging, either," Cunningham says. "We never scrimmaged. You would be on offense to defense or defense to offense. So you'd play half court. And the team would take a shot. If you made it, you'd press them. If you missed it, the defense would break, and then, when it got down at the other end, if they didn't get a quick shot, then he'd blow the whistle, and the same team would be on offense and the same team on defense as before. We never had full-court scrimmages. The only full-court scrimmages that we had were the games. Where a lot of coaches say we're going to have a scrimmage on Wednesday or Friday, we never did, other than the first week of practice.

"He always wanted to end practices on a high note. It didn't always happen that way, but the majority of times it did. You know, he could be tough on you, and he could get on you, but at the end of practice, he wanted to do something that was kind of fun. So we'd shoot free throws and have contests and things like that. He might pick out one guy and say, 'Jim, come on over here. If you make this free throw, everybody gets to go home.' And so everybody is going, 'Come on, Jim! come on, Jim!' and if you missed it, he'd give you kind of a reprieve. You'd get to do another one. In his mind, these were fun things to do."

According to Cunningham, little changed in the ten years he spent with Wooden. "People can know what you're doing, but if you execute right," he says, "it's just like you draw a football play. If everybody blocks the way they should, you should gain ten or twelve yards on it. It works. So that was his whole philosophy: Keep it simple—but be fundamentally sound and have counters to what the defense does."

Wooden would lecture his players and explain his philosophy in the first few days of practice. "When you come to practice, you cease to exist as an individual," he would say. "You're part of a team." He felt that being on UCLA's team was something his players should savor. "Basketball is a privilege, not a right," he often said. "They didn't have to be out there, and if they can't go along with the one in charge, I felt they would be better off if we parted company."

Steve Lavin, a head coach at UCLA for seven years, might have studied Wooden more closely than any of his predecessors. "He was smart enough to take psychology courses at UCLA," Lavin says. "He was always growing, adapting, and adjusting to the times. That's how he stayed ahead of the competition. Besides his strategic and technical gifts, he coached in a broader concept. He was a stickler for details, but he could adjust. His teams were always so different, from the Eddie Sheldrake days to the Bill Walton Era. At the same time, his players had to adjust to him. There was no middle ground.

"When you think of the range—he coached five or six decades, starting back from when people were driving Model-T cars to Vietnam, from the pre-jump shot days to coaching Lew Alcindor and Marques Johnson. The fact was, he was always able to adjust, to adapt to his players. If one of his players was interested in Far Eastern religion, he'd read up on it. Yet all his players reflected his coaching and his obsession with details. Everyone from Goodrich to Kareem to Walton to Marques, they all said they realized how much more fundamentally sound they were than almost all other players in the NBA."

It wasn't only the great players who realized what Wooden was doing. Andy Hill, a reserve who saw little playing time in the Walton Era and later became a good friend and even wrote a book about his experience with Wooden, still talks about the remarkable manner in which the man coached. "I was there; I know," Hill says. "We did change of pace and change of direction without the ball. That's how we started every practice. You'd run a dummy offense with nobody defending, and it seemed silly. You were moving the basketball and making your cuts, but no one was on defense. But there were two things that would be essential to our success coming out of that. With no one on defense, you were forced to pay a lot of attention to setting up the outlet pass. You learned what to do when the first option wasn't available. In his regular offense, you'd look for the cutter first, then you'd look toward the post, and

COURTESY OF UCLA ATHLETIC DEPARTMENT

John Wooden poses in front of some of the more prominent trophies and plaques he has received in his memorable career as the greatest, most successful coach in college basketball history.

next you'd look for the other guard at the top of the circle. It was all about timing. He wanted you to get your timing down.

"The other thing he always drilled you on was placing the pass on your teammate's outside hand. The guy receiving the pass has an obligation to make the right target. The guy throwing the pass has an obligation to hit the target. It sounds simple. But you'd be surprised how many teams you watch these days don't understand that concept, whose players have no idea where to put the pass.

"It was impossible for fans to understand how much time went into preparing fundamentals that looked second nature on the floor," Hill says. "I coached for a while at Santa Monica City College, and the head coach there was a big UCLA fan. He thought it would be a good idea to shoot bank shots at the end of our fast breaks, the way Wooden's teams did. I told him, 'Great, but if you want to do it, you've to do it every day in practice.' That was the kind of commitment to everyday fundamentals you just didn't see at other places. Most coaches would spend a lot of time talking about those things. Coach always spent no time talking and all his time doing. He wouldn't sit the team down lecturing. We spent very little practice time talking. He once explained it was all about repetition, repetition, repetition."

Hill was fascinated at what he saw transpire on the court. "There was an unspoken transfer of power at game time," he says. "Very few coaches or managers ever do this. It involves the T-word—trust. It was never said, but there was a clear transfer of trust from Wooden and his assistants to the players once the game started. No one ever called the players to the bench. No one ever said, 'Give the coach a minute, he'll think of something.' It was not about smoke and mirrors once the game started. It was about execution."

Eddie Sheldrake, Wooden's first point guard at UCLA in 1948, still marvels at the coach's attention to the little things. "He was a big baseball fan, and he'd sit and talk about percentages for hours," Sheldrake recalls. "He used to keep stats during practice. I'm talking about real detailed stats with charts about everything. He'd know how many times this guy got offensive rebounds and how many times this other guy turned the ball over. He made a lot of his decisions based on percentages. That's how he'd pick who played. If there was a senior who was not playing well, he wouldn't keep him, because he could be playing someone else in relief, someone younger who might help him down the road.

"Even on the drills we had, he'd have percentages worked out. He had picked out five spots on the floor he wanted you to cover on rebounds. When the ball was in the air, we were supposed to go to those five spots. Each guy knew where they were. You had to go to the closest one, and if someone was already there, you went to the next one. That's one of the reasons his teams always rebounded so well.

"It was the same when we were warming up before a game. With a lot of teams, you see ten guys standing around with two balls to shoot. Not with us. We always had two guys on one ball. There was no fooling around. In practice, there was no time when you weren't doing something. Like when we did a full-court drill, we wouldn't wait around on the other end for the drill to end. We would go all the way around the court so we were always running. Same with free throws. We didn't have four or five guys shagging the ball. At every basket, there were two guys, with one guy shooting. It was all precise, all charted out very carefully."

If UCLA's teams performed well in the clutch, there was a reason. "He drilled on us on emotional conditioning," says Swen Nater, a backup center during the Walton years who would go on to be a top NBA rebounder. "He was always getting on us about losing emotions, about always trying to stay under control."

Hill claims everything Wooden did was carefully plotted, even what he would say in practice. "There were all these little subliminal things," Hill says. "He'd watch somebody throw a crosscourt pass on the break that would work in a game, and he'd admonish the player for it. The player would reply that the pass worked, didn't it? Wooden would smile and say, 'Yes, but it won't work against the best teams.' And the fact of the matter was, he was right.

"He was great at that kind of thing. He would kind of raise the bar without anyone seeing him raise the bar. 'I'm not interested in beating just anybody,' he would say. 'I'm interested in beating the best teams.' You'd do something in practice and he'd say, 'Some of those things might work against mediocre teams, but they won't work in the NCAA Tournament.' One of his favorite sayings, of course, was 'The way you practice is the way you play.'"

Nater noticed one thing about Wooden. Despite his calm demeanor, he was always a fierce competitor. "I'd call him an extremely competitive person," Nater says. "If you'd play him in cribbage or golf or tennis, he's going to find a way to win. He'd get you riled or do something to make you lose your concentration. Whatever it would take, he would do. He used to say one of his assistants played golf with him, and the assistant was a far better player than he was but he never beat him. That was the thing about him: He'd think of every little detail. Remember how stiff the nets were at Pauley Pavilion? That was legal, but Wooden kept them that way for a reason. He thought the stiffness of the nets gave us another half-second to set up for the rebounds."

Hill tells a story about the time he took a graduate education course in learning theory. "The instructor explained: If you want to train a pigeon to peck on the bar, you have to give him positive and negative reinforcement. But if you want him to keep pecking on the bar, you have to do it the same as you would with a basketball player. The positive and negative reinforcement has to be slowly removed over time. After the class, I realized it was the same with Coach Wooden's teams. By the last practices of the season, there were not a lot of 'atta boys' or sharp criticism. By then, he would have you just doing what you do.

"The same was true in games. Whatever else happened, Coach's teams just kept running their offense. They never got panicky. They continued to execute. That's why, I think, they were able to win so many of those close games through the years. Anyway, after I completed this graduate class, I couldn't wait to go see Coach and tell him about this reinforcement theory I'd just learned. Coach smiled when I told him, and then he said, 'Yes, Andy, I know.' I walked away thinking, *What a clever dude he is.* As it turned out, this was just another detail he already had covered."

Fate—And Indiana

"I've never told anybody this story," says Jerry Tarkanian, "but I don't mind telling you this now."

Tarkanian, one of college basketball's most successful coaches, was a rival of John Wooden in the late 1960s and early '70s, when "Tark the Shark" was at Long Beach State. But this story precedes a 1971 NCAA regional game between UCLA and Long Beach State, one of the biggest tournament scares a Wooden team would ever have.

"It was the day before the game, and we were at an NCAA Tournament media function there in Salt Lake City," Tarkanian remembers. "Coach Wooden stops me and says, 'We have to be back here in an hour for another press conference, why don't we stay here instead of going back to the hotel and the two of us can just talk?' Well, you don't turn down Coach Wooden when he asks you something like that. So we went to a wing in the hotel, we sat down and then he hit me with it.

"He said he'd been offered the Indiana [head coaching] job [pre-Bobby Knight]. They were going to pay him back all his retirement that he had accrued at UCLA and make it very lucrative for him. But he told me he didn't want to go back and be that far away from his children and grand-children. Then he starts telling me how great a job it is and everything. And then he tells me he recommended me for the job and that the athletic director wanted me to call him. I was really excited about the idea. I knew what kind of hotbed [Indiana] was for basketball.

"I rushed back to the hotel to tell my wife, and we talked about it the rest of the night," Tarkanian says. "We were really interested. Well, turns out, we had an unbelievable game the next day [UCLA won, 57–55, but only after Long Beach State blew a lead in the final minutes.] We lost, but when we flew back, there were several hundred people waiting to cheer us at the Long Beach airport. Now, there really hadn't been any great interest in college basketball at Long Beach until that time. I felt so good about the way we played and the reaction we were getting from the city, I never bothered to call the athletic director. I think if we had played poorly and lost big, I definitely would have called and flown back there for an interview. Again, I've never told anybody this before, but I guess it's time."

The story is confirmed by a close friend and sportswriting mentor, Loel Schrader, who worked as a columnist for years at the *Long Beach Press-Telegram.*

"I was interviewing Wooden in his office the Monday after that regional game in Utah," Schrader says. "The phone rings, and Wooden says, 'Yes, this is Coach Wooden.' Then he listens for perhaps thirty seconds, then says, 'No, no, I can't do that.' He listened some more, then says again, 'I said I can't do that. Besides, I've already recommended someone else for the job—Jerry Tarkanian of Long Beach State.'

"After hanging up, Wooden figured I would be curious about the call. I said I was. He said, 'Well, that was a friend of Bobby Knight. As you know, I'm sure, the Indiana job is open and Bobby's friend wanted me to recommend Bobby for the job. I said I couldn't do it. I'm sure you heard what I said about Tarkanian.'"

Those close to Wooden figured there were different reasons for his recommendation of Tarkanian. One is perhaps that Tark had become his fiercest rival in the West. Another is that he held, and still holds, Tarkanian in high regard as a coach of the sport. Wooden says of Tarkanian now what he has always said about Knight: "I don't always agree with his methods, but I don't think there is any question about his ability to coach the game."

PART III

THE BOYS
OF WOODEN

Five Hundred Boys

SWEN NATER

Class of '74

Because of you five hundred boys have grown to men;
They took the golden words you speak and gave them life again.

Because of you five hundred boys have walked the walk;
They watched the careful, cautious way you practiced all your talk.

Because of you five hundred boys have learned to give;
They watched the sacrificing, selfless, gracious way you live.

Because of you five hundred boys can teach our youth;
They saw the detailed, thorough, loving way you drill the truth.

Because of you five hundred boys have learned success;
They saw you strive to be your best and spurn the tiredness.

Because of you five hundred boys learned to lead;
You lead them by example for that's what they really need.

Because of you five hundred boys have grown in grace;
And with you, made this world a little better, nicer place.

If the true measure of a coach is in the quality of the people he coached after they leave him, there is no question about John Wooden's mastery of his profession.

Many of his players, the great ones, went on to enjoy distinguished careers as basketball professionals. But many others thrived in different areas, where their specific on-court skills weren't as important as the lessons Wooden provided them while they played for him at UCLA. The reason this coach, this man, is still so relevant today is that most of his ex-players have come to realize that what Wooden taught them was invaluable not only in their chosen professions but in their daily lives.

Although there are hundreds of stories to chronicle, the following are some of the chosen few who played for him and came to know him later as a friend and, in many cases, as almost a father figure. How John Wooden influenced them as college students and how he continues to influence them even today is as fascinating as any of the precise reports of UCLA's great victories.

Great coaches are supposed to build great character, and after reading about some of these remarkable men who played for him, you will have little doubt that Wooden succeeded as much, if not more, in this area than he did in the searing spotlight of the NCAA Finals.

Included in this group are Hall of Famers, All-Americans, Academic All-Americans, a player who didn't blossom until he left UCLA and moved on to the pros, and in one case, a frustrated benchwarmer who never made it onto the floor for more than a few precious minutes during his career at UCLA. All have been deeply affected by the man they have come to respect and revere more than ever.

The Boys of Wooden offer an intriguing and insightful look at what John Wooden is truly about and why his impact today is as strong as ever.

The Runt

One of the many subtleties of John Wooden's genius is his knack for spotting potential talent. People often overlook the fact that besides the Alcindors and Waltons, the players with overwhelming ability, many of Wooden's UCLA teams were infiltrated by kids who never would have been called blue-chippers in their high school days. There were all sorts of them through the years, from the less-than-pure athletic types, like Lynn Shackelford and Jack Hirsch, to the slow and hardly physically imposing players, such as Terry Schofield and John Ecker. There were always kids this coach took, believing he saw traits in them none of his peers could see. More often than not, he was right.

The best example was a five-foot-eight, 120-pound runt of a high school junior Wooden noticed while at a Los Angeles city basketball tournament to scout other players in 1960. Sitting in the stands, watching Poly High that day, Wooden turned to a friend who had come with him and said, "See that little left-hander over there? He's the smartest one out there. If he grows, he has a chance to be a really good player." No one was there to document his friend's reaction, but he must have thought something was wrong with Wooden's glasses. "That skinny kid who looks like he hasn't eaten in a week? You've got to be kidding!" he must have muttered to himself. But Wooden wasn't kidding.

Neither was the friendly woman who just happened to be sitting in front of them. She turned around, smiled and said, "You know that little left-hander you were talking about? That's my son." Which is precisely the moment Wooden began to recruit Gail Goodrich, the quintessential basketball gym rat who would grow enough the next year to blossom into the L.A. City Player of the Year. Now, suddenly, other coaches and other schools were interested. But it was too late, because Wooden already had formed a relationship with Goodrich and his parents.

"All my life I had wanted to go to USC," says Goodrich, reminiscing from his home in Connecticut. "My father had gone there and played basketball. I used to go to sleep with my dad's letterman's jacket next to me in bed. As it turned out, my only two real big-time scholarship offers came from UCLA and USC. But USC's came late. By then, I was already going to UCLA practices with my dad. We liked how organized Coach Wooden was, how much he stressed fundamentals. It became clear that, as much as I had always wanted to go to USC, I ought to go someplace where I really wanted to play and where I thought I'd improve."

You could say it was a decision that turned out well for both Goodrich and Wooden, who eventually blended their considerable talents to begin what would be the greatest dynasty in the history of college basketball. A starter for much of his sophomore year (1962-63), Goodrich didn't fully mature until he was a junior, when he teamed with Walt Hazzard to form the finest, most complementary backcourt in UCLA history.

Hazzard, the kid from Philadelphia, had arrived two years earlier to send the program into spasms of both confusion and delight. He was a flashy player with a pure East Coast style that emphasized the type of passing nobody in California had ever seen. This was a young man who could thread a basketball through a knot hole, and it took some time for the Bruins, and Wooden, to adjust to his skills. But they did.

Besides his wondrous passing ability, Hazzard was a terrific ball handler and dribbler and a great floor leader. By the end of that first season, he had taken a modestly talented Bruins team to the Final Four, where they lost to Cincinnati by two points in the semifinals. As a junior, Hazzard and his teammates didn't do quite as well, failing to make it past the first round of the NCAA regionals.

But when Hazzard entered his senior year, there was Goodrich, a little taller, a little stronger and considerably more mature, to play alongside him on a team that, to this day, Wooden still admits is his all-time favorite. It was a team without a real big man. Fred Slaughter, at six feet five, was the center. Lanky, six-foot-five Keith Erickson, a great volleyball player, was at one forward and six-foot-three Jack Hirsch, all angles and elbows, was at the other. On paper, it was not a particularly imposing team. On the court, however, meshing together to execute a blur of a 2-2-1 zone press, it proved to be the surprise team of college basketball.

"None of us were really highly recruited," Goodrich says. "Erickson was probably the best athlete of any of us. He was the safety man in the press, and he was absolutely fearless. Hirsch, at six feet three, was the best forward in America. He just had a knack for getting the ball. He couldn't really jump, but he had long arms and he was very hard-nosed. Slaughter was another great athlete. He could run the hundred [yard dash] in 9.9 [seconds] at 240 pounds. He was the fastest guy we had, and he could set huge picks. Then there was Walt. He was the best passer in college basketball and a great leader and floor general."

Together, they started modestly, barely squeezing by at Kansas State, 78–75, in their third game. But after that, they were never seriously challenged in an almost surreal season. Their final record was 30–0 after they dispatched Duke, 98-83, in the NCAA Finals at Kansas City. What Wooden admired so much about this group was its amazing selflessness. None of his future teams, some of them vastly more talented, played together game-in and game-out as well as this one. And none of them had so many players who sublimated their personal skills for the good of the group.

"I know I had a big adjustment to make," says Goodrich. "In high school, I had the ball all the time. In Wooden's system, you had to be more balanced. And, of course, with Walt on the floor, he controlled the ball. I didn't realize it at the time, but it turned out to really help me, because I learned how to play with Walt. Wooden taught me how to move without the ball. And any time I would get open, Walt would get me the ball."

A year later, Hazzard, Hirsch, and Slaughter graduated, and only Goodrich and Erickson would return as starters. But anyone who thought UCLA wouldn't be formidable didn't understand the dynasty Wooden was beginning to build. "We had Kenny Washington and Doug McIntosh, who had played big roles off the bench for us in winning the first title," Goodrich says. "Then Freddie Goss, who hadn't played the previous year, came back, and we added Edgar Lacey, a sophomore with tremendous talent. We still ran the press, but we changed it from a 2-2-1 to a 1-2-1-1. But, really, after the first pass, it was the same press."

COURTESY OF UCLA ATHLETIC DEPARTMENT

Although he was never the biggest guard around, Gail Goodrich could always get off shots like this. Goodrich helped UCLA win two national titles and was the star of the 1964-65 team.

Opponents weren't happy about that. You had to observe the UCLA press in person to fully understand how it changed games. You had to see the look of panic in opposing guards, who would be trapped with nowhere to go with the ball. You had to watch the exasperation on the faces of coaches, who were trying to stem the momentum the press would generate. The Bruins would regularly go off on 12–0 and 16–2 runs, turning close games into instant routs. More important, the press would change the tone of a game, forcing it to speed up, which only gave the quicker, more polished UCLA players an added advantage. The faster the game, the better they liked it.

Whenever Wooden talks about the press now, he mentions Goodrich as the perfect "No. 1 man" in the alignment. "He fooled people because of his size and his boyish demeanor," says Wooden, "but he was very intense, a great competitor. He also had very long arms for someone his size, and he was always knocking down balls and making steals and converting them into easy baskets. It helped that he was left-handed, too. That made him ideal for that spot."

If the public didn't realize how effective Goodrich was on defense, it certainly knew how good he was on offense. Without Hazzard, Goodrich became the focal point of that 1964–65 team. It was a club that wasn't as perfect as the previous year's championship team. This one lost to Illinois and Iowa early, but by tournament time, it was on a roll that was just as impressive as its predecessor's. In the

NCAA Finals, against Michigan and Cazzie Russell, Erickson was injured, and some felt his absence would be too much to overcome.

Goodrich made sure it wasn't. Taking over that game in Portland, he broke his personal scoring record, pouring in forty-two points in his final collegiate appearance, to lead the Bruins to a 91–80 victory and their second NCAA title in a row. Princeton's Bill Bradley, the future Senator, had a brilliant tournament and was named MVP. But Wooden still smiles when you ask him about it, adamant that Goodrich should have received the honor.

Goodrich went on to have a distinguished professional career. He started with the Lakers, who drafted him in 1965. He was traded to Phoenix three years later, where he began scoring the way he did in college. Two years after that, the Lakers reacquired him, and he immediately became the star he was at UCLA. He averaged 25.9 points per game for L.A.'s Bill Sharman-coached NBA Championship team in 1972, the one that rattled off a league record thirty-three victories in a row. He averaged twenty-two or more points for four consecutive years in L.A. and eventually had his uniform retired. It now hangs in the rafters at the Staples Center, alongside those of Jerry West, Elgin Baylor, Wilt Chamberlain, Magic Johnson, and James Worthy. Goodrich also was inducted into the Basketball Hall of Fame a few years ago. Why UCLA still hasn't retired his number remains a mystery. He belongs right there with the Waltons and Alcindors and the other Bruin greats.

Now sixty-one and living with his second wife in Connecticut, where he moved twelve years ago, Goodrich is a semi-retired golf course consultant who still tries to follow the trials and tribulations of his alma mater in basketball. He also attempts to stay close to the man who taught him so much about the sport.

"I'd say I talk to him about once every quarter [of the year]," Goodrich says. "I had breakfast with him at his favorite spot in L.A. the last time I was there.

"You don't realize it until later, until after you've been away from UCLA for a few years, but it was not just basketball he was teaching you. He was teaching a philosophy you could apply to everyday life. Anytime I was faced with a crisis, like, say, something in raising your kids, I'd think, *This is how Wooden would handle this.* It really does apply to other things. You know, it is interesting, but he really forces you to think. A few years ago, I accepted an award for him at the New York Athletic Club. He couldn't travel at the time, and he asked if I would accept in his behalf. I said of course. But I asked him if there was anything special he wanted me to say. His answer was, 'No, I think you'll do just fine. You'll figure it out.' And I did.

"It is the same way when you ask him his opinion on something. He might suggest something. But he'll never tell you what to do. He is a very wise man. Sometimes, I think his greatest trait is his ability to communicate with people. He always says he is still learning. Every day, he says he learns something new. But really, he is the ultimate teacher."

For those who think Wooden was always a quiet, composed man, Goodrich begs to differ. When he was coaching, he was often a different personality. "He could be critical in practice, very critical," Goodrich says. "I saw him run Fred Slaughter out of the gym one day, and Coach was running with him, jawing nose to nose the whole way. He was tough as nails.

"One day, it would be pick-on-Walt [Hazzard] day. The next day, it would be pick-on-Gail. He'd usually wait until you were the star of the team to do that, but we all had our turns. You really couldn't argue with him, either. Because he could outshoot any of us. No, really, at age fifty or whatever he was, he'd challenge you to a free-throw shooting contest, and he'd hit nine out of ten shooting in that weird underhand style every time. He was a better shooter than any of us. He'd take his first shot underhanded, and the guys would all hoot at him—until the shots went in every time. Then they stopped hooting.

"There were certain things he would go crazy about, too. The one thing you never wanted to let happen was for some defensive guy to post you up. Oh my God, then he'd blow the whistle. 'Goodness gracious sakes alive,' he'd scream. 'You do not let him do that. You never let *anyone* do that.' And you know, after that, you never did."

In his office, at home in Connecticut, Goodrich has Wooden's Pyramid of Success on his wall. "You know, when I was in school, I was not that close to him. He was always someone who was more like a father figure. By my senior year, I guess I had more communication with him off the court. But he was a teacher, and he taught and I listened. Later, after I got to the professional level, it really hit me. That's when I realized what a great coach he was. How he had taught me the game from the ground up. His preparation, compared to other coaches, was remarkable. I looked around at other players who weren't as versed in fundamentals, and I realized how well coached I'd been. And he cared for his players. I mean, he really cared for them. He still does."

What Goodrich came to realize later was that Wooden also was something of a leader in integrating black players into his program. "I saw Kenny Washington from South Carolina and Henry Bibby from North Carolina and began to understand that they were not recruited by certain schools because they were black. I think UCLA, because of Rafer Johnson and Jackie Robinson and, yes, Coach Wooden, became a place where blacks knew they could come and be treated fairly. In my freshman year, I roomed with Fred Slaughter and thought nothing of it. In L.A., you played with or against black players all the time. But in the South, it was different for a long time."

After he left UCLA, Goodrich marveled at the success Wooden forged. "I remember the first time I saw Lew [Alcindor]," he says. "He was the best basketball player I'd ever seen at the time. He was so agile and mobile for his size. After a while, I just began to accept that UCLA was going to be good every year. I became surprised anytime they would get beat.

"People have to understand what Coach Wooden accomplished is never going to happen again. First of all, not many players hang around for four years anymore. And there are a lot more good players now than there were then. But all those people who think it was easier to win the NCAA back then, they forget that you had to win the conference to even get into the tournament. That makes a big difference. Now you can finish fifth or sixth in your conference and still get in. Back then, some great teams finished second and didn't even make the tournament.

"The thing about Wooden is, he won with all kinds of teams. He won with teams that had great centers and others that had great guards. He won with big teams and little teams. He'd be the first to tell you he had great players. But he also developed some great players who might not have been as good somewhere else."

Nowadays, even after all these years, just the thought of Wooden brings a smile to Goodrich's face. "He's such a smart man, such a great man," he says. "I'm blessed to have had the opportunity to play for him. I didn't realize it at the time, but one of the best things I did in my life was go to UCLA and play for John Wooden."

You could say it worked out well for both parties. Especially once "the Runt" grew up, in more ways than one.

The Prodigy

eBron James is nothing compared to him. Oh sure, LeBron came dribbling into basketball's glitzy new world with great skills and probably more hype and media coverage than any other player who's ever slam-dunked his way out of high school. But as good as he is, as celebrated as the athletic shoemakers and the sports drink companies have made him, James is no Ferdinand Lewis Alcindor Jr.

Lew Alcindor is the standard against which all others have to be measured. Coming out of Power Memorial Academy in New York, he was a prodigy unlike any previously seen, more famous than Wilt Chamberlain, more advanced than Bill Russell. He was a seven-foot-one (and maybe taller) wonder with the kind of agility and coordination that hadn't been observed before in a man that size. Chamberlain was stronger and Russell was better defensively, but not even those two future Hall of Famers had as complete a game as the most coveted high school player in America. If James had allowed himself to be recruited, every major college in the country would have been interested. He would have filled their arenas and been an immediate media magnet.

But Alcindor, in the spring of 1965, was so much more than that. He was, almost every basketball scout agreed, an immediate ticket to the

NCAA Finals. Get this guy, they said, and you could win the national championship, maybe several times. That is how skilled and polished he was and how much better he already seemed compared to every other center at the collegiate level.

This was the era before cable TV, before ESPN, before the Internet. And yet, even then, the hype was overwhelming. With the help of his coach, the late Jack Donahue, Alcindor finally narrowed his choice of colleges to five: Michigan, Holy Cross, Boston College, St. John's, and UCLA. Newspapers, especially along the East Coast, were covering his recruiting sessions as if they were major events. Every trip was chronicled, every word was analyzed in an attempt to figure out where this celebrated phenom would decide to go.

Not surprisingly, John Wooden maintained a lower profile than most of the coaches trying to land perhaps the most sought-after prep player in the history of the game.

"I first met Coach Wooden when I came out to UCLA on my recruiting trip," says Kareem Abdul-Jabbar, who was known as Lew Alcindor before he embraced the Muslim faith and changed his name. "Lewis," is what Wooden preferred to call him. "I remember thinking he was kind of quaint," Jabbar says. "He reminded me of the midwestern stereotype, even an archetype, you could say. But you could tell right away that his basketball knowledge was very sound. I'd already been very impressed by the way UCLA's team played basketball. I liked the way they pressed and ran with the ball, and I really enjoyed watching Walt Hazzard. I also admired the team concept and the balance they demonstrated. Wooden talked very honestly to me. He stressed that academics were important and how much he wanted all his players to graduate. Everything he had to say about what my life would be like at UCLA I responded to."

The school was smart, too. Knowing Alcindor was deeply interested in the history of black America, it had Jackie Robinson and Dr. Ralph Bunche send him letters extolling the university. "Then I saw Rafer Johnson on the *Ed Sullivan* TV show and found out he was student body president at UCLA," Jabbar says. "That really impressed me, that a black man could earn that position, that he could excel beyond sports."

Later, for perhaps the only time in his legendary career, Wooden traveled across the country to meet Alcindor's family. Not surprisingly, they were duly impressed. "Once my parents met Coach Wooden, they wanted me to play for him," Jabbar says. "They realized he would be someone who wouldn't exploit me. And he didn't need me to guarantee his success. He'd already won two national championships, so his success was assured.

"What he had to say to both my parents and me was very compelling," Jabbar says. "Some people thought I wanted to go somewhere I could set new scoring records. But that wasn't the case at all. I wanted to go somewhere I would learn the game and play on a winning team. I wanted to be able to cut down the nets [at the Final Four]. That's what I really wanted."

He must have thought Wooden would give him the best chance, because on May 4, 1965, in front of a huge media gathering at Power Memorial Academy's gymnasium, with coaches across the country holding their collective breath, he made it official: He would attend UCLA. And college basketball would never be quite the same again.

Alcindor was the bridge between the Hazzard-Goodrich championship teams and the Bruins' star-spangled future. He was the one player most responsible for the dynasty that was to come. He was the one who made every great high school player in America sit up and begin to consider UCLA. Before he arrived, the Bruins were the small, gifted, overachieving team that stunned the nation. Once Alcindor strolled onto the court and began to showcase his breathtaking ability, the tall, intimidating kid turned UCLA into a monster favored to win every game.

Almost as if it had been preordained, Alcindor's arrival coincided with the opening of Pauley Pavilion, the glittering, new basketball palace on campus that Wooden had been promised for years. It was, at the time, a $5 million facility with more than 12,000 seats—all of which would soon be filled once people got a load of the gangly new kid who would enthrall fans and boosters for the next few years.

If there were any doubts, Alcindor erased them in Pauley Pavilion's opening game, a match between Wooden's still-talented defending NCAA champions and the Lew-led freshmen. The best way to describe Alcindor's debut was spellbinding. He didn't play with the defending champs. He basically toyed with them, scoring thirty-one points, gathering twenty-one rebounds, blocking shots from everywhere, and forcing the varsity into an embarrassing 35 percent shooting night. The varsity tried to utilize its famed zone press to get back into the game, but with Alcindor stationed at mid-court, his frosh teammates merely had to lob the ball high in the air and that was the end of that. The press and maybe the varsity's spirit were both broken. The freshmen won, 75–60, and the varsity never quite achieved the success many had predicted for it as the season progressed.

Maybe that was because the fans and most of the basketball public already were looking ahead to the 1966-67 season, Alcindor's first with the varsity. No one wanted to put too much pressure on the Bruins, but in the first national poll that season, they were ranked No. 1 before the heralded sophomore had even put up his first shot. It was, they were soon to discover in Westwood, all part of the package that comes with a player of this magnitude. The expectations and the pressure had quickly been dialed up several notches.

Life would change for UCLA, and Wooden, too, would be forced to change, in more ways than the coach could have anticipated. First, he had to alter his mindset. He had to accept the fact that he'd be going into every game as the favorite for the next three years, a concept that could intimidate even the greatest coach in any sport. Before, Wooden would go into every game always trying to win. Suddenly, in this strange new rarefied world, the priority would be to try to avoid losing. The difference was difficult and not nearly as much fun.

Next, he had to alter the familiar high-post style of offense he always loved. Putting Lew Alcindor at the high post would have been like putting Sandy Koufax in center field. With potentially the greatest center the game had seen, Wooden had to switch to a low-post offense to take advantage of his sophomore's obvious talent in the paint.

If the coach had any doubts he was doing the right thing, they were quickly dispelled the night of December 3, 1966, when Alcindor made his varsity debut against UCLA's crosstown rivals from USC.

"I still remember that opener as one of the most memorable games of my college career," Jabbar says. He should. He poured in a school-record fifty-six points. "I don't think Coach Wooden wanted me to come out of the gate that way, but there was nothing he could do," he says.

But if people thought that would be the norm, if they assumed Alcindor would lead the nation in scoring, they were mistaken. That is not the way he or Wooden wanted it. The more the finest player in the sport observed the team-style basketball his coach taught, the more impressed he was with it.

"The whole idea of team efficiency, as opposed to having a high scoring average, appealed to me," Jabbar says. "I was primed to play that way. Back home, I used to go to the Garden [Madison Square Garden] and watch the Celtics play the Knicks. I loved the way they played so unselfishly. I'd come back the next day to school, and Coach Donahue would ask me, 'OK, how many of those guys on the Celtics got twenty [points]?' I'd say, 'None.' He'd say, 'Exactly. But they still killed them, didn't they?'"

Later, Alcindor would be just as eager to inhale Wooden's theories. "It really was enlightening to me to see how he would break down the game and all its elements," he says. "He had a way of stringing fundamentals together that gave us a tremendous advantage. He taught me how all positions were supposed to relate to each other."

What Wooden couldn't teach him, not by himself, anyway, was how to cope with the attention and adulation and, yes, the lack of privacy he would have to endure. "There was a lot to deal with," Jabbar says. "Just the idea of puberty and trying to become an adult was a lot by itself, then on top of that I had all the rigors of college athletics. What's the old saying? When you're polishing a diamond, you either destroy the stone or it comes out a brilliant jewel. Well, Coach Wooden's positive attitude helped me come out of it all in good shape."

Off the court, the Alcindor Era was not a joyous time at UCLA—not for Lew, not for Wooden, not for the media, not for anyone. It soon became clear this was an intelligent, but complex young man who was not entirely comfortable living in his seven-foot-one body. How could he be? Everywhere he went, people stared and gawked and pointed at him. I remember the thing that struck me most was that, even in airports, he would rush to find the nearest seat, settling into it with a slouch and hoping that when he was seated, at least, he wouldn't be so conspicuous.

As a sophomore, Alcindor lived by himself in a Westwood apartment, and although he had some friends on the team, he came off more as a loner who liked to read and listen to jazz. Even then, he was a student of black history and an admirer of Malcolm X. "I wanted to know all I could about my people," he says. When the civil rights issues began to dominate the news, he became even more engrossed. There were some who later would say Wooden couldn't deal with all that, claiming that he never understood his young superstar. Abdul-Jabbar says that isn't true.

"Coach Wooden was very supportive of my views," he says. "You know, the [Ku Klux] Klan was very active in Indiana, where he was from. He'd seen it as a young man and thought that it was ugly. So, it was not a great leap for him to understand what was happening around the country. He also played basketball against the Harlem Rens, a team I had researched and knew a lot about. He told me about it, and I think that brought us closer. The whole brotherhood of basketball thing Coach Wooden was connected to in positive ways. And we talked about it often in those days."

Wooden was getting an education on race relations, too. "Once I walked into a restaurant with Lewis," the coach says, "and this woman shouted out: 'Oh, look at that big, black freak.' I could feel Lewis go rigid, and I tried my best to tell him that it was just a demonstration of ignorance. But I learned a great deal about the inhumanity of man from being around him. What he had to go through wasn't easy."

Alcindor was quietly changing along with the world around him. "Between my freshman and sophomore years, I had read the biography of Malcolm X and pretty much made up my mind I was going to be a Muslim," he says. "It was no big deal to Coach Wooden. He understood. I didn't want to join the Black Muslims, or anything. I wanted to still try to fit in and be a good citizen. Besides, we had a lot of different religions on that team. We had Donnie Saffer, who was Jewish, and several players of Christian faith. We also had some guys who thought they were hippies, even if they weren't."

Alcindor and the media didn't get off to a good start. Whether he had struck a deal with the school before signing or not was never determined, but UCLA decided it would close the Bruins locker room after games. Some perceived it as a way to protect the introverted Alcindor. But Wooden, who always worried about the team first, explained he was doing it because if he opened the locker room, the only player writers and broadcasters would rush to was Alcindor and the rest of the team would feel slighted. So, near the end of games, UCLA's sports information director, the late Vic Kelley, would send an assistant through press row asking which players the reporters would like to interview. Then Kelley would choose two to bring outside in the hallway.

Writers sneered at this policy, and after a while, some of us would pick the last guy on the bench who never got into games, just to demonstrate our disgust. It was a frustrating time. Here you had the finest basketball team in the country, a raging dynasty unlike anything the sport had seen, and there was no access after regular-season games to the player everybody wanted to read about.

"I still feel I did the right thing in that regard," Wooden says. Many of us still feel he didn't. The result for Alcindor was that the public never really got to know how intelligent and articulate he was, even at that age. He was sheltered throughout his college career, and when he moved on to the NBA, he never appeared comfortable in interviews, especially in the locker room.

At one point early in his collegiate career, rumors circulated that Alcindor wished he'd gone somewhere else to play basketball. They said he was unhappy with the general atmosphere at a "commuter school" like UCLA. "What that really was," Jabbar says today, "was a kid bellyaching whenever things got difficult. You want to be a man and sometimes you need guidance. It's funny, but

I look back now and those were the good old days. You never get to do that again, to experience college life. It is sad to see that, for most college basketball players today, it's less than the norm. Now kids want to play a year or two and jump to the NBA. It's too bad, because they're missing out on the greatest years of their life."

Alcindor's greatest years began with his sophomore season on a team with three other sophomores and a junior. Of course, all four sophs had been high school All-Americans, including guard Lucius Allen and forwards Lynn Shackelford and Kenny Heitz. The leader was Mike Warren, the junior guard Wooden still describes as "the smartest player I've ever had." Allen was a satiny smooth kid who looked like a future NBA star. Shackelford had the game's most unorthodox, left-handed jump shot, but the funny thing is that it almost always went in. Heitz would develop into one of the better defensive players of the Wooden Era.

So despite its youth, there was no stopping this team with Alcindor in the middle and so many weapons around him. It coasted to a perfect 30–0 season, and Alcindor was named MVP of the NCAA Tournament, an honor he would win all three of his seasons at UCLA.

Strangely, though, the public reaction to this championship was one of general indifference. Of course this team won the national title, what did you expect? That seemed to be the general tone. And as Alcindor's career progressed, the only time the national media took notice was when the Bruins had a close call or on that rare occasion when it actually lost. "People were expecting us to win." Abdul-Jabbar says. "It was almost as if we didn't win three national titles, we'd be considered a failure."

As it was, all they did was go 88–2, losing for the first time in Alcindor's junior year in that monumental match in the Houston Astrodome in the game that changed the scope of college basketball. Elvin Hayes went wild that night, delivering jump shots from somewhere out in center field, or so it seemed, and the Cougars won a thrilling, close game, 71–69. Although Alcindor played hurt, suffering from a scratched eyeball that prevented him practicing all week, Houston took over the No. 1 national rating, and Wooden was gracious in defeat. Quietly, however, the Bruins simmered about the loss and couldn't wait for a chance at a rematch.

It arrived in the NCAA semifinals at the Los Angeles Sports Arena, and with Alcindor and his teammates as emotionally ready as they'd been for any game, they blew Hayes and the Cougars away, winning, 101–69, in probably the greatest team performance of the Alcindor years.

"I certainly think we enjoyed that game more than any game we played at UCLA," Jabbar says. "The press really wore them down, too. It was quite a game and very fulfilling."

The only other loss came in Alcindor's senior year when USC's Bob Boyd, an excellent coach forced to spend most of his career operating in Wooden's shadow in Los Angeles, designed a slow-down, or "stall," strategy in an attempt to offset UCLA's dominant player in the middle. It worked, too. After much booing and catcalling from the faithful at Pauley Pavilion, Boyd's Trojans managed to keep the game close throughout and in the final seconds, won it, 46–44, on a shot by senior Ernie Powell to register the first defeat for UCLA at Pauley.

The Alcindor Express recovered quickly from that slight diversion and rattled on into another NCAA Tournament where, in perhaps the scariest moment of the big center's collegiate career, Drake University almost produced an upset for the ages in the NCAA semifinals in Louisville, Kentucky. They caught the Bruins possibly looking ahead to a match with Purdue and Rick Mount in the Finals, although UCLA did hang on to win. The final score was 85–82, and for one of the few times after a game, Wooden appeared ashen-faced and relieved.

"I remember thinking, *What's going on here?* during that game against Drake," Abdul-Jabbar says. "I think for one of the few times we had some problems with team unity. I remember one of our players, Bill Sweek, got into a deal with Coach, and we just never really seemed in sync."

The Bruins made it through to the game with Purdue, and in his grand finale, Alcindor was rarely better. He scored thirty-seven points and snapped up twenty rebounds in the 92–72 rout, and you could almost sense his relief, the huge burden of expectations he was shaking off his shoulders. He had done what had been expected: He brought an unprecedented three consecutive national championships to UCLA and was named MVP of the tournament all three years. No one, not Wilt Chamberlain, who never won the national title at Kansas, or Bill Russell, who won twice at USF, had won three in a row before. Now Alcindor and Wooden had done it.

"Later on," Abdul-Jabbar says, "I would look back and think, *Wow.* We were the first team to win three in a row and be part of a dynasty that would go on to capture seven in a row. We belonged right up there with the Yankees dynasty or the Celtics. Some of us had to go through a lot to get there, but now, as I look back, it was worth it. It is something they can never take away. You know, I broadcast some college games for CBS, and I've had a chance to see the game up close. And you realize what we accomplished is never going to happen again. You are just never going to see a dynasty like the one we had."

Abdul-Jabbar has also come to realize something else: The game never will see a coach like Wooden again, either. "He was the ultimate," he says. "He was a teacher above all else. He taught us about life, as well as sports. I was an English major, and he was a former English teacher. So I could ask him anything, and he'd have it on his fingertips. What he did was challenge us. And he did it without taking away our spirit. What he did has helped me in so many ways, especially in being a parent. He taught me how to instill confidence in others. He made me understand that everything is a learning game. It's all learning about yourself and learning how to be successful."

Like other former UCLA players who moved on to the pros, Abdul-Jabbar realized he had an immediate advantage, thanks to Wooden. "All of us who played for him were so sound fundamentally," he says. "We understood the game so well, and that really helped us be successful in the NBA. It was amazing, but Gail Goodrich and I played together my first year with the Lakers, and although we went to UCLA in different years, it was as if we'd been on the same team. He knew where to pass the ball and how to find the slots when people were double-teaming me. And I knew how to get him the ball when he was open, because both of us were trained by Coach Wooden. It was as if were on the same wavelength, which I guess we were."

Just as in college, Abdul-Jabbar's interests range beyond the basketball floor, even though he still would like to coach an NBA team some day. He just completed writing a book about an all black unit, the 761st Tank Battalion in World War II. "Jackie Robinson was in that battalion for a while, and he was court-martialed when he wouldn't go to the back of the bus," Abdul-Jabbar says. "Patton eventually called the unit up, and they were one of the first units to invade the German heartland. I've really enjoyed writing the story, and I'm also working on a movie script."

Like most former players, he has remained in contact with Coach Wooden. "I see him at special events," says Abdul-Jabbar, who now works as a scout for the New York Knicks. "We're often honored together. He is as amazing as ever. Even at his age, he can recite his favorite poems or scriptures. He'll remember something about our second game against Cal in my sophomore season, and I'll say, 'Whoa, wait a minute. How does he do this?' I just hope I can be that sharp at that age. When you look back at his legacy, at the players, the children, grandchildren, and great-grandchildren he has produced, it's just remarkable. I always speak of the privilege of playing for him. He was a person who cared and taught people proper values. And he was always genuine about it. He got rich from it. Not in material wealth. But he got rich from it. It boggles your mind to think what he would be worth in today's market. His value as an educator, you just can't quantify that.

"You know, Charles Barkley said he was born too soon. And I realize someone with my talent coming out of high school today would be a very wealthy man. I missed out on some of that. But I got to go to UCLA and play for Coach Wooden, and to have that experience was truly extraordinary."

Two years ago, Abdul-Jabbar coached the Oklahoma Storm in the United States Basketball League. "The toughest thing for me was to get the players to realize they didn't have to be flashy and showboat to win," he says. "They actually think they should hot dog it. That's the problem. They see the whole thing as a means of self-expression. Teaching them to lay it up instead of windmilling a dunk, that's a hard value to get across. They want attention so badly. But we did win the league, though. I was happy about that. I tried to teach them that winning for the team was the most important thing, not putting the spotlight on individuals. Even then, in our championship game, we were down sixteen points."

That's when Abdul-Jabbar called a timeout and switched to a ploy he'd learned from his mentor at UCLA. "We went into a 2-2-1 zone press and turned the game around. I thought about that later. I thought that if Coach Wooden had seen that game, he would have been proud."

The Disciple

When you choose to interview Bill Walton, you know it is bound to be different. It has to be, or it wouldn't be him. Even the precise directions he gives you to his house are, well, pure Walton. "Park in the street and walk up the driveway," he wrote in his carefully constructed e-mail, "but make sure you go past the tennis court and the teepee before you get to the front door."

Yes, he has a teepee in his backyard. Would it be Walton if he didn't? From the beginning, this tall redhead with the ingratiating smile was the free-spirited, free-thinking symbol of American youth in the 1970s. Full of fun, full of mischief, but a young man whose mind was always as fertile and far-ranging as his basketball skills.

He hasn't changed now, as he glides gently into his fifties, his hair slowly turning from red to gray. There is the sprawling, stylish house near the Hillcrest section of San Diego, located on three flowing acres, with a backyard full of trees, fountains, and rock formations that could pass for the lush courtyard of a Hawaiian hotel.

Inside, the home is decorated in early Grateful Dead. Walton's infatuation with the rock group is well-known by now. He might be the original

Deadhead. And there are enough souvenirs and artifacts strewn throughout his house to make you think the late Jerry Garcia lived there.

"I don't know who we have more pictures of around here," says Lori Walton, Bill's vivacious wife, "Jerry or Coach Wooden."

Of all John Wooden's former players, Walton is probably his leading disciple. Part of the reason is that Walton is more visible in his growing role as a loquacious color commentator on nationally televised basketball games, often interrupting play to mention, "As Coach Wooden always used to tell us . . ." Some enjoy the references to his legendary former coach. Others are infuriated by his constant rants about Wooden and his homespun philosophy. None of that matters to Walton. He worships at his mentor's shrine. He is so taken by the man and what he stands for that he can't wait to spread the gospel of Wooden everywhere he goes.

"For me, playing basketball at UCLA was perfect," Walton says. "Playing for Coach Wooden was perfect. I signed a contract with the Portland Tail Blazers making me the highest paid player in the history of team sports at the time. And the quality of my life actually went down. That's how great it was to play at UCLA for Coach Wooden.

"But you know, it didn't dawn on me until I got to the NBA how special Wooden really was. And I think I am learning more from him today than I did when I was playing. I must, because whenever I see him, he says: "Walton, you're the slowest learner I ever had."

It is clear Walton is one of Wooden's favorites, too. But this is a relationship that wasn't always as smooth as one of Bill's turnaround jumpers. Walton was a child of the Vietnam era, and, like so many of his peers, he wanted to wear his hair long and his shirts tie-dyed and chose to protest against the war, all while playing for the conservative coach who grew up in the heartland in a much simpler time.

"In some ways," Walton says, "I was his worst nightmare." But he was also an extraordinarily talented basketball player, one many still consider to be the finest all-around center in the history of the college game. The best part was, it didn't take much to recruit him. Every major school in America was after him, but he had made up his mind years earlier that UCLA was where he wanted to play.

"We grew up in a house without television," Walton says. "But I can still remember, as a thirteen-year-old, going over to a friend's house to watch UCLA play Michigan for the national championship in 1965. It was the first basketball game I'd ever seen on TV. Michigan had Cazzie Russell and Bill Buntin and all these studs. The Bruins had Gail Goodrich, Kenny Washington, and all these skinny, scrawny guys. I looked at them and figured no way UCLA could win this game. But then they went out and were quick, and they exuded teamwork and ball movement. They were playing John Wooden basketball, and right then I knew. That's what I wanted to do. That's where I wanted to play basketball."

COURTESY OF BILL WALTON

Bill Walton and Wooden remain close to this day. The former star turned broadcaster and the coach talk at least three times a week, and Walton never fails to visit when he attends UCLA games.

Walton's parents were convinced three years later. They'd been inundated by college coaches calling and stopping by the house, offering scholarships and making promises. "Some of the promises were off the charts," Walton recalls. "The things these coaches were saying I could have. Let your imagination run wild and you still wouldn't come close. I couldn't believe it."

Then, one day, Wooden arrived at the Walton home in La Mesa, where his parents still reside. "Coach Wooden comes in and says, 'I'm aware of what other schools have promised you. I won't promise anything. I won't even promise you'll make the team. First, you'll have to prove you are a fine young man with good personal values. Then you'll have to demonstrate you can do well in the classroom. If you can do that, we'll give you a practice jersey and allow you to try out for the team.'"

"I'm fairly sure," Walton says, with a smile, "my parents pretty much were sold right there."

So Bill Walton, hotshot recruit, the most sought-after high school player in America, shows up at UCLA in the fall of 1970 and strolls out to his first practice at Pauley Pavilion. To this day, he still remembers his first impression of Wooden at practice.

"I thought he was nuts," Walton says. "Coach Wooden comes out, this little guy, dragging one leg, squinting through his glasses, and he says, 'OK, you new guys come with me.' I figure he's going to let us play by ourselves to see what we've got. Instead, he takes us into the locker room. He comes in and says, 'This is how you put on your shoes and socks.' We all look at each other in disbelief. Then he took off his own shoes, and you could see his varicose veins and his hammertoes. He even had some fungus growing on one of his nails. It was gross. But he showed us the right way to do it to avoid blisters and other problems with our feet.

"Then, for the next four years, he proceeded to show us everything we needed to know. He would eventually show us how to eat properly, how and when to sleep, how to warm up, how to shoot, how to organize our day. Nothing was left to chance. Basketball was his link, but he was really teaching life. He never talked winning or losing, only about giving our best effort. There was no hype, no ego out of control. He was the most selfless person I'd ever met. His whole thing was about giving up accolades in his own life to make other people's dreams come true. And you know what? He still has those same varicose veins and hammertoes today. And he's still outthinking all of us."

If Walton has become a complete convert today, he wasn't back then. He was young and headstrong, intelligent, but still as immature as most of us were at that age. "I think the only real mistake I made at UCLA was having Bill as my best friend," says Greg Lee, chuckling. Along with everything else, Walton had a severe stuttering problem that made him feel self-conscious, especially in front of the media. But even that wouldn't stop him from speaking out when he thought something was wrong.

"Walton was different than the rest of us," says Sidney Wicks, who had been the precursor at stirring things up in Westwood. "He actually went to jail. He did things the rest of us couldn't. Bill forced Coach to do things we never even thought about. Bill never did back off, and I respect him for that. But those were different times."

The most famous story revolves around Walton's urge to let his hair grow long, as was the style in those days. He arrived on campus one day with his red locks at shoulder length. "He told me," says Wooden, "that I didn't have the right to tell him how to wear his hair. I said, 'You're right. I don't. I just have the right to set rules for my team. I want you to know I fully understand your feelings. And we're going to miss you, Bill.'" Walton had his hair cut later that same day.

"It was a changing world," Walton says. "We thought what was going on with the war was ridiculous. We didn't challenge authority, necessarily. We challenged the structure."

And in so doing, Walton challenged his coach. When he wasn't practicing basketball, he was protesting in the streets. One day, he and his fellow protesters proceeded to lie down on Wilshire Boulevard, the busiest, most congested street in west Los Angeles, not far from the UCLA campus. With traffic snarled and chaos ensuing, the police soon arrived, and Walton and his friends were arrested. When Wooden arrived to help bail him out of jail, it didn't take long for Bill to realize how disappointed the coach was in him.

"We were driving back to school," Walton says, "and I can still remember what the coach said. 'Come on, Bill,' he asked, 'what do you think you're doing? You're the NCAA Player of the Year, representing UCLA. What do you think you're doing?' I told him I couldn't help it. 'Coach,' I said, 'a lot of my friends are coming back [from the war] in body bags.' He said he knew that. 'I'm against the war, too,' he said, 'but protesting is not the right way.' His parting shot to me was, 'Bill, I know you firmly believe in all that stuff. But I'm appalled at your course of action.' Then we parted as we got to my dorm room."

If you knew Walton, you realized he couldn't leave it at that. "I went back to his office. He wasn't in, but his secretary was. I asked her if I could have some of the coach's stationary. She said sure. So I took this sheet with Coach Wooden's picture on it and I wrote this script of a letter to President Nixon, demanding his resignation. I had it all typed up and brought it to our locker room later that day. The whole team proceeded to sign it. It was almost like our own declaration of independence. Then I took it to Coach Wooden's locker. I showed him the letter and said I'd like him to sign it. I remember him holding up the letter. You could see he wanted to tear it up. Then he looks up at me with the sad, soft eyes of a father who'd been let down. He said, 'You're not going to send that in.' He gave it back to me, and I did send it. The funny thing was, not long after that, Nixon resigned."

Walton's political beliefs were not the only thing that drove Wooden up the wall. Bill and his friends on that team, including Lee, Larry Hollyfield and others, were all into experimenting and pushing the envelope. Wooden couldn't understand the way they dressed, the way they looked, their strange eating habits (several were attempting to be vegetarians), and he certainly wasn't a fan of their music.

"Once, when we were having some give and take with Coach, we threw back a couple of [Bob] Dylan lines at him," Walton recalls. "He got so mad. He said, 'If I hear any more of that Dy-land—that's how he pronounced it, Dy-land—crap from you guys, that will be the end of it.' Well, we couldn't believe he'd used the word *crap*. It was the only time he'd come even close to something that could be called a cuss word. We were amazed, and that's all we could talk about for days."

Walton's game, punctuated by an unfettered joy for team basketball, already was impressive when he arrived. But it continued to grow at UCLA, even if he wasn't playing where he wanted to on the court. "I wanted to be near the basket, where I could shoot more," he says. "Coach told me I also had to play the high post, where I could pass and see more efficiently. I didn't understand, but he was right, of course."

UCLA went 30–0 in each of Walton's first two seasons (freshmen weren't eligible for the varsity at the time). "No one dominated the sport the way Bill did," says Lee, who fed him many of his passes. "If he were around today, there's no way he would have stayed his senior year. He would have been long gone." But Walton did stay, and in his senior year, the Bruins were overwhelming favorites to win again, although the team's incredible 88-game winning streak was stopped early in the season at Notre Dame. And later, in the semifinals of the NCAA Tournament, UCLA was shocked by David Thompson and North Carolina State. Walton is convinced bad karma had something to do with it.

"Before the start of each season opener, Coach would always come into the locker room and talk about the importance of a good start to insure that undefeated season," Walton says. "Then he would glance toward the corner of the room, as if he had spied something out of place. We would follow his gaze until we saw a penny sitting on its edge. "'Men,' he would say, holding the coin up for all to see, 'this penny means good luck.' The first time I heard the speech, we finished 30–0 and won the national title. The second time I heard the speech, we finished 30–0 and won the national title. The third time was different. By now we knew the speech by heart. We also knew that Coach Wooden had instructed an assistant to place the penny in the corner. Before Coach entered the locker room, I snatched the lucky penny, put it in my pocket and watched as he tried to find the coin on the ground. Something was obviously wrong.

"'Coach,' I said, as I stood up in the center of the room, 'We're a great basketball team. We don't need luck. We know what to do.' At least we thought we did. Coach Wooden had always told us how important it was to be able to look everyone squarely in the eye after a game with the confidence that we had done our best, that we did not beat ourselves. He was right again. Beating yourself is the worst kind of loss to endure. The kind you never get over. The kind you never forget. We learned the hard way; we usually do: You can never discount the power of luck. And you should never fool with John Wooden's penny."

If it didn't end as well as everyone had hoped, Walton's college career was still an overwhelming success. During his three All-America years, the Bruins went 86–4 and won two NCAA titles. He averaged 20.3 points, about half what he might have averaged had he gone somewhere else, where they might have allowed him to shoot at will. But for averaging 15.7 rebounds per game and shooting a remarkable 65 percent from the floor, he was a three-time winner of the Naismith Player of the Year award, and he was also an Academic All-American. He appeared on the cover of *Sports Illustrated* eight times.

Everyone agreed he was the best "white center" they had seen. Others went even further. "He's the best college basketball player I've ever seen," says Carroll Williams, the coach at Santa Clara. "He's better at both ends of the court than Lew Alcindor was. He dominates like no college player in the history of the game. And that includes Bill Russell, whom I played against."

Unquestionably, Walton's signature game came against Memphis State in his junior year, when Walton made twenty-one of twenty-two shots and finished with forty-four points, breaking the NCAA record set by Gail Goodrich in the game that was the first Walton had ever watched on television. Walton's performance that night, in the Bruins' 87–66 victory, is still generally considered the greatest in NCAA history.

"People don't remember that we were tied at the half, and I had picked up three first-half fouls and had to be pulled from the game," Walton says. "But the second half was different. Memphis State used a questionable zone [defense] against us, allowing Greg [Lee] and Larry Hollyfield to keep laying the ball in my hands at the rim. We ran the same play over and over and scored virtually every time.

"I remember Greg yelling over at one time, 'Hey, Coach, how about calling another play so somebody else can shoot?' Coach Wooden just looked at Lee and said, 'Why?'"

The relationship that Walton and Wooden have now is more than just one of successful student and proud mentor. They have forged a friendship steeped in mutual respect and warm humor. And yes, the coach still continues to amaze his former player.

"In 1994, Coach Wooden, me, and my parents all flew to Washington for an Academic All-American Hall of Fame induction. Both he and I were inducted. That day, he, my mom, and I go to the Lincoln Memorial. We all know how much he admires Abraham Lincoln. Anyway, now we've spent considerable time there and we're coming down the steps from the memorial and Coach says, 'Let's go over here to the Vietnam Memorial.'

"Well, I don't know if you've ever been there, but it's the saddest place on earth. When we get done, we're coming out on the White House end of the memorial, and Coach Wooden, without any prompting, begins to recite this poem. I'm not sure of the name of the poem, but it's all about the evils of war. He didn't say anything else. He just recited the poem. It was incredibly powerful."

You suspect it was also Wooden's unique way to letting Walton know he understood what he was so angry about during his student days. This wise coach, who didn't believe in protesting, still realized why his best basketball player wanted to vent against a war he felt was wrong and unjust.

These days, the mood between coach and player is much lighter. Walton, the fun-lover, calls Wooden two or three times a week, usually with a joke or a mock attempt to make light of one of the coach's habits. Wooden, with a more subtle sense of humor, always manages to get in a few shots of his own.

While conversing about Walton and other players in his condo, Wooden will often pause and tell one of his favorite stories.

"You know, Bill Walton's mom called me the other day," he'll say, with that sly twinkle in his eye. "She told me she was so happy that those sportscasters and speech therapists had taught Bill how to speak. But she said there was only one problem. They didn't bother to teach him how to stop."

13

The Role Model

Whenever John Wooden is asked to name the greatest player he coached, his answer is always the same. He regards Lew Alcindor as "the most valuable player I've ever had." He adds that Bill Walton "would have graded out the highest on an overall test of basketball skills." He describes Mike Warren as his smartest player, Walt Hazzard as the best on the fast break and groups Gail Goodrich, Keith Erickson, and David Meyers among his most competitive. Then he always adds: "And if you considered everything—athletic, academic, and citizenship skills—Keith Wilkes might have topped them all."

It is the perfect way to honor Wilkes, who later embraced the Muslim faith and changed his first name to Jamaal, because he, in many ways, was the ideal Wooden player: so smooth, so elegant, so beautifully understated. Unlike many of the other great UCLA players in Wooden's time, Wilkes always seemed to be under control, both on the court and off. The son of a Baptist minister and a mother who was a bookkeeper in education, Wilkes was the quiet, All-America complement to the fiery, redheaded Walton, who played alongside him. Walton was always animated and emotional. Wilkes was cool and composed. Both proved to be Academic All-Americans as well, but while Walton was likely to be out on Wilshire Boulevard protesting, Wilkes was more apt to be in the university library studying.

Yet it is interesting that, of all Wooden's former players, it is Wilkes he perhaps helped the most after his UCLA playing days were over. It is Wilkes, the inquisitive kid who used to come to his office and listen to the coach recite poetry, who would later seek out this man to aid him in a time of personal distress.

"I was going through a difficult divorce," Wilkes says. "My second wife now is a great lady, but at the time, I was having problems and I went to see him. Sometimes, all you need is a little nudge, but Coach would listen and not be judgmental. He is a master at saying so much with so little words. I don't think he'll ever know how much he helped me at the time. The thing about it is, he honestly feels like it is an obligation to help his former players. He wants to make a difference in young peoples' lives. It is serious for him. He doesn't grandstand about it. But you can see it is very important to him.

"There is a quality, kind of like an aura, about him that is really, really strong. I don't know what to call it, but it is special. I know, for me, I love my dad. He's a great man. But I can go to Coach Wooden for a more honest, detached perspective. When you go to Coach, you don't even have to say you have a problem. You can just say, 'What if?' And he'll understand. He won't press you for the details. He will just listen and try to help you solve it."

Keith Wilkes grew up in Ventura County, about sixty miles north of Westwood. He attended Santa Barbara High as a senior, where he developed into a thin, almost slinky athlete who moved and scored easily at the high school level. He had soft hands, a delicate shooting touch, and the kind of quickness Wooden always coveted in his players, so it wasn't long before UCLA took notice.

"I think Coach [Denny] Crum did most of the recruiting. I didn't meet Wooden until I took my official trip to UCLA. When I finally made my decision, it was the first opportunity to really see this person I'd heard so much about. I mean, to a kid of seventeen, this was like meeting the Wizard of Oz. He was already such a legend and all. I thought he would be superhuman, but my first impression was that this is a nice, friendly man. He was like one of the neighbors, or something."

Wilkes's opinion quickly changed after his first contact with the coach as a freshman. "I have to admit, it was baffling," he says, echoing so many other players' views, when the famous coach first showed them how to wear their socks properly and how to tie their shoes. "Lots of guys were making fun of him, but I wasn't," Wilkes says. "I felt it was such a privilege to be there, I didn't want to call any unnecessary attention to myself. Besides, even early,

I knew there something special about this guy."

Once practice started, Wilkes, like so many before him, discovered what it was. "Every drill, every word had a purpose," he says. "The confidence he instilled in you through conditioning was amazing. You believed it. You believed that you were in better condition than your opponents. Our practices were extremely well organized and competitive. They were a lot more competitive than some of our games."

This was in the midst of UCLA's golden era, at a time when the Bruins were rolling up their 88-game winning streak, and Walton, Wilkes, and Company seemed like they were completely unbeatable. Some critics scoffed and called them robots, but they weren't. They were just young kids lucky enough to be playing for a coach and a system that was probably the finest in college basketball history.

COURTESY OF UCLA ATHLETIC DEPARTMENT

Coach Wooden presents Keith Wilkes with his Academic All-American award at the Hall of Fame. The coach was, and still is, a great admirer of his star forward, both on and off the basketball court.

"I can't say that by my sophomore and junior year I understood all that was going on," Wilkes says. "I was like your normal college student, just trying to get through school and have some fun. But by the time I was a senior, I grew to have complete confidence in this man. I also knew he was there for help if you needed it. I grew up in a relatively small city, and I would often feel overwhelmed by Los Angeles and student life. When I felt that way, I would go by his office and sit down with him, and he would start reciting poetry. It was a very positive thing, but it was intimidating. I had some trepidation about not being able to please him; I wanted to do that so badly. Yet, every time I would leave his office, I would feel totally exhilarated and inspired. I didn't always know why. And sometime the things he said even sounded corny. But it was genuine. That's who he was. And he made it feel like my personal moment with him. I will always cherish those times."

For all their success, the 1973–74 senior season for the Walton Gang proved more than a little chaotic. Off the court, the Vietnam War was a subject of great debate throughout the country. And at UCLA, as on most college campuses, students were railing against the government, demanding that America get its soldiers out of Southeast Asia and stop killing innocent people. Walton, of course, became something of an athletic symbol for protest in America at the time. Wilkes did not.

"I wasn't one of those demonstrating," Wilkes says. "Bill always pushed the envelope. Because he was so out front, he had a lot of people in his ear. We had a lot of guys on our team experimenting with vegetarianism and transcendental meditation, things like that. The world was changing, but I was just a twenty- or twenty-one-year-old kid trying to get though college. I didn't get arrested on Wilshire Boulevard like Bill did. But I did come to realize how crazy the times were. Looking back, I marvel now how this coach, this guy from Martinsville, responded to so many challenges. Before this Vietnam protest thing, he had [Sidney] Wicks and [Curtis] Rowe and a lot of civil rights issues. But he was always in a bend-but-don't-break mode. He managed to stay open-minded, but at the same time he was extremely consistent in his beliefs."

In many minds, the Walton-Wilkes teams were, at their apex, the finest of Wooden's record-breaking era. They cruised undefeated through their first two seasons, but soon after that surreal 88-game winning streak was broken by Notre Dame in one of the most memorable games in NCAA history, some small cracks seemed to develop in their blue-and-gold veneer.

"We lost four games, all in our senior year," Wilkes says.

The worst loss, of course, was the last one—the crushing, overtime 80–77 defeat to David Thompson and North Carolina State in the NCAA semifinals that cost the Walton Gang its opportunity to win three national championships in a row. To this day, Bill Walton says that if there is one thing he could do over in his life, it would be to replay that game. Wooden won't say that, but he will say it was one of the biggest disappointments in his coaching career.

"I think it was very hard on him, because it was very hard on us," Wilkes says. "As kids, we were really depressed. I think we had begun to believe that we were invincible."

You really couldn't blame them. Pauley Pavilion was a grand place to be in those years. It was the Taj Mahal of basketball palaces. The championship banners were draped on the walls, the stands were filled to capacity, the national TV cameras were everywhere. "It was just a great atmosphere," Wilkes says. "In three years, we never lost a home game. And you know, I don't ever recall

Coach saying we've got to win this game. He never made an issue of our [88-game] streak. But at the same time, he was the greatest motivator you ever saw. Not that he ever gave emotional speeches, because he didn't. But he had all these little sayings that sounded corny, but they stuck with you. You began to think about them in different ways. You began to apply them to what you did."

What Wilkes did after leaving UCLA was become one of the NBA's great forwards, first with the Golden State Warriors, with Rick Barry, and then with the Los Angeles Lakers, where he teamed with another all-time Bruins great, Kareem Abdul-Jabbar, the former Lew Alcindor. Next to Jabbar, Wilkes probably enjoyed the most productive professional basketball career of all of Wooden's former players. He was the prototypical small forward who could operate smoothly in the paint. His skills were so understated that the late Lakers announcer Chick Hearn gave him the perfect nickname—"Silk." And that's how he played, silky smooth, always getting his points, always being in perfect position to grab more rebounds than a skinny player like Wilkes should collect.

"As a pro, I started out with the Warriors opposite Rick Barry," Wilkes says. "The only way I could have done that was to be perfectly prepared to play the position. I knew how to move my feet and how to get to certain spots on the floor. I realized it was because of Coach Wooden's training. The more I played, the more I realized the brilliance of his coaching. I would instinctively do things without thinking. And that's because of all those drills that reinforced what you should do. I was succeeding because of all those repetitions he put me through. Somehow, I would always open up properly to the ball; I would always block out for rebounds. You could see it in all his former players. It was pretty amazing to watch."

Although he went on to become a perennial NBA All-Star, Wilkes continued to follow his alma mater. When the news arrived a year after he graduated that Wooden had retired, his reaction was the same as most.

"He had some heart problems my junior year, but I was still shocked," Wilkes says. "You knew it had to end some time, but you hoped it could go on forever."

What didn't end was Wilkes' relationship with Wooden. As the years drifted by and he grew into a mature adult, Wilkes began to appreciate even more what this man meant to him.

Remarried and owner of his own firm, Advanced Financial Services, Wilkes today has three teenage kids: Omar is a sophomore basketball player at Kansas University; Sabreen is in her final year at UCLA; and Jordan is a young, gifted high school player the scouts are already talking about. As busy as Wilkes's life is, though, he still reserves time to call Wooden every week or two.

"It means a lot to me personally to still stay in contact with him," he says. "You can always call him if you want to talk about something. He is always there for you. As an ex-player, you're always talking to other former players, and not many of them can communicate with their old coach.

"You talk about givers and takers in this world. Well, this man is definitely a giver," Wilkes says. "He has never been interested in a big house or having a fancy car. What he has is comfortable to him. He is more about giving. And when you look around the busy world we all live in, you realize that this kind of person just doesn't exist much today. Oh, there are some teachers here and some ministers there who are into giving. But for the most part, you don't see that many people. Especially those like him, who give so freely. It is almost like he has a need to give.

"You read about him as a patriarch, and I don't know what that conjures up in your mind, but to me, it is a very endearing term. To Coach, his players are all part of his extended family. And if you know anything about the man, you know he loves his family. I think that's why, for me and many of the players, our love for him continues to grow. We realize he gave us the essence of himself. And a lot of his philosophy applies to your daily life."

For many, it remains a highlight to visit Wooden in that tiny Encino condo. It is almost like a daily parade, with exceedingly tall individuals stooping down low to squeeze into the small elevator that leads to his floor.

"When you leave after seeing him, you somehow always feel better," Wilkes says. "I don't know what it is. Everyone talks about having consideration for others, but then you see him showing it. He always said if the leaders of the world had more concern for others, there would be less problems. He didn't say *no* problems, but *less* problems. His favorite American is Abraham Lincoln, and Lincoln supposedly once walked a mile to return a penny. Coach Wooden is of that ilk. In this day and age of self-hype and people being self-driven, he is so genuine, it is scary.

"You know, he was such a dominant basketball coach, but what he has to offer now has nothing to do with basketball. It has to do with how you live every day. He is truly unique. He is a treasure. That's what he is. He is truly an American treasure."

The Wild One

Sidney Wicks was one of those special players, a "can't-miss" prospect who was making the all-city team as a fifteen-year-old sophomore at Hamilton High School in Los Angeles. He was bigger, stronger, and quicker than everyone else, and although every college scout in America knew about him, they also knew he was "raw."

Translated, that means he wasn't very well coached in high school, where he was allowed to play on the perimeter, take ill-advised twenty-five-foot shots and fail to dominate games in the paint the way he should have. In his senior year at Hamilton High, Wicks's team didn't even finish first in its conference, let alone the city. Because his grades weren't good enough to get into UCLA, Wicks spent a year at Santa Monica City College, where he was taught by a very good coach named Bobby Dye, who would later take a little-known commuter school, Cal State Fullerton, to the Final Four. But one year under Dye couldn't make up for those three years in high school, and when this six-foot-nine potential wunderkind arrived in Westwood as a sophomore, John Wooden took one look at his undisciplined game and realized there were problems.

"Who was the toughest player you ever had to motivate?" Wooden is asked regularly these days. "Probably Sidney Wicks," is his answer. "He wound up as the best forward in the country his junior and senior years, but his first year with me he sat on the bench. As far as motivating Sidney, the bench was my best ally. The key was to get him to be a team player."

More than thirty years later, Wicks sits in a stylish Beverly Hills restaurant and reminisces about those early, confusing days at UCLA. "My sophomore year, Lew [Alcindor] was still there, they had a lot of talent, and Curtis Rowe and some of the others were coming up from the freshman team," Wicks says. "First time I saw Lew, I thought he was phenomenal. He was so poised, and his demeanor was so amazing, along with all that talent. I'd seen Wilt [Chamberlain] and [Nate] Thurmond, and for his age, he knew he could play against those guys right then. Since I came in from junior college, I was almost like a freshman. It was a completely new season to me. But once I got out on the floor, I realized I was as good as they were, and I thought I was playing well."

But playing well to Wicks was different than playing well for Wooden. While Sidney was remarkably quick and agile for someone his size, he was also too engrossed in making one-on-one moves. Wicks was all about being flashy. Wooden was all about being effective in the context of the team. It hardly came as a surprise that a clash between the two would soon develop.

"Coach would take stats of practices," Wicks says. "I was leading in almost all of the statistical categories, but unfortunately I was also leading in turnovers."

When the season started, Wicks was sitting, while his fellow sophomore and best friend, the more technically sound Curtis Rowe, was starting alongside senior Lynn Shackelford, a great shooter who wasn't nearly as athletic as Sidney. "It was difficult for me to deal with," says Wicks, who had always been the star of the show since he first picked up a basketball. "I figured Shack was a senior and Curtis had been there a year longer than I had, so I was the new guy coming off the bench. I went out and played hard, and, yes, I made my share of mistakes. But I still didn't get it.

"Midway through the season, I went to Coach Wooden's office and asked what was going on. Coach said, 'You're doing well, but I have the luxury of playing players who make the least mistakes. Right now, you lead the team in all categories, including turnovers. You will have to come off the bench until you understand what I'm saying. Once you overcome that problem, you will be OK.' I told him it would be hard to overcome the problem if I didn't play. He said, 'Sidney, if you correct what you are doing wrong, you'll do well.' I said that I still hadn't got the answer I came in for. 'Yes you did,' he said. 'I need to know the players I put out on the floor don't make mistakes. Any other questions?' I said, 'I guess not.' So I left feeling frustrated."

Wicks's frustration would continue for most of that first season in 1968-69. "I didn't enjoy not starting, but I resigned myself to the fact there was nothing I could do," he says. Rowe, who wasn't as skilled as Wicks, was nonetheless far more polished, both offensively and defensively, at that point in his career, while Shackelford was a deadly outside shooter who could help discourage opponents from collapsing inside on Alcindor.

"Many times during practices, I would look over at coach, and he would look back at me as if to say, 'If you understand our conversation, you'll be fine.' Then he'd just sort of smile. By the time the NCAAs came around, I was really, really upset. When I'd get into the games, they were usually over already. And when we played Rick Mount and Purdue in the Finals, I basically didn't even play in that game. But at the end, I realized I'd been part of a successful UCLA season, a championship season. I even managed to make honorable mention all-conference as a second stringer, so I must have showed something."

He had shown plenty. Anyone watching UCLA that season could see that Wicks was the Bruins' future. Only he, among those who would replace Alcindor the next season, had the ability to take over games, to be potentially dominating.

"A lot of people were saying we'd fall apart when Alcindor left," Wicks says. "The other schools may have thought they could come in and kick our booties, but we didn't think so. That summer, we all hung around L.A. and played together as much as we could. Henry Bibby came to town, and he joined us. We went to all these different gyms to play as a unit. We had Rowe, [John] Vallely, and me back, three of our top six returning, and we knew Bibby could play, and we were confident that Steve Patterson would be a good college center."

But the major revelation for Wicks was in his own play. "I was so much better," he says. "I didn't get it at first, then it was like it all clicked in. I wasn't making the same mistakes. You know that phrase Coach Wooden always used, 'Be quick, but don't hurry'? Well, I finally understood it. I knew I had to cut down on my mistakes if I wanted to be starting, so instead of forcing things, I began to let the game come to me."

The more the season progressed, the more Wicks' game began to blossom. By the time the NCAA Tournament came around, he was clearly the go-to player on the team and one of the finest forwards in the country. But with Alcindor gone, most of the national publicity centered on Jacksonville University's upstart team. People were calling Artis Gilmore, Jacksonville's seven-foot-plus center, the "new Alcindor," and Gilmore and his teammate

Rex Morgan were nicknamed "Batman" and "Robin." By the time the Batmobile motored its way into the NCAA Finals in College Park, Maryland, Wicks and UCLA were waiting.

In the game that solidified Wicks's status as the country's next great player, he outperformed Gilmore at both ends of the floor, even rising high into the air to block five of the huge center's shots, helping the Bruins overcome an early nine-point deficit and leading them to a convincing 80–69 victory and a remarkable sixth national championship in seven years. Batman, you could say, had been supplanted by UCLA's latest Superman. Sidney Wicks, had arrived.

"You know, when that Jacksonville game started," Wooden recalls, "we had Sidney fronting Gilmore, and Curtis playing him off to the side. I told Curtis that any pass that went over Sidney, think of it as yours. I thought that defense would work. But it didn't. Gilmore hurt us early. Then we called time out, and Sidney said, 'Let me go behind him.' That's actually what I wanted to try, but I wanted Sidney to suggest it. I said, 'Now, Sidney, you know you can't guard him from behind.' I was trying to motivate him a little. 'Yes, I can,' he insisted. So that's what we did, and Sidney blocked several of Gilmore's shots. In the end, that was the whole key to that game, Sidney accepting the challenge and then going out and showing me he could do it."

"We had a lot of fun that season," Wicks says. "It was Coach Wooden going back to the high-post offense, the style people had always liked about UCLA basketball. It made me realize, hey, this guy [Wooden] is so cool. He can win with any kind of team, with a small center, a big center, or a medium-sized center like Patterson. Back then, we dictated the way games were going to be played. We would look at opponents and say, 'You guys have to adjust to us.' Coach Wooden wouldn't even spend much time on scouting reports or looking at opponents on film, or anything like that. Once in a while, he'd come up to you before a game and say, 'Sidney, this guy you're playing likes to go to his right, so watch out for it.' But that was about it.

"He installed the thought in us that if we played our best, nothing else mattered. We were going to win. I'm telling you, it was just so cool. Playing basketball at UCLA then was the most exciting time in my life."

Wicks managed to make it exciting for Wooden, as well. Sidney's personality was as flamboyant as his game, and he always pushed the envelope. His chirping voice could be heard above all others in practice. And while many of the players were intimidated by Wooden, Wicks never was. He regularly engaged the coach in conversation, even in the midst of practice, while many of his teammates would stand there, staring open-mouthed.

"I was edgy," Wicks says. "I'd always greet him with, 'Hey, Coach, what's going on?' Everyone else was afraid to talk to him. I thought it was good for someone to exchange with him."

Before games, Wicks and Rowe made it a habit to stroll in proudly, like a pair of young peacocks, often dressed less than conservatively, and walk directly in front of the UCLA rooting section. The students would react with hoots and shouts and wild applause. Wicks was a showman, a Reggie Jackson type. He played to the spotlight but often performed his best under pressure. He loved being the guy everyone watched, the one nobody could take his eyes off.

Before the start of their junior year, Wicks and Rowe appeared in

COURTESY OF UCLA ATHLETIC DEPARTMENT

Sidney Wicks came into his own when he outplayed Jacksonville's highly touted Artis Gilmore in the NCAA Finals in 1971. Wicks was the NCAA Player of the Year as a senior.

the locker room for the freshman-varsity intrasquad game. "They were always dressed immaculately, but they hadn't shaved," says Gary Cunningham, who was an assistant coach on that team. Apparently, according to Wicks, the two hadn't cut their Afros down to the size preferred by Wooden, either.

"Wicks comes in and says, 'How you doing, Coach?' Cunningham says. "This is before the game, and Coach says to him, 'You've got five minutes.' Wicks says, 'What do you mean, five minutes?' Coach says, 'You've got four and a half minutes.' This is in Pauley [Pavilion] before the intrasquad game that we used to have. Remember, a lot of people would come out to watch that game. And Coach says, 'You've got four minutes.' Wicks was still puzzled. 'What you mean, Coach?' he asked. 'You've got four minutes to shave that off your face and cut your hair, or your season is over.'

"In Pauley, you know, the locker rooms are downstairs, and there's a training room up at the top. They run up there, and they get the electric shears that you would use to shave the hair off your ankles in order to tape them. It's the kind a barber would use to cut your hair. It was brutal. And they run that thing over their face. And they come down and they've got cuts and everything else, but it's off."

Wicks still remembers that when he and Rowe raced back downstairs, clean-shaven and with their Afros at the appropriate length, they were out of breath. "I looked over at Coach, and he didn't say anything," Wicks recalls. "He just smiled."

Even the next season, when Wicks was an established senior All-American and the clear leader of the team, he had moments when he had to be disciplined. One of them almost cost UCLA a chance at another national championship. The Bruins were playing perhaps the greatest USC team of the modern era. Trojan coach Bob Boyd, with a team led by Paul Westphal and Ron Riley, went 24–2 that season, and the Bruins' crosstown rivals were rated No. 1 in the country, while UCLA was No. 2. When they met for the final time, tied for the conference lead, the stakes were as high as they could get, because back then only the conference champion, advanced to the NCAA Tournament.

"Wicks came late for a pregame meal," Cunningham says, "and Coach goes through the starting lineup: 'Front line—Patterson, Rowe, [John] Ecker.' And Wicks is sitting on the bench. Wooden tells him why. He says, 'You were late for the pregame meal, so you're not going to play.' Sidney says, 'What do you mean, Coach, I'm not going to play?'

"The game goes on, and it's a close game. John Ecker played pretty well. He played very well, actually. I'm sitting there, and Wicks looks down at Coach and says, 'Hey, Coach, I'm ready, I'm ready.' Wicks did that about three times, and he just ignored him. And then he turned around and he said, 'Sidney, you might sit there until you rot.' And he turned his head back toward the game. In the second half, he played Wicks, and Sidney played one of his best games ever. He just took the game over, but he was passing the ball and doing the things we wanted him to do. It was all to teach Sidney a lesson about being on time and discipline. He could have sacrificed the game for that, but Sidney respected him for it."

At the time, on college campuses everywhere, it was an era of protest, with civil rights and the Vietnam War both major issues for students. "We had Angela Davis on campus and student unrest and everything," Wicks says. "Curtis and I joined the Black Student Union. I remember Coach took us aside after he heard. He said, 'I'm not telling you what to believe. You have to follow your hearts. But you can't allow any of this to interfere with your education or playing basketball.' A couple of days later, there was a shooting on campus. Two guys got killed. The next day, we had another meeting with Coach. He said, 'That's what I'm talking about.' We had to refrain from being too active after that. It was hard. But we understood. So did everybody else."

Wooden especially understood. He seemed to allow Wicks more rope than most of his players, in terms of his pranks. "Sidney," says Wooden, "was always great fun. One time, he waved me over after practice, and he had a wrapped gift in his hand. 'Here,' he said, 'take this home to the little woman. She'd like this.' He told me not to unwrap it until I got home. So that's what I did. I drove home and told Nellie, and then we both unwrapped the package. It turned out to be a framed picture of Angela Davis. I laughed and told Nellie that we should have Sidney over and put the picture up in our living room wall. She said, 'We'll do no such thing.' But Sidney and I laughed about it later."

Wicks and Rowe were inseparable in those days. "Yeah, we were as thick as thieves," says Wicks, smiling. "Curtis had a quiet demeanor, but he was very opinionated, although low-key about it. He was a real family person, too. He was like a brother to me. It was like having your brother be the other forward with you on UCLA's national championship team. I mean, you couldn't have scripted it any better than that. Life was good. It was the best time any of us ever had.

"I remember in our junior year, the ABA [the fledgling American Basketball Association] came after us. Coach heard about it, and he said, 'Listen to what they have to say. I can't tell you what to do, but I will say this: Whatever they promise to give you now, they will give you that and more later.' Curtis and I thought about it for about three and a half seconds. Then we said, Hey, we're having too much fun. Why would we want to leave this? We can have all that other stuff later."

It wasn't always fun, though. In Wicks's senior season, UCLA lost to Notre Dame, 89–82, breaking another Bruins winning streak of nineteen games. "It was disheartening to lose," Wicks remembers. "We were just so used to winning. But in South Bend, anything we did, we got called for a foul. Austin Carr had a great game, but anytime you got near him, they'd blow a whistle on you."

Later, back at Los Angeles International Airport on the way home, Wicks was sitting with his head down, appearing totally dejected. "What's wrong, Sidney?" Wooden asked him. "Coach, it just hurts so bad to lose," he replied. "The solution is simple," Wooden said. "Don't let it happen again."

It didn't, either. That team never lost again. Wicks still remembers that quote from his coach. "I thought it was kind of profound," he says. "I figured I can go along with that."

UCLA would win yet another national title in that season, Wicks' senior year. And Wooden's team would do it, typically, emphasizing the team concept. While Sidney had dominated the NCAA Finals against Jacksonville as a junior, the Finals opponent in Salt Lake City in 1971 was Villanova, a team that had decided the way to beat the Bruins was to overload its zone defense to stop Wicks and Rowe. While the Wildcats were busy concentrating on UCLA's forwards, Patterson lit it up for twenty-nine points, saving his best game for last and helping the Bruins to a 68–62 victory and their fifth consecutive national championship.

In the fleeting final moments of that game, as Wicks was coming out to a huge ovation, he went over to the UCLA bench, grasped Wooden's hand and bent down and whispered something in his ear. "I just told him, 'It was my pleasure playing for you here at UCLA,'" Wicks says. "He said, 'Thank you very much.' It was really a nice moment, but it was completely spontaneous. All of a sudden it hit me that this would be my last game at UCLA."

Now, all these years later, the wild kid who had to learn to refine his game and discipline his life has come to appreciate his college coach even more. "You really understand, as you grow older, the things he taught you," Wicks says. "He was so regimented and disciplined. He affected the way I started dealing with things. All that time, he was dealing with the teachings of life. I have a daughter, and she heard many of Coach's sayings through the years. I think it affected her. I also grew to understand his basic philosophy of the game. It was all about team play and mistakes. You play flawless basketball with the talent we had and nobody could beat us. All that talent and no mistakes equated to winning on a consistent basis."

Wicks was equally impressed with Wooden's coaching staff. "We had assistants like Denny Crum and Cunningham," he says. "They were better than good. They were fantastic. Better than you could ever imagine. They would break down the game and tell you how to handle different situations. That was another smart thing Coach did. He always had players who had played for him as assistants. They had been through it before. They knew how to deal with things, and they taught you how to handle it."

When Wicks looks back now, it scares him that in high school he actually considered other colleges. "I'd toyed with other schools, but I don't think I would have made the wrong turn," he says. "I remember being at Hamilton

High and playing a pick-up game, and some guys came in and said, 'Man, you got to see this new player they got at UCLA. He was playing against [Edgar] Lacey and [Mike] Lynn, and he was just killing them. You got to see this guy, man.' And I thought, *Hey, I've got to hop in a car and go take a look.* So I did. The guy they were talking about was Alcindor. I guess I knew right then that I had to go to UCLA.

"You know, I realize there have been some great coaches in college basketball. But I don't think any other coach affected his ballplayers the way Johnny Wooden affected his ballplayers. I don't mean just at the time. I mean for the rest of their lives. He didn't just make you a better player. He made you a better person."

Divorced with one daughter, Wicks, who had an eventful but less than great NBA career, is in the real estate business. Although he spends as much time in North Carolina as he does in Los Angeles, he remains a UCLA basketball season ticket holder and booster. "I still like to go to games, to see everybody and catch up," he says. "Life is sweet.

"When I think back now, I'm just so glad I made the right choice. I don't know what would have happened if I'd gone somewhere other than UCLA. I probably would have scored a lot of points, but I never would have understood how to win. I realize now he was right about me. The things Coach said about my game when I first got here, he was right. If I'd gone somewhere else, I wouldn't have had everything I had at UCLA.

"Hey, I'm a lucky guy. Playing for UCLA back then, having John Wooden coach you, with those great games at Pauley and all those others on national television . . . hey, it just doesn't get any better than that."

The Convert

Andy Hill was like so many of the thousands of young men growing up in Southern California in the 1960s. He loved UCLA basketball. He loved everything about it, from the powder-blue uniforms to the blurring fast breaks to the beautiful cheerleaders. He would stand out in his backyard, like many of us, and dream that he was a Bruins point guard, dribbling the ball in the final seconds, waiting for the last couple of ticks of the clock before going up for the winning jump shot. More often than not, in the quiet confines of his backyard, the ball would swish through the hoop. Andy would smile and hold up his arms and imagine the fans, his teammates, and of course the girls mobbing him on the court in jubilation.

The only thing that made Hill's dream different is that the fates teased him into thinking it could actually happen. The hours of practice in his backyard helped him develop skills that allowed him to become a star at University High School in west Los Angeles, just a ten-minute drive, depending on traffic, from the UCLA campus. A relatively small but good-shooting guard for the Uni team directed by Courtney Borio, a terrific high school coach who had played briefly for Wooden's Bruins in the 1950s, Hill averaged twenty-seven points a game as a senior and

COURTESY OF UCLA ATHLETIC DEPARTMENT

Andy Hill wanted to dribble his way into UCLA's starting lineup in the worst way, but it wasn't to be. A fine high school player in Los Angeles, he played three years in Westwood without starting.

made all-city, an impressive feat in a town noted for its deep basketball talent pool.

Several colleges were interested in recruiting him, including Stanford. But once UCLA called, Hill was overwhelmed by the thought of actually living out his dream. John Wooden met with him, he sat at the same table as Kareem Abdul-Jabbar during a meal on his recruiting visit, and he was generally swept away by the idea of getting to play in Pauley Pavilion.

"I was a kid," Hill says. "What did I know?"

It is a mistake hundreds of thousands of potential athletes have made across the years. Their goal is to play at the very top level of their sport, but even while they are being recruited, no one explains the odds against them. No one tells them they will be competing with some of the most gifted freshmen in America. The Andy Hills of this world could have started for any number of schools in the country. But this was UCLA, and thanks to John Wooden, it was the nation's No. 1 basketball program. And to start for this team, you had to be more than just very good, you had to be extraordinary.

Andy Hill wasn't. He was too small and not very quick, and although he could always shoot some, it wasn't enough to beat out quality, blue-chip athletes like Henry Bibby and Larry Hollyfield. Although he had an excellent season on the freshman team and, for a brief few weeks, looked like he might break into the varsity rotation as a sophomore, Hill's dream slowly dissolved into years of sitting on the bench, wallowing in frustration, even though UCLA won the national championship in all three seasons he was on the team.

It probably didn't help that this clean-cut, shorthaired kid proved to be something of a rebel. This was the 1960s, and Hill was deep into the student anti-war movement. So deep, in fact, that he found himself in an awkward position on the very first day of varsity practice his sophomore season, the day he'd been practicing and planning for all those years. As it turned out, it was also the day of the first national moratorium to protest the war in Vietnam.

Hill and his two closest friends on the team, John Ecker, who was a year ahead of him at University High, and Terry Schofield, from nearby St. Monica's High, went to Wooden and asked him to cancel practice in support of the moratorium. Wooden refused, and Hill's status with the coach got off to a shaky start and would only grow worse in ensuing seasons.

"It was a revolution we lived through," Hill says. "It was a cultural earthquake with this sixty-ish guy from Indiana. I remember Coach saying, 'I don't think this is a good thing.' Looking back today, I think he was probably right. We showed lack of respect for authority. I don't think that was a good thing."

The ensuing months only became more difficult for Hill. "I wanted to play so badly, and my youth made it easy for me to mistake my enthusiasm for talent," he says. "When you're overlooked like I was, it can be really frustrating. And when the person overlooking you is someone like Coach Wooden, someone you always looked up to and even idolized, it can be pretty devastating."

Again, Hill's off-the-court activities didn't help. His role in writing a letter of protest to President Nixon's top aide, H. R. Haldeman, forced the coach to call him in his office and read him out, in the quiet, polite way only Wooden could. In his junior year, not learning his lesson too well, Hill challenged the coach's authority again, arguing that basketball players shouldn't be forced to cut their hair as short as Wooden wanted. By the time he was finished at UCLA, Hill realized he had created more of a stir by his protests than he did with his shot-making. He played very little, usually coming in after the Bruins had built an insurmountable lead late in the second half and the crowds were already filing out of the building.

"I soon came to realize my dream was never going to be fulfilled," Hill says. "Even though I got to play on three national championship teams, by the time my senior year was over, I was more than ready to leave and do something else with my life."

It is safe to say that in the years immediately following, Hill was still bitter about what happened to him at UCLA. If someone was looking for an endorsement for Wooden and his program, Andy would not have been the first to approach. Happily, in the business world, Hill fared much better. After supervising movies and miniseries at Columbia Television, he formed his own production company and produced a Disney-style family movie called *Three Wishes for Jamie* in England. He then started a television production arm for a major theatrical film producer and made three more television movies. By that time, CBS became interested and hired Hill to run the network's in-house production company. As president of CBS Productions, he helped create such hit TV shows as *Touched By an Angel*, *Dr. Quinn, Medicine Woman*, *Caroline in the City*, and *Walker, Texas Ranger*, among others.

Hill had displayed exceptional management skills and had begun to wonder just how such a gift had developed when, one day on a golf course, he had what he describes as "an epiphany." About to hit a shot, his playing partner said, "You're hurrying; slow down and get some balance." To Hill, it was as if his partner were spouting Coach Wooden's words. The fact Hill then hit a beautiful shot was overshadowed by the revelation that much of his success in business could be directly related to the lessons Wooden taught him all that time he was angry and frustrated at UCLA.

"You can imagine how I felt when I realized this man who I was so bitter at was actually responsible for all my success since leaving," Hill says.

So, ten years after he had last spoken to Wooden, Hill decided to call him. With much trepidation, he dialed the number, eventually got through, and asked if he could come out talk with him. Wooden's answer was the same as it always is with one of his former players. "Of course," he said. Hill went to Wooden's condo in Encino, sat with him, and explained the wild emotions he was experiencing and the gratitude he was feeling toward a coach he wasn't always happy with in his playing days.

"Coach nodded at me as I told him," Hill says. "And then he said, 'So you did learn something after all.' I couldn't believe it. Here is this man I fought against, a man I feared much of my time at UCLA, someone I actually despised at times, and we were sitting there talking like old friends."

The story only gets better. Hill was so impressed, he began visiting Wooden regularly. Eventually, he was so overwhelmed by the experience, he decided to write a book. It is called *Be Quick—But Don't Hurry!*, one of Wooden's favorite phrases and one that is recognizable to every player who ever wore a Bruins jersey during the coach's years on the job. Published in 2001 by Simon & Schuster, the small, readable book has done well and has brought the coach and his formerly disgruntled player even closer in the months since it first came out.

While much of *Be Quick—But Don't Hurry!* details Wooden's coaching methods from a player's standpoint, the really interesting segments arrive in the first sixty pages, when Hill writes of his own personal thoughts of this legendary man.

"Before we dive back into the abyss of conflict that characterized my memories of Coach Wooden," Hill writes, "it is important for you to have a clear picture [or at least my clear] picture of this seemingly simple man who many have made out to be almost saintly. John Wooden is not a saint. . . . He genuinely cared that his players get an education, which he considered much more important than playing basketball. . . . It is also true that this outwardly gentle and soft-spoken man might just be the toughest man I ever met. I am sure that many of his former players would concur. No matter how many times this guy got knocked down in his athletic days, there was simply do doubt he was getting back up. He was a tough taskmaster in practice, demanding full attention and effort at all times. . . . While many of Coach's staunchest admirers make a big deal out of the fact he never swears, and it's true that Coach never uses profanity, it is simply ridiculous to say he never swears." Hill goes on to write that Wooden's favorite stern admonishment of 'Goodness gracious sakes alive!' proved he knew how to cuss without using profanity."

It is now several years later, and Hill and Wooden have the kind of warm relationship neither would have imagined back in Andy's playing days. When I contacted Hill and told him I wanted to include his story among those in a section of this book called "The Boys of Wooden," he chuckled. "I'm the most unlikely of all of them," he says. But at the same time, he was glad to share the observations and views of this man that have changed dramatically in Hill's older, more mature eyes.

"First, I have to tell you he is more amazing than I ever thought by a factor of about 100," Hill says. "I've spent a lot of time in the entertainment business with a lot of impressive people, but John Wooden is as smart a guy as I've ever met. His mind is so facile, it startles me. What's clear is that, at age ninety-four, he is still so flexible. Then there is that twinkle in his eye. I never saw that twinkle as a player. He was stern. 'A leader's job is not to be liked,' he always says. When I played, he didn't seem like a guy I'd like to hang out with very much. Now I love to go over to see him as much as I can. Of all the famous people I've known, Coach is the only one who, the more time I spend with him, the more I like him. He is the only one who seemed worthy of his reputation."

Like many of us, Hill realizes that Wooden continues to have a huge impact, even though it's been almost three decades since he coached his last game. "I think Coach became even more relevant on September 11," Hill says, referring to that dark day in our history in 2001. "The terrorist attacks made us look at what's important and relevant, and in many ways he embodies that. Because his philosophies are really powerful, nothing gets pounded into you. It is absorbed in almost a very organic way. He is this quiet, centered, twinkling, engaging, bright guy. If you wanted a Rorschach of what an American is, he is a pretty good place to start. Hardworking, modest, successful, he values family above all else. And he is always happy to do something for someone else.

"The thing with Coach is, he's still getting better. Isn't that what we all want to be like? We all want to feel we keep getting better. Most people don't. But he actually works on stuff to get better. So many people in your lifetime turn out to be not who you thought they were. Coach is who he is. That's unique. Coach isn't situational. He is who he is all the time."

Hill still shakes his head whenever he discusses his new role as an author who has written about Wooden and as a friend who now sees him regularly. "It's such an improbable turn in my life," he says. Some of it has been cathartic. Once he felt comfortable enough, Hill told Wooden that there were times when he was sitting on the bench that he needed a pat on the back or an occasional word of encouragement in practice. He explained that he thought too often the coach paid little, or no, attention to his reserves. To Hill's surprise, Wooden thought about it and eventually agreed with him. "He told me he had made some mistakes like anyone else," Hill says. "He told me he wished he had done better. I felt that was a pretty big admission from someone of his stature."

Hill and Wooden have grown so close that when Wooden was honored with the Presidential Medal of Freedom and was summoned to Washington, D.C., for the presentation in July 2003, he asked his two children and their spouses to join him. Then he asked Hill and his wife, Alex, to go along. "It was the thrill of a lifetime for me," Hill says. "Coach was deeply moved. He is an American in the deepest sense of the word, and I think the gravity of it all really impacted him. He's gotten every award available in sports, but I think this one was special. President Bush was obviously excited to meet him, being the big sports fan that he is. I think we were all moved by the ceremony."

As much as Hill enjoyed being there for the presentation of the Medal of Freedom, it was a seemingly routine drive with the coach a few weeks later that brought him to tears. "Coach and I were doing a power-lunch show somewhere, and we were crossing the 405 Freeway, near the intersection of the 134," Hill says. "Suddenly, out of the blue, Coach says, 'Andy, have I ever told you how much I love you and how much I appreciate doing this book with you?' I was so shook up, I thought I was going to crash the car. 'You know, Coach, I think I sensed that,' I said. 'But to hear you put it in words means more to me than you'll ever know.' Coach said, 'You know, I've been working on that. I'm better at expressing things like that now.'

"To me, that's Coach. Still working on it, still trying to get better. He truly is an amazing man."

BEYOND THE BASKETBALL
Swen Nater

Beyond the grand Pavilion,
Where Bruin banners span
Beyond the accolades, I learned
To be a champion man

Far beyond material,
Or book on any shelf,
Beyond the break, the pass or play,
I learned about myself

Beyond the fundamentals,
Or how to work the task,
Beyond the "how," I learned the "why"
And learned to think and ask.

Beyond the Bruin uniform,
Beyond the Blue and Gold,
I gained a pride in who I am,
That lasts until I'm old.

And far beyond instruction,
Beyond the hardwood class,
Beyond the game and all the tests,
Beyond the fail or pass

The Teacher loved me, so he coached
Beyond gymnasium wall.
I thank my God, the Teacher taught
Beyond the basketball.

The Poet

You would never have guessed that Swen Nater would some day become the poet laureate of UCLA basketball. You would never have figured that of all the Bruins players through the years, this huge, perfectly sculpted, prank-loving athlete would be the one whose beautiful poetry would touch John Wooden so deeply.

When Nater arrived in Westwood, he wasn't a star. He was a project. "I was born in Holland and never even heard about basketball until I was nine years old," Nater says. "I'd only seen a soccer ball, and later football was probably my strongest sport. My family moved to Long Beach, California, and I was a mixed-up kid. I came from a divorced home and lived in an orphanage in Holland for three years. I was here with a mom and a step-dad, and I got kicked out of junior high for fighting all the time."

He first tried out for basketball as a junior at Wilson High School in Long Beach. He didn't make it. "I was the tallest kid in school at six foot seven," Nater says, "but I just hadn't played basketball much at all." From there, he moved on to Cyprus Junior College, where the head coach was Don Johnson, a former UCLA player under Wooden. Nater began to improve slowly at first. "I worked really hard my first year, then I became a JC All-American my second year," he says. It wasn't long before Johnson tipped his old coach about this young, studly kid who stood six feet ten,

167

COURTESY OF UCLA ATHLETIC DEPARTMENT

Swen Nater was a young, gifted, but unpolished player when he arrived at UCLA. Although he never started, because he played behind Bill Walton, he went on to a solid pro career.

weighed 240 pounds, and had all the potential in the world.

"First time I saw him," says Wooden, "I saw this big fella who was as beautifully proportioned as any big man I'd ever seen. I already knew we had Bill Walton coming in, and I was honest with Swen. I told him if he came to UCLA, he probably wouldn't play that much. But I also told him if he came, he would have the opportunity to practice every day against Bill Walton. I told him that if he wanted to play professionally one day, this would be the greatest preparation he could have."

Nater, happy to just have a scholarship to such a prestigious university, agreed. He transferred to UCLA as a junior in 1972. But at that level, he was exposed for what he was: a still-raw, inexperienced player with few, if any, accomplished skills.

"Playing at UCLA wasn't easy," Nater says. "I admit I got mad sometimes. I wanted to play more in games. But then I'd see incredible players like Sidney Wicks, who wasn't getting to play much, either. I remember Sidney going to Coach and complaining, saying he should be playing more than Shack [Lynn Shackelford]. Coach said, 'Too bad you're letting him beat you out, then.' The truth was, Shack played more in the team concept, something Sidney hadn't learned at that time. That's what Coach was all about. He was all about the team. I had to learn that, too. I was six foot ten, 240 pounds and I could run, jump, and shoot. I actually led the Olympic Trials in scoring one year. So, yeah, I thought I should be playing more. But I had to decide to give 110 percent at practice first."

Wooden remembers what kind of player Nater was when he arrived. "He was kind of pitiful at first," the coach says. "But by his senior year, he was a lot better, and he was good for Bill, too. Bill used to say nobody gave him more trouble on a basketball court than Swen did in practice. I can honestly say I never had a player improve as much as Swen did. But let's face it, he had the farthest to go."

Wooden's promise proved true. After graduation, Nater signed with the Virginia Squires of the American Basketball Association, where he played briefly before being traded to San Antonio, where he wound up the ABA's Rookie of the Year. He played alongside Julius Erving with the Nets, then, after the NBA-ABA merger, went to Milwaukee, where he started for three years and developed into one of the most consistent rebounders in the sport, leading the NBA in that category one year in San Diego. Nater finished up playing one season on the Lakers with Magic Johnson, James Worthy, and Michael Cooper. He traveled to Italy to play one additional season before retiring.

BE QUICK BUT DON'T HURRY

If you wish to be successful
To be all that you can be,
Take a little piece of wisdom
That was handed down to me
"Be quick but don't hurry"

Every task must be accomplished
Well, exact and never late
So in every deed, act quickly
Execute and never wait
"Be quick but don't hurry"

For an act performed too slowly,
Excellent, though it may be
Will come later than it's needed
And is valueless, you see
"Be quick but don't hurry"

On the other hand, don't hurry
There are errors made in haste
And the errors cause the detour,
Inefficiency and waste.
"Be quick but don't hurry"

To be quick without the hurry
Requires work, for gracious sakes.
You must practice, practice, practice
Till you're quick, with no mistakes
"Be quick but don't hurry"

"Be Quick But Don't Hurry" was and still is one of Wooden's favorite admonitions—rules by which Nater learned but never realized how much until he left UCLA.

"Wooden was only the second coach I ever had. What did I know?" Nater says. "I thought they were all like this." He soon found out otherwise. In the pros, he began to understand. "There were all these different styles," he says, "but none was like Coach's. What I came to realize about Wooden is that each practice, each learning session was like a masterpiece. You talk about preparing someone for competition. We never ran without a basketball. Everything we did, even the usual weaves and fast breaks and cuts, were all part of his conditioning drills. He would script his practices. They were set to begin at 3:29 and end at 5:29, and they never went over. I mean never.

"When I started at UCLA, I didn't know much about Wooden. But I learned quickly. I noticed you couldn't get away with anything. He was always one step ahead of you. During practice, he allowed you to take two sips of water. If you took three, he knew somehow. I don't know how, but he did. He used to attend psychology classes at UCLA to help him get to know us better, to find out what makes us tick. I always sensed an incredible deep caring from him toward me and my welfare. I think one doesn't necessarily feel that if you haven't really talked to him. But I sensed a deep love and an incredible amount of professionalism. He was very, very humble. You never sensed he was trying to make you think he knew it all or he was smarter than us in any way.

"But once practice started, the guy was an animal. Practices were extremely intense. He would raise his voice at times. He was not very patient if you made the same mistake twice. But at the same time, he demonstrated patience in your development, although he praised very little. It was mostly correction. 'NO, NO, NO! How many times do I have to tell you NO?' I can still hear his voice in my head.

"We were definitely well-conditioned," Nater says, "but there was more than just physical conditioning. There was mental conditioning. We would practice a lot of pressure situations, especially when we were tired. Like at the end of practice, we'd work on a special inbounds play, like we would at the end of a game. And all our practice free throws were under game conditions. We never just stood around and idly shot free throws like so many other teams you see.

"There was emotional conditioning, too. He was always getting on us about not losing our emotions. He wanted us always under control. By example, he never gave us a pep talk. Not ever. He said he didn't want us too high or two low before a game. He always wanted us on an even keel."

MY CHILD

I'm your teacher, I can't teach you.
I can reach, but I can't reach you.
You, my child, a price must pay.
And I must meet you at half way.

I will walk and I will lead you.
I will serve but I can't feed you.
I will prompt but I can't make you.
I will drive but I can't take you.
You, my child, must bear your load.
And meet me half way down the road.

I can show but I can't do it.
I can only lead you to it.
I reveal and you uncover.
I present and you discover.
You, my child, must labor bear.
And must dispense an equal share.

I'm your friend and I'm your neighbor.
And together we will labor.
Working side by side we tarry,
With an equal load to carry.
You, my child, if you would know.
Must take the scythe and the hoe.

I'm your teacher, I can't teach you
All the wisdom that must reach you.

171

I request for your assistance,
So that we can go the distance.
Then, my child, you will recall,
That it was you who did it all.

"It wasn't until I started teaching myself that I realized some of what Coach Wooden was doing all those years," Nater says. "The research, the details, the planning, the striving to improve—that's when I learned. You know, the funny part is, he never thought he was very good at coaching. He used to say that he learned how to coach by teaching high school English.

"As a man, as a human being, there is a tendency to put him on a pedestal," Nater says. "When you compare him to most other people, that's how he comes off. He is extremely loyal as a friend, and the funny thing is, he's always teaching. I remember once I was at a banquet with him, and as a joke, before he saw me, I came running up in my tuxedo and came to this giant jump stop right in front of him. He looked at me as if he wasn't even startled, and before I could say anything, he said, 'Get your chin up.' When he talks to you, he makes you feel like you're the only person in the world. President Bush could walk by, and he wouldn't break the conversation.

"In many ways, I consider him like my Dad. His priorities are family, faith, and friends, and he often talks about the mystical law of nature and the three things mankind craves most—happiness, freedom, and peace. He says none of these can be obtained without giving them to someone else first. It's not just what he says, either. He backs it up. He walks the walk. That's the power of his teaching. First of all, he loves what he teaches. He has a passion for it. He is extremely interested in people and how you can learn more about them. But most of what he talks about he can back up, because he's already done it. 'You can't impart what you don't possess,' he says. And he's obviously right."

The nice thing is, Nater has been able to express his feelings for this man who has meant so much to him through his poetry. So how did this impressive hulk of a jock take to the intellectual pursuit of reading and writing poetry? Nater says it began early in his life.

"When I attended ninth grade at Jefferson Middle School in Long Beach, California, I had the privilege of being in a poetry class taught by one of the best teachers I have ever known, a Mrs. Roche," he says. "As she taught the poem 'Richard Cory,' I became hooked. Although I did not write a great deal of poetry during my teens, twenties, or thirties, I read it and loved it.

"After graduating from UCLA, I got to know John Wooden much better and, in doing so, discovered his love for poetry. We have shared many poems since then, sometimes just sitting in his living room and reading them to each other. About six years ago, I got the notion to write a poem which, in rhyme, echoes something he believes and has taught, such as 'Be Quick But Don't Hurry.' He loved it and it gave me great satisfaction to be able to give something back to a man who has given me so much. Since that first poem, I have probably written a hundred more.

"A poem is usually initiated when I see or hear something that has a message. It might be an article, something someone says, a movie, a television show, or something Coach says to me. I then turn it into a poem. I have learned different styles of rhyming, and rhythm should be used to help bring out the true meaning of what's written. The goal of poetry is to bring out the emotion of the reader.

Nater certainly has brought out the emotions in Wooden. Anytime friends drop by for a visit to the coach's Encino condo, he refuses to let them leave until he pulls out a pack of papers and begins reciting some of his favorite Nater poems. When he is finished, he looks up and beams, like a father who couldn't be more proud of a son. If his visitor is really lucky, Wooden will take out a tape recorder, slip in a cassette, and play a song Nater wrote and sang himself. It is a version of the old Bette Midler hit song "Wind Beneath My Wings." Only the words have been changed to pay homage to the coach and friend Nater has come to respect and love. When the tape is finished, both the coach and the visitor usually have tears in their eyes.

Of all Wooden's relationships with former players, this one with a gifted center who hardly played significant minutes in his UCLA career might be the deepest and most emotional. Most of Wooden's former players feel the same way as Nater. It's just that none of them is able to express it in words quite as well.

I SAW LOVE ONCE

I saw love once,
I saw it clear.
It had no leash.
It had no fear.

It gave itself
Without a thought.
No reservation,
Had it bought.

John Wooden

It seemed so free,
To demonstrate.
It seemed obsessed,
To orchestrate.

A symphony,
Designed to feed,
Composed to lift,
The one in need.

Concern for others,
Was its' goal,
No matter what,
Would be the toll.

It's strange just how,
Much care it stores,
To recognize,
Its neighbor's sores.

And doesn't rest,
Until the day,
It's helped to take,
The sores away.

Its joy retains,
And does not run,
Until the blessing's,
Job is done.

I saw love once,
'Twas not pretend.
He **was** my coach,
He **is** my friend.

— *Swen Nater for Coach Wooden,*
   Christmas, 1998.

The Pyramid of Success

Almost as much as his remarkable string of basketball championships, John Wooden has become known for his Pyramid of Success.

The Pyramid represents everything Wooden believes, everything he has tried to teach over the years. It is a tool that transcends basketball, because it is utilized by teachers, businessmen, religious leaders and just plain people all over the world. "Not a day goes by," says Wooden, "that I don't get at least one piece of mail concerning the Pyramid and asking if I could autograph and send that person a copy."

Many of his former players admit, as Gail Goodrich does, that they keep a copy of the Pyramid close by in an office at home and utilize it as a tool when confronting problems in their daily lives. Amazingly, the Pyramid did not begin in any specific shape or form.

"There were a lot of things I thought about that I wanted to organize in some way," Wooden says. "In 1934, I first coined what I felt was the definition of peace of mind: It is a direct result of self-satisfaction in knowing you did your best to become the best you are capable of becoming. Slowly, many of my thoughts on this subject began to evolve, but even several years later, it wasn't quite right. I began to think it would be more effective if the thoughts could be represented in something you could see. I'd seen something called the Ladder of Achievement, in which some traits or characteristics were noted that you would take to get to the top of the ladder. Sometime between 1934 and '48, I came up with the idea. I came up with the Pyramid. It still took time to develop, though. I don't think it was completed until 1948, when I had just completed coaching at Indiana State, before I came to UCLA.

"I have to admit, I had no idea it would get this much exposure. It's very surprising to me. It helped me become a better teacher. I think it gave many of my athletes something to aspire to, besides being just a top scorer or a respected scholar. I think, overall, the Pyramid epitomizes what I've tried to teach through the years. I'm very proud of it."

John Wooden's
Pyramid of Success

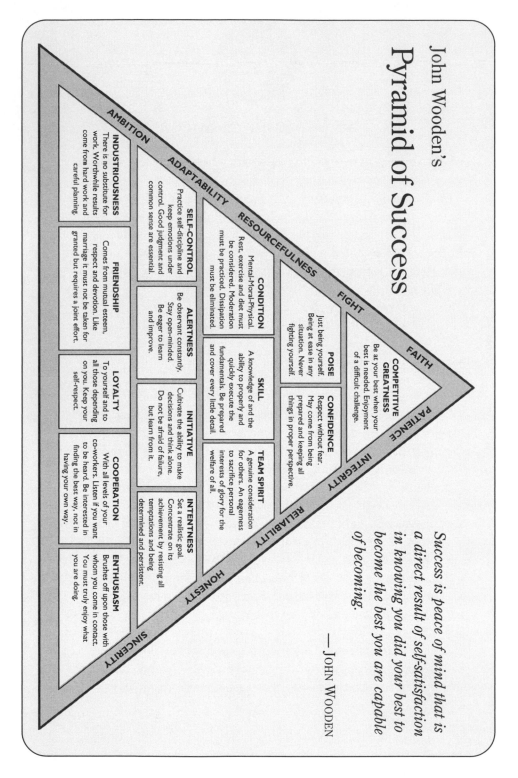

INDUSTRIOUSNESS
There is no substitute for work. Worthwhile results come from hard work and careful planning.

FRIENDSHIP
Comes from mutual esteem, respect and devotion. Like marriage it must not be taken for granted but requires a joint effort.

LOYALTY
To yourself and to all those depending on you. Keep your self-respect.

COOPERATION
With all levels of your co-workers. Listen if you want to be heard. Be interested in finding the best way, not in having your own way.

ENTHUSIASM
Brushes off upon those with whom you come in contact. You must truly enjoy what you are doing.

SELF-CONTROL
Practice self-discipline and keep emotions under control. Good judgment and common sense are essential.

ALERTNESS
Be observant constantly. Stay open-minded. Be eager to learn and improve.

INITIATIVE
Cultivate the ability to make decisions and think alone. Do not be afraid of failure, but learn from it.

INTENTNESS
Set a realistic goal. Concentrate on its achievement by resisting all temptations and being determined and persistent.

CONDITION
Mental-Moral-Physical. Rest, exercise and diet must be considered. Moderation must be practiced. Dissipation must be eliminated.

SKILL
A knowledge of and the ability to properly and quickly execute the fundamentals. Be prepared and cover every little detail.

TEAM SPIRIT
A genuine consideration for others. An eagerness to sacrifice personal interests of glory for the welfare of all.

POISE
Just being yourself. Being at ease in any situation. Never fighting yourself.

CONFIDENCE
Respect without fear. May come from being prepared and keeping all things in proper perspective.

COMPETITIVE GREATNESS
Be at your best when your best is needed. Enjoyment of a difficult challenge.

AMBITION · ADAPTABILITY · RESOURCEFULNESS · FIGHT · FAITH · PATIENCE

INTEGRITY · RELIABILITY · HONESTY · SINCERITY

Success is peace of mind that is a direct result of self-satisfaction in knowing you did your best to become the best you are capable of becoming.

— JOHN WOODEN

176

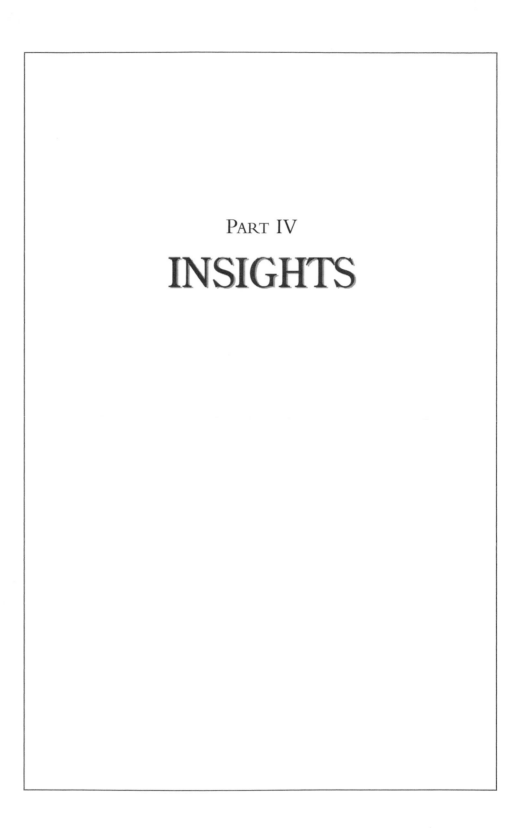

PART IV

INSIGHTS

The Family Man:
Father, Grandfather,
and Great-Grandfather

Prominently displayed in the den of John Wooden's tiny condo in Encino, California, is a framed picture of his late wife, Nellie, holding a basketball. Underneath it, in large letters, are the following words: "God never closes one door without opening another."

Deep in despair over losing his wife in 1985, the legendary coach was searching for a reason to go on, to be encouraged about the future, when Cori, his first great-grandchild, was born. "It kind of gave him a new lease on life," says his daughter, Nan Wooden Muehlhausen.

"I believe in those words," Wooden says. "I believe God never closes one door without opening another. Cori was like another door opening for me. She was a great blessing, and having more great-grandchildren only made it better."

Family was and still is at the center of Wooden's world. "My father used to tell me to hold sacred my faith, family and friends," he says. "I always put family first, although I know faith probably should be. But I think He [the Lord] will understand." Wooden has two children, seven grandchildren, and twelve great-grandchildren, with more probably on the way. In the midst of becoming the greatest coach his sport has known, he always made sure to spend much of his time in and around his family.

THE FATHER

Both of Wooden's children realized their father knew best when it came to basketball. But what about away from the game? Away from the cheers and the championship banners? What about when he put down his whistle and clipboard and strolled through the front door? What was he like at home? How difficult was it growing up the daughter and son of one of America's few living treasures?

"It wasn't difficult. It was nice," says Jim Wooden, John's sixty-eight-year-old son. "Dad was a strict disciplinarian in a sense, but not in a standard sense. He rarely raised his voice, but you always knew what he wanted of you. And you always knew he could get it without yelling."

Nancy Muehlhausen, or Nan as everyone calls her, was the elder of the two Wooden children by two and a half years. Now, at age seventy, she remembers the early years in Indiana when life was simpler. "We didn't have a lot of money," Nan says, "but we never wanted for anything. I remember that I always felt very loved. But when Dad had to go into the service, I was very unsettled. He wouldn't have been drafted, because he was a teacher, but Dad felt very strongly about serving his country. He felt he had to go. I was only five or six years old, but it bothered me. I remember I had bad dreams. Mother worried a lot about it, and I think it rubbed off on me.

"We had to move a lot when Daddy was in the Navy, and when we were in the South, Mom always butted heads with some of the locals about the way they treated blacks. Mom always said she didn't understand. 'They won't sit and eat with them, yet they allow them to serve food and nurse their babies. It doesn't make sense,' she said."

Probably the biggest event in both children's' lives was the family's move from Indiana to California when their father took the head coaching position at UCLA. "I was just excited about it," Nan recalls. "I was in the ninth grade at the time, and to me, California meant Hollywood. I was busy the whole time looking for movie stars, thinking I would be discovered."

Jim remembers the house the family bought. "It was the only one we ever had," he says. "It was in west Los Angeles, and Dad borrowed money from his father for the down payment. People don't know this, but Dad had to take a night job at a dairy farm while he was coaching in order to pay back the money for the down payment on that house."

It was a house based on middle-class values, where they went to church regularly on Sundays, and Wooden's famous homilies could be heard daily by his two children. "One of my Dad's favorite sayings was, 'The best thing a parent can do for his children is to love their mother,'" Jim says. There was never any doubt about that in the Wooden household.

Once they settled into the Southern California lifestyle, the family acclimated nicely. "It was fun," says Nan, "but when Daddy was coaching, it was nerve-racking, too. We'd all get real nervous before his games, and superstitious. Funny what you remember, though. I remember watching Dad after games, and he'd sit down and eat a Chili Size and a hot fudge sundae at the same time. I used to think that was so gross."

Jim says theirs was a close family, with the doors always open for friends and, yes, Wooden's players. "I played in high school, although I really

COURTESY OF NAN MUEHLHAUSEN

The whole Wooden clan, except for its most famous member, gathers at a family function. Overall, there are two children, seven grandchildren and twelve great-grandchildren, and all are very proud of "Papa."

wasn't very good," Jim says. "Mom would always make my friends and I her version of a pregame meal, just like the college guys. Many of the UCLA players we had over made it feel like we had a lot of brothers. But I never felt left out."

Although Dad often had the last word, Mom was the one generally in charge at home. "We got more of our disciplining from Mom," Jim says. "She was the one who was on us about doing homework and picking up our clothes. He'd back her on everything. But we'd be more apt to tell Mom something and then have her tell Dad about it in her way."

Jim was a typical teenager, learning as he went along, making his share of mistakes. "I remember a week before I left for the Marine Corps, I was hanging out with a bunch of friends at a Beverly Hills drive-in when one of my buddies got into it with some guy and we all wound up getting into a fight. I remember it was real foggy, and the cops came and took us all down to the Beverly Hills jail. We couldn't get hold of anybody's dad but mine. Well, Dad came down and got us out. He was kind of chuckling in a sense. Later, I asked him if he was worried. 'Oh yes,' he said, 'I would rather that would have happened to someone else.'"

Another time, Jim convinced his father to let him take the family car, the only one they had, on a date. "My girlfriend talked me into letting her drive, and we got into a head-on collision. Nobody was hurt, but my dad's radiator was ruptured. When I got home, I told him I was driving. Well, my girlfriend confessed to her father, and he called Dad and told him he wanted to pay for the damages. I remember Dad saying, 'No, Charlie, that won't be necessary. Jimmy will be paying for this.' Dad wasn't mad about the accident. He was mad that I didn't tell the truth. I had lied, and he said that wasn't right. I can tell you this much: I don't think I ever lied to him again."

Luxuries, such as a fancy car or expensive clothes, were not a staple in the Wooden home. "Dad was never motivated by money," Jim says. "The one car we always had was a four-door, powder-blue Chevy. The only fancy car we had was a Mercedes that a bunch of old players chipped in to buy Dad. It was a 450 SL, but you know, Mom hated that car. She never felt comfortable in it. So, Dad finally traded it in for a Ford Taurus."

Game nights were a family experience. "We went to almost all the games," Jim says. "Then we'd go out afterwards and have ice cream together. UCLA used to play in a lot of places—at Venice High, Santa Monica City College, the Pan-Pacific. But it was the campus gym, B. O. Barn, that I remember most. We used to call it the sweatbox. The rumor was, we'd turn up the heat and sweat the other team up real good."

Unfortunately, coaches work long hours and travel more than most people. "Dad was away a lot," Nan says. "But the only time it bothered me was during the Final Four, when all coaches went, even if their team wasn't in it. It always seemed to come on my birthday, and I wasn't happy about that."

It took Wooden sixteen years to win his first national championship, but for many of those years, there was less pressure and a more relaxed atmosphere. "It wasn't until after Nancy and I left home that he started to win the national championships," Jim says. "But if he ever felt frustration about not going higher, I didn't see it."

Nan didn't, either. "He won a lot of conference titles," she says, "and he's made the statement that maybe he was trying too hard and lost his focus. But, you know, winning was never his thing. He just wanted the team to play as well as it could, although everyone wants a shot at the big cheese."

As the children grew into adults, Jim was the more laid back of the two, more like his father, while Nan was more fiery, like her mother. As adults, Nan encountered more troubled times. "I'm a rescuer," she says. "I've always loved men who were needy. I guess because I had all this love in my background. Well, I managed to find some who couldn't be helped. My second husband was an alcoholic and an abuser, but each step in life has made me a better, stronger person."

It also helped that she had the support of her family. "My parents helped me through a lot of it," Nan says. "I remember asking Dad: 'When does life ever get easier?' His answer was: 'Who says it does?'"

Now a big part of Nan's life is taking care of her father, who still lives alone at age ninety-four and refuses to move. "He thinks it is a burden on me, but it really isn't," she says. "I think it's hard for him sometime because I look like Mom and remind him so much of her. But I try to take care of him and sort through all the things people want him to do. You can't believe all the people who want to make money off his name. I get so mad at all the mail he gets. He gets big boxes of basketballs people expect him to sign. I can't believe people are that stupid. People think he should have a full-time assistant. He tells them that I take care of everything. Well, sometimes I think I want a raise. Honestly, I don't know how he does it. He stays so busy and does so many things at his age. He complains his memory isn't what it used to be, but he just rattles things off. It's just amazing."

You won't find many daughters more loving than this one. "I'm happy he still enjoys life and his family, but I worry about him," Nan says. "He hasn't fallen lately, but he has a couple of times. The latest thing he talks about is getting in his Taurus and driving across country by himself. We told him he can't do that. But he still drives to breakfast or to church."

Nan lives not far from her father in Reseda. Jim lives fifty miles away in the Orange County town of Irvine. But the family gets together for special occasions and Jim visits his dad at his condo regularly. "He was here just the other day," John says, smiling, as he tells a visitor. "He even stayed overnight with me. We had a great time."

Jim is as awed by his father's ability to get around as Nan is. "Dad's amazing," Jim says. "He still somehow gets to charity functions and The Tradition Tournament in Indianapolis and things like that. A couple of years ago, we took all the kids back to Indiana for that tournament. We went to

Martinsville High, and the gym now named after my dad. He really enjoyed it. All the girls back there were asking to kiss him and wanted to have their pictures taken with him. I think he got a real kick out of having his whole family with him."

Nan is more talkative than Jim, but like his father, the son tends be more introspective. "I'm proud of my dad, and I love him dearly," Jim says. "To me, he's always been someone who practices what he preaches. It's funny, people come up to me all the time and tell me what a great coach he is. I thank them, and then I tell them he is more than that. He is a great man."

THE GRANDFATHER

They call him "Papa," and to many of his seven grandchildren, John Wooden is simply the nicest, kindest relative they could ever imagine.

"Growing up, we never realized how famous he was. We were just happy to be with our grandfather," says Greg Wooden, the forty-one-year-old son of Jim. "I guess later on we felt more lucky than anything. I mean, how many kids get to travel with a team like UCLA? When I was a teenager, my cousin Cathleen—she's Nan's youngest daughter—and I got to go on some road trips with our grandfather. We got to see some of San Francisco on what turned out to be his last year of coaching, and it was great."

Greg remembers listening to "Papa" talk about the Pyramid of Success when they were young. "We never really thought anything of it," he says. "It wasn't until later on, when we had kids of our own to raise, that we realized how much some of what we learned helped us in living our lives."

Eventually, once they were old enough, the grandchildren began to understand how famous their "Papa" was. "But whenever we got together, the conversation was never about basketball," Greg says. "It was always about doing the best you can do and making the best of a situation that comes across."

Not that they didn't get to their share of basketball games along the way. "Oh, yeah, we went to the games," Greg says. "We always went out for ice cream or pancakes after the games, too. It was kind of a tradition. I remember as I got older that I admired him even after UCLA got beat. He always acted the same as if they had won."

One of the perks of being a Wooden relative was free entrance to the coach's summertime basketball camps. "I went to all the camps," Greg says. "I used to stay at his house some of the time. The other kids at the camp, they knew who I was, because I always ate breakfast and lunch near his table. The kids would say, 'Gosh, you're lucky.'"

Greg was indoctrinated early in his grandfather's world of poetry. "He told us that he taught English and showed us a lot of poetry," Greg says. "I think he really enjoyed listening to poems. He would end all his basketball camps by reading 'The Little Fellow Who Follows Me.' It is a poem about someone who follows in his dad's footsteps. Obviously, he was very, very close to his dad. He credits his father for making him the man he is. He much prefers telling stories about when he was growing up on the farm to stories about basketball."

One of Greg's favorite moments growing up was the time Lew Alcindor came to his house on a weekend. "That was cool," Greg says. "It was also fun to talk baseball with Papa. Baseball is his favorite sport, you know. He likes showing an old picture of Babe Ruth and Lou Gehrig with both their signatures on it. He loves Abraham Lincoln a lot, too. Lincoln is definitely his favorite American. I think he likes him for his ability to say so much in such few words."

As Greg grew into an adult, he grew even more fascinated by his grandfather. "I was amazed, because he became much more famous after he retired," he says. "I think it is because he stands for all the good things in sports or life. He always wanted his players to do their best, and he was happy if they did, whether they won or lost. I don't think you see that anymore. When you're around him now, he always has a wise thing to say. I think that's why women relate to him as well as men. Whenever he is speaking somewhere, it's always the women in the crowd who come up after."

Like all members of the family, Greg found it difficult to watch his grandfather after his wife died. "He is such a proud person," Greg says. "It was hard to see him hurt as much as he was. I know he still writes letters to my grandmother once a month. They were so close. I know from when I lived there. She took such good care of him. She pulled the clothes out he would wear; she poured his cereal in the morning; she always got him going. And when she was upset about something, she let him know how she felt.

"I think my grandfather turns to Nan now for some of the things my grandmother used to do. He has a real hard time saying no to people. I think he commits to things he really shouldn't. But that's just him. He believes in sticking to his word.

"A lot of us would like to see him slow down at his age. But, you know, maybe he shouldn't. Maybe that's what keeps him young and sharp."

THE GREAT-GRANDFATHER

Cori Nicholson was John Wooden's first great-grandchild. Now she is identified more as the oldest of twelve. She is the one whose birth allowed her grieving great-grandfather to realize that a new door in his life had opened. She is the one who made it possible for him to smile again.

"We have a special bond," Cori says. "I'm his baby."

The two seem to have grown closer than most children and their great-grandparents. "I think he's just wonderful," says Cori, a twenty-year-old sophomore at the University of California at Riverside. "I get a big kick out of him. We like to hang out together. We go to lunch a lot. He loves to go to Fromin's [a deli near his home]. I like Islands [a franchise hamburger restaurant]. We usually trade off. We like to kid around a lot. He gives me a hard time because I just got my earring holes. I kid him about his big ears and tell him he could get them pierced a lot. He likes to play pranks, too. When I was little and I was afraid to go in the house, I'd ask, 'Anybody there?' And Papa would make this weird chicken voice, and he'd say, 'Nobody here but us chicks.'"

All of Wooden's great-grandchildren arrived long after he left coaching. They never saw him roll up his program and direct players from the bench. They didn't watch him win any national championships or see him smiling next to a huge trophy.

"But I've always grown up knowing about him," Cori says. "Everyone idolizes him. It's an amazing thing. A couple of boys in my dorm hall saw his picture in my room and got really excited."

The funny thing is, Cori isn't really a basketball fan. She is a biology major who is part of a biomedical program that will send her to UCLA after two years at UC Riverside. She is much more into plants and bugs than she is dunks and dribbles. "Honestly, I'm not into sports," she says. "I'm not too coordinated. I have read a lot of articles and books about him, though. I did my project in eleventh grade on him, and he came and spoke to our class. That was a neat thing."

Cori has made some trips with her great-grandfather, as well. She traveled to Utah once when he had a speaking engagement and flew to Seattle with him on another occasion. Her favorite, though, was the trip back to Indiana for the Wooden Tradition a couple of years ago.

"That was really great," she says. "We saw the house where he grew up. It was amazing. The toilet wasn't even in the house. Then you remember, he's ninety-four. You don't think about how different things must have been back then. We went to the cemetery to see where his sisters were buried. We saw the John Wooden Gym, where a statue of him was built. At least it was supposed to be of him, except it looks like someone else's head. I'm serious, it's not his head."

The more personal memories are the ones Cori prefers to talk about. "Once I spent the night at his house," she says. "I fell asleep on his bed. And when I woke up the next morning, I realized that he had slept in the next room

COURTESY OF NAN MUEHLHAUSEN

In one of his more touching family photos, Wooden nuzzles his great-grandson, Cameron, who suffered disabilities at birth. Wooden describes him as the family's "special child."

on the couch. I guess that's why I think of him more like a best friend.

"I'll tell you what, I wish I had his memory," she says. "He's always bringing up his favorite poems, and then he'll recite the entire poem. He likes to give us advice, giving us his father's creed: Be the best you can be, take advantage of things when they come your way. But he doesn't force any of it on us. All I know is that when I'm around him, he always brightens my day."

His first great-grandchild is special to him, but if you know Wooden, you realize he never will play favorites. He loves them all equally. But there is one that generates more emotion from him than the others. His name is Cameron Trapani, and he is eleven years old now. Cameron suffered a stroke in the womb about five months into the pregnancy of his mother, Cathleen Amy, who is Nan's daughter. Doctors weren't sure he would survive, and he had to undergo heart surgery at age one and a half.

"He had some brain damage at birth, and he has no words to this day," Nan says. Yet, both Wooden and Nan are proud that Cathleen Amy refused to institutionalize Cameron. "She said no, she was going to keep him at home,"

187

Nan says. "She's a teacher, and so is her husband, Paul. Now Cameron is walking and able to feed himself."

Wooden's eyes grow teary when he talks about it. "I couldn't be more proud of Cathleen Amy," he says. "When she found out how severely disabled Cameron would be, she didn't say, 'Why me?' She said, 'Why not me?'" Wooden keeps one of his favorite poems nearby and reads it every time he comes home after visiting Cameron. He says he gave the poem, called "Heaven's Special Child," to Cathleen Amy, who also became a fan of the words written by Lou Franchini. The poem's final lines read:

> And soon they'll know the privilege given
> In caring for this gift from Heaven.
> Their previous charge, so meek and mild.
> Is Heaven's very special child.

Nan, too, gets emotional when talking about Cathleen Amy and Cameron. "What he taught us is priceless," she says. "But I wouldn't wish this on anybody."

Cameron's older brother, Tyler, often complained to his mom that life wasn't fair. "No, you're right," Cathleen Amy told him. "Life's not fair." But one day, according to Nan, Tyler finally agreed.

"I know Mom," he said to Cathleen Amy. "Life is not fair. Our family should know that better than anyone. You know why?" His mother gulped and then hesitatingly asked, "No, why?"

"Because," said Tyler, "everyone in the world wants to be related to John Wooden, and we're the lucky ones."

The Understated Play

John Wooden is a big fan of what he calls "understated play," and not just in basketball but in all sports.

"I've always liked those who did it effortlessly," Wooden says. "It's why I always loved Joe DiMaggio. Willie Mays was spectacular, and I understand those who pick him as the best player ever. But I honestly believe I saw DiMaggio wait for balls to catch that Willie made look spectacular."

It is the same reason Wooden prefers Oscar Robertson over Magic Johnson, when it comes time to naming his favorite all-time guards. "Technically, Magic was great," Wooden says. "But I still think he thought more of Magic first. He handled the ball a little more than I preferred. Oscar was so superior to all the others, and he did it so effortlessly."

It is the same reason his favorite players of this era are not the Tracy McGradys or Kobe Bryants or Shaquille O'Neals. For years, Wooden said the only NBA player he loved to watch was Utah's John Stockton. When Stockton retired, he had to choose another player of similar style to be his favorite. If you're an NBA fan, the selection really shouldn't surprise you.

"It's Tim Duncan," Wooden says. "I love the way he gets everything done in such an understated way. I also think he's a fine young man. I've met him before, and I think he has high moral values off the court, as well."

Casting a Giant Shadow

On any list of impossible jobs, it has to rank right near the top. Trying to replace John Wooden at UCLA was like to trying to follow Bear Bryant at Alabama, or Vince Lombardi in Green Bay. It couldn't be done. There was too much success, too many expectations, too much pressure. Talk about placing the bar too high. This time the bar was so high, you couldn't even see it.

Not that the job itself still didn't seem like one of the more cherished positions in sports. There was no question it was. In baseball, it was the equivalent of managing the New York Yankees. In the NFL, it was like coaching the Green Bay Packers. In college basketball, it was directing the UCLA Bruins. It was the pinnacle, the highest you could go. And even though the thought of following Wooden seemed daunting, there was no lack of candidates eager to apply for the job.

The surprise was that Gene Bartow was picked as the first to take a shot at it. Most university alums and boosters wanted it kept in the family. They would have opted for Denny Crum, who had already established himself at Louisville, or Gary Cunningham, Wooden's trusted aide for so many years. Instead, J. D. Morgan, the athletic director who always had a mind of his own, chose to go outside. Bartow had impressed him in taking a

Memphis State team to the NCAA Finals against Wooden a few years earlier, and although the quiet, bespectacled coach had moved to Illinois and coached there only for a year, Morgan knew UCLA would interest him.

Bartow could coach. After accepting the job amid much surprise in Los Angeles, he proved his skill in two brief seasons at Pauley Pavilion, going 28–4 and 28–5, taking the Bruins to the Final Four in his first year, only to lose to Bobby Knight's eventual national champions from Indiana in the semifinals. What Bartow couldn't do was handle the anxiety of working in Wooden's shadow.

"For me, coaching basketball always had been a pretty relaxed job that I enjoyed," says Bartow, some twenty-nine years later. "But out there, I found myself not enjoying it. I was feeling the stress and strain and the importance of winning every game. It had taken the fun out of the job for me. I felt for us to have a successful year, we would have had to win the national championship. If I'd stayed another two years and we'd won one, it still wouldn't have solved anything, because I still would have been nine short."

In the post-Wooden Era, one needed thick skin to coach basketball at UCLA. Bartow seemed to lack that quality. "I felt the media, or at least the beat writers, were extremely professional and fair," he says. "But a lot of the columnists who didn't see our games butchered me every time we lost. A radio guy, Jim Healy, was tough on me. But apparently he was tough one everyone. Hey, I coached at Memphis State and played for a national championship. I didn't come in from high school, or anything. I paid my dues."

Surprisingly, Wooden doesn't think Bartow had it so hard trying to follow his act at UCLA. "I think he was fortunate in a way," Wooden says. "I'd like to go to a place with the material I left there, with all the history and tradition in place at Pauley Pavilion. Bartow and [Gary] Cunningham, in the four years after I left, had the best winning percentage ever at UCLA. I think they won something like 85 percent of their games."

But it's what they didn't win that mattered. They didn't win a national championship.

Marques Johnson played on Wooden's last team and Bartow's first one. He is quick to tell you the new coach didn't have it easy. "We were constantly comparing him to Coach Wooden," Johnson says. "Coach Wooden was such a model of sophistication. Now, suddenly, it was like we had Jed Clampett or something. It was all so foreign to us. Coach Bartow thought he had a honeymoon period at UCLA. He thought everyone would love him. But he wound up wearing his every emotion on his sleeve. He'd throw things; he'd slam papers down. He was so unlike Coach Wooden. He'd hand us extensive scouting reports on our opponents. We'd never, ever had that before. We always felt we didn't need that. I remember having breakfast with him at a pregame meal, and I had the sports section in front of me. 'What's it say?' Bartow asked. 'I swore never to touch an L.A. paper again. Would you read it to me?'"

The deeper he went into his time at UCLA, the worse it got. "I remember seeing him at a banquet once wearing a fedora pulled down on his head, with dark shades and a tan overcoat with the collar pulled up, so no one would recognize him," Johnson says. "He used to call the media *kooks*. 'The kooks are after me! The kooks are after me!' he'd say. The level of paranoia was amazing. He was a nervous wreck. His face was pale, and he looked like he was running from a demon or something."

Bartow looks back now and he utters a long sigh. "I actually liked living in L.A.," he says. "I still have a house in Palm Desert. But being the first coach after John, for me, was not much fun. Maybe if I'd been No. 3, the third guy tried, I might have made it. I spent thirty-four years coaching college basketball, and thirty-two of them were pretty enjoyable. The two at UCLA were not. I've had people infer that if John had not been so close to the situation, it might have been better. I never gave any thought to that. I've always felt John Wooden was a friend of mine and a great person. In my twenty-eight months there, we had many visits. He was a fine friend and still is.

"Some of UCLA's powerful boosters weren't as friendly," Bartow says. "There was one in particular who didn't want me there in the first place. I'm not getting into names." Asked if it was the infamous Sam Gilbert, Bartow reiterates, "I won't comment on that."

Bartow's own actions often didn't help. He walked off an L.A. sports-talk radio show one night, generating a new wave of criticism. "Someone had been butchering me on his talk show, so I went on with him," Bartow says. "I actually had a dinner engagement later that night, but agreed to go on from 5:00 to 5:30. But this guy and his listeners just wanted to chop on me about recruiting. Finally, I told him, 'You don't need me here for this. Let them keep on butchering me.' And I left early."

Asked if Crum or Cunningham would have been granted a year or two of immunity by Bruins fans and boosters, Bartow acknowledged it was possible. "They were family," he says. "I think a family member might have had a little better reception. Maybe J. D. should have given it a little more thought. But you've still got to win. Anything less than a national championship might not have been good enough for a lot of people. I'm convinced UCLA and

Kentucky in basketball and Notre Dame and Alabama in football are just special situations. The expectations at those places are just greater than they are anywhere else."

It shouldn't have come as a surprise that when Bartow was offered the job as athletic director and coach at the University of Alabama at Birmingham, with the prospect of shaping his own program, he quickly snapped it up. "J. D. Morgan was a friend and a great athletic director," Bartow says. "But this was a chance to start my own program, serve as AD, and earn a lot more money. My ego didn't need to remain in that high-profile of a job."

As soon as he accepted the position and moved back to the South, Bartow knew he had done the right thing. "I lost all the stress and the pressures," he says. "All of that left me immediately."

In the twenty-seven years since Bartow departed, there have been seven more head coaches, with only one, Jim Harrick, managing to win a national championship, in 1995, before being fired in a blaze of NCAA violation-stirred controversy two years later. Some of these coaches have had UCLA ties, some haven't. All have been earnest, well-meaning gentlemen who have done their best. And all of them have come to realize that the giant shadow of Wooden still hovers over the program.

Cunningham was probably the most low-profile of the bunch. Larry Brown swirled in and out in typical Larry Brown style, then briefly accepted the job a second time eight years later, before changing his mind at the last moment. Larry Farmer was simply too young and inexperienced. Walt Hazzard worked hard and was determined to do well, but he proved to be a far better player than he was a coach.

Technically, Harrick ranked just below Brown as a coach. But there were too many incidents when he blurted things like: "All these players are running around with my paycheck hanging out of their mouths." As he would establish at future coaching stops, Harrick had a strange knack for saying or doing the wrong thing at the wrong time.

Steve Lavin, who followed him, was the rawest of the bunch, a well-meaning kid who was making coffee runs under Harrick when suddenly he was named interim head coach and then inherited the position full time. Image-wise, handsome with slicked-back hair and an ingratiating smile, he was perfect. He was the coach every UCLA alumni mom wanted her daughter to date. But coaching-wise, Lavin was never quite up to the task, and eventually it showed. What he never seemed to let bother him, however, was the presence of Wooden.

"I think it was because of my background," says Lavin, who was fired two years ago after taking more flak than any of Wooden's eight successors with the possible exception of Bartow. "I was an assistant for five years, and I'd already spent so much time around him. If I'd come from outside, it might have been different. As it was, you knew the legacy could make it difficult, but having him here could be helpful, too. Being the basketball coach at UCLA and having Coach Wooden around is the equivalent of a young political leader being able to call up Jefferson or Washington or Franklin. It's like picking up the phone and having a direct line to Mount Rushmore. He is the equivalent of the pope in college basketball. It's like you're a young cardinal in the Vatican with the pope in the audience watching everything you do."

Cunningham, who followed Bartow, didn't feel the same strain when he took the job. "Any pressure I felt was self-imposed," he says. "I think Gene felt tremendous pressure. I didn't, because I was family. Either that, or maybe I wasn't smart enough to figure it out."

But even this blond former assistant, who went 40–8 in two years and never made it to the Final Four, found some hints of the expectations associated with the job. "I had people come up to me and say, 'I don't think I'll bother with getting tickets to the regionals. I think I'll just go ahead and buy them for the Final Four.'"

When Cunningham, now the athletic director at UC Santa Barbara, walked away after two seasons, many assumed it was for the same reasons Bartow gave. Cunningham says it wasn't anything like that. "I told J. D. before my second season that this was my last year," he says. "He tried to convince me otherwise. It wasn't that I didn't like it. It was just that I didn't want to coach. I still have people coming up to me all the time and asking me about it. They want to know if I miss coaching. I tell them, no. I'd rather build programs and buildings.

"UCLA is a prestigious place, no question about it. But you really weren't rewarded as you should be," he says. "When I left to become the athletic director at Oregon State, I made the same base salary that I made at UCLA. When we went 25–3 and won the Pac-8 my first year [at UCLA], I got a $3,000 raise, from $33,000 to $36,000, then I was told I couldn't have a summer camp on campus. It wasn't worth it. The head coach at Long Beach State was making more than the head coach at UCLA. If it had been more lucrative, I probably would have stayed."

Ben Howland, fresh from his first, somewhat shaky season as UCLA's latest coach with a much bigger salary, grew up in Southern California watching

Wooden's teams play on television and following them as a young basketball fanatic. "I remember those late-night delayed telecasts," Howland says. "I used to watch them with my dad in Goleta [near Santa Barbara]. He had a television room in the back of the house. Sometimes I'd stay up late by myself and watch. I remember the Goodrich and Hazzard teams. I recall the teams with Kareem. And when I got older, I remember rooting for Jamaal Wilkes, because he was from the Santa Barbara area. I always wanted to be a coach, even at the age of eleven or twelve. I told my friends. I always was around basketball. To me, doing something that you love to do, well, there are not many jobs like that."

Howland didn't watch Wooden as much as study him. "I thought of him as the great taskmaster," he says. "He was so good at teaching fundamentals. I marveled at how fundamental his teams were at passing, shooting, shot selection, and how unselfish they were. They had all the attributes that you wanted. He was a great recruiter, too. If you had told me back then I would someday be the coach at UCLA, I would have thought of it as a dream come true."

But along with the dream comes extraordinary pressure in Westwood. "Sure, you have pressure created by the success of the past," Howland says. "Anytime a program has a legacy like UCLA does in basketball, there is a certain standard of excellence. That's what we have to fight to get back to. But I don't think we'll ever see his kind of domination again. There will never be another Michael Jordan, and there will never be another John Wooden. Of course, we'll never see those great players staying four years, as they did then, either. If you had a Jabbar now, he'd go straight to the NBA. A Walton, maybe he stays one year. It's a different era now and a different culture. Given that, what Coach Wooden accomplished will never be repeated. Nobody will ever win seven in a row again. It's inconceivable in this day and age. It will never happen. People say never say never. Well, I'm saying never. I call it a trillion-to-one shot."

Like most of the men to succeed Wooden, Howland has spent some time with the man. "We visited a couple of times," he says. "It's been very cordial. I look to him for advice. I talk to him about how important recruiting is. He talks about how important talent is to success. I've gone to his house with my family, too. It was fun. He took his children's book out and read it to my kids. He was great to us. Some people ask if I worry about him sitting behind me during games. I really don't. I think of it as him being supportive. This is his baby. He wants it to be successful."

Once he took the job, Howland also went out of his way to speak with some of the others who preceded him. "I talked with Lavin, with Bartow, with Harrick. We went into some of the history. It always helps to get perspective, to find out what's happened before."

There are some who feel Howland doesn't have to approach Wooden status, he merely has to restore the program back to where it is competitive nationally again. But others think differently.

"I think the new guy they have there now is a brilliant coach," Bartow says, referring to Howland. "He might think he's following whatzhisname . . . you know, the last guy there, Steve Lavin. But he's not. He is following John Wooden."

At UCLA, whether they want to admit it or not, everyone is following John Wooden.

A Love for Lincoln

Spend any time around John Wooden, and you'll soon know the name of his favorite American.

It is Abraham Lincoln, first and foremost, and no one is even close for second. "I guess I became interested in Lincoln as a youngster, but I really became fascinated with him later," Wooden says. A visit to Wooden's condo will support that fact.

Collecting Lincoln memorabilia has become almost an obsession for the coach. He has books, paintings, newspaper clippings, and anything else you care to mention about the famous president. On a recent visit, I noticed one stack of books just outside his den that included the following: *The Living Lincoln, The Lincoln-Douglas Debates, Dear Mr. Lincoln, The Lincoln No One Knew, The Inner World of Abraham Lincoln, Lincoln's Virtues, Lincoln,* and *Lincoln on Leadership.*

Once, after one of Southern California's more vigorous earthquakes caused some damage to Wooden's condo, a contractor came to do the repairs. He also happened to be an artist, and he later presented the coach with a painting of Lincoln and Wooden together in a depiction of great men from separate eras. It remains one of the coach's prized possessions.

"I think I like Lincoln most for his humanity and his concern for others," Wooden says. "He was a remarkable man. At Gettysburg, his entire address was 272 words, but it says more than some volumes."

Wooden's likes and dislikes, in general, are hardly surprising, considering his midwestern roots and simple, churchgoing style. Some of his favorites include: Restaurant—Knott's Berry Farm Chicken House (where the fried chicken is the style he used to love in Indiana); Books—The Bible and *The Servant* by James Hunter; Movies—*Shawshank Redemption, Goodbye Mr. Chips,* and *It's a Wonderful Life;* Movie Stars—John Wayne, Katherine Hepburn, James Stewart, Cary Grant, and Spencer Tracy.

Tony Spino, the UCLA assistant trainer who visits Wooden three times a week for light workouts that include stretching and massages, has a fitting quote after spending many hours around the man. "Coach Wooden's favorite American is Abraham Lincoln," Spino says. "But I think Coach Wooden should be everyone's favorite American."

A Classic Weekend
and a New Court
at Pauley

I t is ten o'clock in the morning on the day before the tenth John R. Wooden Classic at the Arrowhead Pond in Anaheim, and four of the best coaches in college basketball, some of them yawning, others just appearing tired and fighting off jet lag, straggle into a room for a media conference.

Minutes before they are about to start, there is a stir off in one corner as the elderly gentleman whose name is attached to the tournament shuffles in slowly, with the help of a cane and an usher the size of a middle linebacker.

John Wooden glances over and smiles, and the four coaches look as if they are cardinals in the Catholic Church and the pope has just walked in. A tournament official carefully helps Wooden up the steps of the podium, and he settles into a seat at the far end of the table. Stanford's Mike Montgomery, Kentucky's Tubby Smith, Kansas's Bill Self, and Ben Howland, in his first season at UCLA, the school Wooden put on the basketball map, realize it is time to pay homage to the man before they discuss anything about their teams or opponents.

"It is a great honor," says Howland, "to participate in a Classic named after the greatest coach in the history of college basketball."

Self, who has succeeded Roy Williams at Kansas, says, "Anything that has Coach Wooden's name on it figures to be first class. Certainly, this is a great event."

Montgomery, whose father used to work at UCLA when Wooden was coaching, knows the legendary coach better than the other three. "Anytime you have a chance to see Coach Wooden and be around him, it's a great opportunity," he says. "He tells me that fifty-six years ago he held me when I was just a kid, but I don't remember."

Smith's remarks echo the others. "It's a real privilege to be part of something named after the man who is said to be the greatest coach college basketball has ever seen," he says.

As usual, Wooden looks embarrassed by all the kind words. "I always appreciate flattery," he says, "but I don't like it. I've always felt uncomfortable when people talk about the best. Merely to be considered one of the best ones is pleasing to me."

The four men who have studied his teams and records know better. They are asked to comment on his ten national championships, including seven in a row, and are asked if they think anyone can ever repeat that accomplishment.

"No, I don't think we'll ever see anything like that again," Montgomery says. "I was around here back then, watching most of those games on television. It was really pretty simple. What he did was what we all would like to do. He took great talent but made them play the game the right way. That's very difficult to do, and it's not going to happen again. But it was a remarkable run and fun to watch."

Self considers it, then shakes his head in admiration. "Now it's unthinkable to win back-to-back national titles, and we're talking ten of twelve. It's never going to happen again," he says. "Nobody is even going to sniff that. When you watch tapes, it is amazing how he gets all those great players to play unselfishly. You can tell a lot about a coach by the players who come back and talk about the coach years later. His all say such great things, it is remarkable."

Smith, like the others, doesn't believe such a basketball dynasty will occur again, but he prefers to dwell on other parts of the Wooden magic. "He did so many innovative things with his squads," he says. "He was able to make adjustments every year. And he did it at all levels. Then to go on and do it at the highest level is just remarkable. I have so much respect for what he stands for."

Howland smiles at reporters and talks about the legacy the man left at UCLA. "I know our alumni expect it to happen again," he says, as the reporters laugh. "I have fond memories of the games I used to watch on late replays on KTLA in Los Angeles. I grew up wanting to be a Bruin and enjoyed the way they played the game. Just look at his stats. They went something like 100–2 [88–2, actually] in the Alcindor years, then with Walton they went 86–4. Those are unbelievable numbers. And remember, for part of his career, they didn't even have Pauley [Pavilion] yet. He won with different ways with different teams, and that's truly a sign of a great coach. You'll never see it again. You'll never see anything close."

Wooden, sitting next to Howland, moves the microphone back over in front of him and, with a twinkle in his eyes, addresses the new Bruins coach. "Ben, it happened at UCLA once, and it can happen again," he says. "We, the alumni, expect it, you know." Again, the room erupts in laughter. "Thanks a lot coach," Howland says, with a smile.

When the formal conference is over, the reporters, many of whom have come from different parts of the country, gather around Wooden to ask more questions of the legendary coach they know their editors would like them to write about.

"Do you really think what you accomplished at UCLA can happen again?" a writer asks. "You can never say never," Wooden says. "Would you have said a shortstop could one day break Lou Gehrig's consecutive-games record? No way. Absolutely not, especially not a shortstop who is asked to play such a demanding position. You would have said no chance. But [Cal] Ripken did it by a considerable margin."

Wooden is asked if he enjoys watching professional basketball. "I watch the pros," he says, "but if I want to see wrestling, I'll go to a wrestling match. If I want to watch traveling, I'll go to a track meet. And if I want to see showmanship, I'll go see the Globetrotters. I think the athleticism of today's players is unbelievable. But it has had a negative effect on team play."

A tournament official taps Wooden on the shoulder. "Coach, it's time to go out for our clinic now," she says. The Classic schedules a clinic with some of the competing players and a group from Special Olympics, one of the charities the tournament benefits. Wooden makes his way to the court, where he is seated on a barstool waiting to address the Special Olympians after the clinic is finished.

"Would you like a doughnut?" asks one of the tournament assistants. "Are they Krispy Kreme?" the coach asks, grinning "They sure are," the assistant says, bringing one over. Wooden wastes no time in devouring the doughnut. "Umm, ummm," he says. "I don't know if it's good for you, but it's mighty good."

On the floor of the Pond, the players from Kansas, the No. 1-rated team in the country at that moment, are having a grand time playing basketball with the Special Olympians, offering tips and encouragement. They pass the ball generously, allowing their guests, many of whom are physically handicapped, to cast off well-intended but often awkward-looking shots. The kids from Kansas whoop and holler and shout out compliments. When an occasional shot goes in the basket, they scream and slap palms with the Special Olympian, who beams as if he had just won an NCAA Tournament game. Laughter and good vibes permeate the place, and when the clinic is over, the players and the Special Olympians gather around Wooden's chair to hear words of wisdom from The Master. The facility becomes so quiet, you can hear a wristband drop.

"First, I want to say hello," Wooden says. "Even though it's been twenty-eight years since I've been teaching, I still enjoy coming to practices. It was wonderful sitting here and watching you have so much fun. My Dad used to tell me when I was in grade school, 'Never try to be better than anyone else. Just try to be the best you can be.' We're not all the same in ability, but as long as we're having fun and doing our best, that's what really matters. Any handicaps we have, we should still try to do the best we can."

An official says they will open it up for questions now. "When you played at Purdue, did you consider playing in the Olympics?" asks one Kansas player.

"I graduated in 1932, and the first Olympics basketball team was in 1936," Wooden says.

"How did you get Kareem to come all the way out to Los Angeles from New York?" asks a smiling Special Olympian.

"To me, he'll always be Lewis Alcindor, not Kareem," says Wooden. "He and his coach watched us play when we won our first national championship. And then I had a speaking engagement at Valley Forge in Pennsylvania, and Lewis asked if he could come there and speak to me about UCLA, and he did. Eventually, he came and helped us dedicate Pauley Pavilion. He was on the freshman team that trimmed the varsity in the very first game at Pauley. And Lewis definitely had something to do with that victory."

Another Olympian asks Wooden who was the hardest player he ever had to recruit. "Paul Westphal, who eventually went to USC," Wooden says. "But he never beat us, so it turned out all right."

After the question-and-answer session, Wooden is surrounded by Special Olympians for a group picture. Self, the Kansas coach, asks if Wooden wouldn't mind having picture taken with his players. Wooden happily obliges and then is taken by golf cart away from the court and back out to the parking lot, where he is driven to a nearby hotel to rest for a few hours.

That night, he is the guest of honor at the John R. Wooden Classic dinner at the Anaheim Marriott, where once again, before a large crowd in a ballroom the size of the Pond, the competing coaches are asked to say a few words about the man.

"As much as I respect what he did as a coach, I didn't realize what a treasure he is as a man," says Stanford's Montgomery. "He claims to have held me when I was a baby. I think maybe he dropped me, I don't know. And if he did, it was his first turnover."

Self says he had the opportunity meet Wooden at an awards function three or four years earlier. "As great as his accomplishments as a coach, it pales in comparison to his accomplishments as a man," he says.

Kentucky's Smith talks about what an honor it has been to spend time with Wooden, then adds: "He's the one person in the coaching ranks you could put on the same level with some of the greatest people of the world."

Jim Hill, sports anchor for the Los Angeles CBS affiliate, is the emcee for the evening, and after the dinner is completed, he and Wooden sit down in large, cushy chairs behind a couple of microphones for an informal interview.

"How big an adjustment was it for you to leave Indiana to come to UCLA?" Hill asks.

"If I hadn't insisted on a three-year contract at UCLA, I would have left after two years," Wooden says. "But I had insisted. And I believed in honoring a contract." You can almost hear the sighs of relief from the UCLA fans in the audience.

"How big of an honor was it for you to receive the recent Medal of Freedom from President Bush?" Hill asks.

"I didn't really earn that. My players earned it," Wooden says. "That doesn't mean I'm not proud. I'm very proud."

Hill wonders what the key to Wooden's consistency was through the years.

"It's been said that consistency is the first refuge of those who have no imagination," Wooden says, smiling. "What is it you miss most since retiring?" Hill asks.

"I love practices," Wooden says. "After twenty-eight years, that is the only thing I've truly missed. I love to teach."

After the interview, a live auction is held, with proceeds going to the Special Olympics. Vacation trips, private suites for Mighty Ducks hockey games, and concert tickets are all offered. But the biggest stir, not surprisingly, is caused by the final prize on the auction list. It is a private lunch with Wooden, along with a trophy case full of signed memorabilia. Before the auction is finished, two different gentlemen bid $5,600 and are both awarded lunches with the man they can't wait to meet. Nearby, at his table, Wooden shakes his head.

"He hates this kind of thing," says his daughter, Nan, sitting nearby. "He gets so embarrassed and thinks having lunch with someone can't possibly be worth that much money."

Now it's Saturday, the morning of the Classic, and Wooden has to rise early. Because of television commitments, the first game, UCLA vs. Kentucky, tips off at 10:30 in the morning. UCLA plays as if it were still sleeping early, falling behind by seventeen points before rallying to make a game of it in the second half. But Kentucky finally prevails, 52–50.

With 3:55 to play, the public address announcer asks the large crowd to look up at the large monitor over the scoreboard, and a long, well-produced segment on Wooden is played, showing him as a young star at Purdue through his winning years at UCLA. After it is over, the crowd rises in en masse to offer a three-minute standing ovation. Wooden, pictured live on screen, looks embarrassed again. Finally, daughter Nan whispers in his ear and helps him stand up to acknowledge the crowd. Smiling, he waves his hand, and the applause grows even louder.

In the second game of the intensely played doubleheader, Stanford knocks off No. 1 Kansas, 64–58, utilizing a well-designed zone defense that shuts down most of the Jayhawks' top shooters. Wooden makes his way down the stairs gingerly afterward to present trophies to the winning teams. Then he is helped back into a golf cart and is on his way out of the arena, pausing to sign autographs and acknowledge well-wishers.

A reporter approaches and asks him what he thought of the games. "They were good, well-played games, very competitive," Wooden says. "I thought Stanford played very well. They play smart for Mike."

So the Classic weekend ends, appropriately enough, with the legendary coach who is still so revered by those in the business pausing to comment on one of the best and the brightest in the profession today. It is John Wooden's way of offering the ultimate compliment, from one teacher to another.

❧

It is exactly two weeks later, five days before Christmas, and UCLA officials have decided on the perfect present for the most respected coach in Bruins' history. They have designated this as the day when they will rename the floor at Pauley Pavilion. They will call it Nell and John Wooden Court and honor the coach in a ceremony before the afternoon's scheduled game with Michigan State.

It seems only appropriate since Pauley is The House That Wooden Built. It was his success in Westwood that prompted construction of the facility and provided UCLA basketball with the type of home it deserved. Even then, Wooden, who honestly doesn't covet the personal attention, wasn't sure he was keen on the idea of naming the court.

"At first I felt no," the coach said, referring to when university officials approached him about it. "At first they didn't mention Nellie. Then I said, well, if they put Nellie's name on it . . ." Turns out, Wooden not only insisted they put her name on it, he made sure they put it first.

So now they are here, gathering on campus on a brisk Southern California Saturday in December. Some seventy-four of the coach's former players and many of his former assistants and team managers arrive for a lavish pregame luncheon in Covell Commons, just a couple of long fast breaks away from Pauley. Sitting there, surrounded by huge, blown-up pictures of John and Nell and so many of his former players, it is like many of those pictures are coming to life. You look around and you see a parade of great players from several generations. There are Walt Hazzard and Keith Erickson here, and Willie Naulls and Morris Taft there. Kareem Abdul-Jabbar and Jamaal Wilkes are greeting each other in one corner, while Mike Warren and Lynn Shackelford are reminiscing in another. Sidney Wicks is introducing his daughter to everyone he can find, while Bill Walton, as usual, is the center of attention, drawing the most interviews and autograph requests. You sit there and you are awed by the collection of talent, clearly the most amazing group of college players ever to assemble in one room.

This is the ticket for the December 20, 2003, game when Pauley Pavilion's court was dedicated in honor of Nell and John Wooden, and seventy-four former players honored the coach.

ABC's Al Michaels, who broadcast games in the Wooden Era for a couple of years after Dick Enberg left, is the master of ceremonies. "This man is unparalleled to me," Michaels says of Wooden. "He is the greatest coach in the history of sports. Look around this room, Coach. There are so many people you influenced over the years."

UCLA Chancellor Albert Carnesale is introduced. "Coach Wooden hasn't experienced success," says Carnesale. "He has defined it. He has had an extraordinary impact on every life he has touched. His legacy certainly endures."

The university's relatively new athletic director, Dan Guerrero, a former Bruin baseball player, talks about how fortunate he feels to have Wooden around to advise him. "I go to him for words of wisdom," Guerrero says. "I don't go for secrets of the universe. It is more about perspective and clarity. One of the joys of my job has been the opportunity to get to know him better."

Wooden sits and listens, sometimes shaking his head as if he is not worthy of all the praise. The shy midwesterner in him doesn't like the adulation, but at the same time, he seems deeply touched. To him, this day is special not because of the tributes he is receiving but because of the tributes directed toward his late wife, Nellie, as he calls her. When he finally approaches the microphone, after the longest of many standing ovations, his voice is choked with emotion.

"I'm having a lot of trouble, kind of filled up," he says. He recites part of a poem about a reunion in heaven with Nellie, then he looks up at the audience with tears in his eyes and adds, "She's waiting for me. I'm sure she's enjoying this day."

A beautifully produced tape, narrated by Enberg, is shown to the audience. Many of the voices and faces on the screen bring back old memories.

"My mother wanted me to have an equal opportunity, to be given a fair chance," says Naulls, Wooden's first great center back in the 1950s, when African-Americans were not that prominent in college basketball. "Coach gave me that. I was the last guy on the team as a freshman, but after three weeks of practice, I moved up to first string. It was a big thing for diversity. Coach started raising the diversity level in Westwood."

Rasheed Hazzard, the former point guard's son, appears along with his father, whose speech is limited after suffering a stroke. "When my father first came here from Philadelphia, Coach let him know not to do all those flashy things," says Rasheed.

Walt, sitting next to him, smiles and shakes his head. "No," he says. "No."

Rasheed just smiles and continues. "My Dad called his father and told him he wanted to come home. My grandfather took it upon himself to call Coach Wooden. He let him know Dad wasn't going anywhere. He'd be staying at UCLA." Walt smiles on screen and shakes his head affirmatively.

Gail Goodrich speaks, and so do Rafer Johnson and Andre McCarter and Lynn Shackelford. It is left for Mike Warren, the player Wooden often describes as "the smartest I've ever coached," to describe what so many others in the audience are feeling.

"He is always there for me," Warren says. "He's my mentor and my friend. Over the years, we've gone from student and coach to simply two people who love each other's company."

Enberg's voice sums it up. "What John Wooden reminds us," he says, "is the best of sport, the best of life, the best of humanity."

After lunch, the proceedings move to Pauley, where the seventy-four players are seated in folding chairs behind one basket, and the official ceremony begins. Two large sections of blue felt covering are removed to show the lettering that appears on two sides of the court. "Nell and John Wooden Court," it reads, and the sold-out crowd of 12,433 rises and applauds as Wooden is led onto the court.

"I'm proud this floor was named for Nellie and I," he says. "But I know what made this day possible. It's those young men down there." And he points his cane at Walton and Abdul-Jabbar and the rest of the players who are now standing there, smiling, and applauding in return. Then, slowly, as Bruce Springsteen's "Glory Days" plays in the background, all the players come onto the new Nell and John Wooden Court and pose for a group picture.

At halftime of a game that first-year coach Ben Howland's team, wearing 1964 throwback jerseys, appropriately wins, 64–58, over Michigan State, Wooden, Walton, Abdul-Jabbar, and Warren are ushered into the UCLA soccer team's locker room for media interviews.

"I was glad they did this in a timely way," says Abdul-Jabbar. "He's not going to be around forever. He's ninety-three years old. I'm glad he could have a day like this."

Warren, more than any of the players, seems to understand the true meaning of the day for Wooden. "For me, it's like having a parent being honored for a lifelong relationship," he says. "I know what a relationship means. My mom and dad were like that, and when my father passed away, it was as if a part of my mother went, too. I know when Nell died, a part of Coach passed. Now many years later, to honor her in perpetuity, I think it means a lot to him. I think today is not only about success on the court but about that relationship. I feel so happy for him. This is not only about him but someone very special to him."

Now the interviews are over, and as Wooden rises to go back to his seat inside the arena, he is met by Abdul-Jabbar, the former player considered stoic by so many who don't really know him. "Coach," Abdul-Jabbar says, his eyes glowing with respect and reverence, "I'd like you to meet my son, Amir."

Wooden smiles and extends his hand. "Nice to meet you, Amir," he says. Then the two happy adults, the best coach and the best player in the history of college basketball, hug each other for several seconds.

"Thank you, Lewis," Wooden says, using the name he always has preferred for the former Lew Alcindor.

"Coach," says the only center to win three national championships, "I wouldn't have missed this for anything." It is this wonderful, freeze-frame of a moment, maybe more than any of the others, that clarifies not only the significance of this day but this man's contributions.

The new imprint on the floor of Pauley Pavilion is nice, but in no way can it compare to the imprint John Wooden has left on so many of his players' lives.

The John R. Wooden Award

What better way to honor the finest college basketball player in America than with a trophy named after the finest college basketball coach ever?

The John R. Wooden Award was created and designed in 1976 by the Los Angeles Athletic Club as an award to honor the outstanding collegiate basketball Player of the Year and the All-America team. The Wooden Award is college basketball's version of the Heisman Trophy.

Each year a panel of more than 1,000 voters [the author is honored to be one], including representatives from all fifty states, casts ballots. State chairmen, who in turn are chosen by area chairmen from the East, South, Midwest, Southwest, and West, select the voters.

John R. Wooden Award voters select the ten-man All-America team. The player who receives the most points from the voters is the recipient of the Wooden Award trophy. The top five All-Americans and their coaches receive special awards and scholarship checks for their schools at the annual televised presentation in Los Angeles.

With Wooden involved, naturally there are some strict criteria for the award. Candidates must have a cumulative 2.0 grade point average since enrolling in their university and "exhibit strength of character, both on and off the court." They also must "contribute to team effort" and "excel in both offense and defense."

The award is held in high esteem and boasts a Board of Governors that includes Wooden, the chairman; Dean Smith, the vice-chairman; and such distinguished members as Mike Krzyzewski of Duke, Lute Olson of Arizona, Roy Williams of North Carolina, Jim Boeheim of Syracuse, and Mike Montgomery of Stanford, among others.

Fittingly, the first winner of the John R. Wooden Award was UCLA's Marques Johnson, in 1977. Two years earlier, Johnson was one of the stars on Wooden's final NCAA championship team, the year the coach retired.

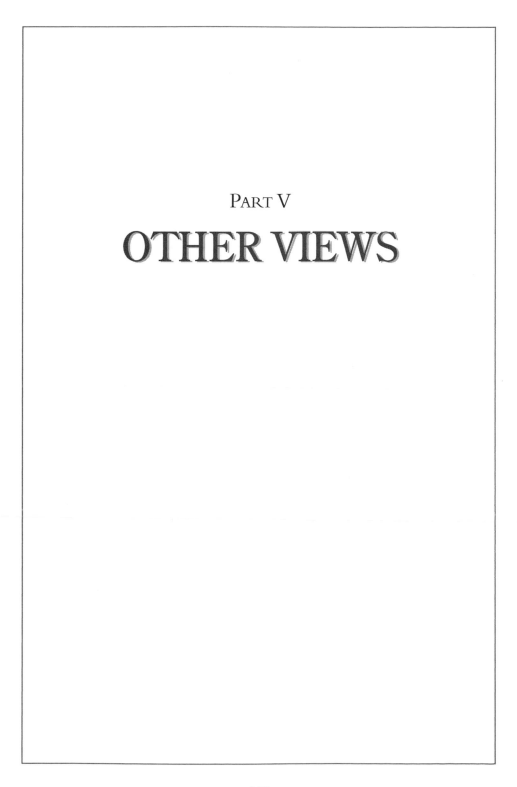

PART V

OTHER VIEWS

The Opposing Coaches

Ask him to pick the most accomplished coaches he competed against in his legendary career, and John Wooden will rattle off a long list of names. He will not, however, select one or two as the finest of the group. It simply is not his nature. He worries that by singling out certain individuals as the best, he would be slighting others. But in attempting to select two who battled him on near or equal terms, two who know him as both an opponent and a man and have closely observed him through the years, it would be difficult to find a pair more suitable, or contrasting, than Pete Newell and Jerry Tarkanian.

Newell has been described as "the godfather of modern basketball." Although, at 89, he is a few years younger than Wooden, he reached the zenith of the college sport at the University of California five years before Wooden won his first national title at UCLA. Newell captured NCAA and NIT championships, coached the United States to an Olympic gold medal, and is in the Basketball Hall of Fame. Of those in his generation, or maybe any generation, only Newell is consistently ranked on the same basketball teaching pedestal as Wooden.

"The chance to spend a week with Pete Newell is like a student of literature getting to spend a week with Hemingway or Frost," says Detroit Pistons coach Rick Carlisle, who has been an instructor at Newell's camp.

Since they competed in the same conference and their teams played each other constantly, Wooden and Newell had some epic battles. If, to the general public, Newell isn't as celebrated as Wooden, it is only because he quit coaching in 1960, in the middle of his career, at the relatively young age of forty-five, due to health problems. He had won the national championship in 1959 and directed Cal to a second NCAA Finals appearance the following season but opted out because of stress and the fact that he was discouraged that the big-business part of the sport had become more important than the teaching aspects.

"My health wasn't good," Newell says. "I couldn't eat from Thursday to Sunday. I was losing too much weight. The doctors told me I had to make changes in my life. I had too much self-induced pressure."

Newell went on to become athletic director at Cal and the general manager of the Los Angeles Lakers and San Diego Rockets, after turning down a chance to be general manager of the NFL's Los Angeles Rams under Pete Rozelle. He retired in 1976 to spend more time with his ailing wife, Florence, who died in 1984. He has since been a basketball consultant at many levels, the acknowledged mentor of Bobby Knight, and the director of the highly successful Big Man's Camp in Hawaii that counts Bill Walton, Shaquille O'Neal, and Hakeem Olajuwon among its distinguished alumni.

Newell's overall basketball résumé is remarkable. Many say it was Newell, not Dean Smith, who invented the four-corner offense. And before Jerry West brought Shaq to the Lakers, Newell brought Kareem. As for Phil Jackson's famous triangle offense, the gentleman generally credited with implementing it, Lakers assistant Tex Winter, broke in serving as a manager on a Loyola freshman team coached by Newell. It is no wonder that Newell is said to offer almost as much basketball wisdom to those who travel south down the 5 Freeway in Southern California to visit him as Wooden regularly dispenses from his condo in Encino.

Tarkanian is well-known as one of the more successful and controversial basketball coaches in the modern history of collegiate sport. He was noted for swallowing up opponents the way he used to chew up all those towels through the years (another habit, by the way, that Newell originated). In thirty seasons of coaching in Division I, Tark's teams averaged a remarkable 25.3 victories a year. His .803 lifetime winning percentage ranks fourth all time. He took his UNLV teams to four Final Fours, capturing the national championship in 1990. In all, he coached in eighteen NCAA Tournaments, finishing with a 38–18 record and, along the way, became famous for perfecting basketball's most effective zone defense. In thirty-seven years of coaching, his teams never had a losing season. Some forty-two of his players went on to the NBA, twelve of them selected in the first round of the draft.

Through it all, Tarkanian battled the NCAA as hard as his opponents. His programs were under constant surveillance. The NCAA began investigating him at Long Beach State and continued its probes when he moved on to UNLV, eventually putting the Rebels' program on probation. Whatever Tark did or didn't do, it was well known that he had a knack for stretching the rules, for squeezing underprivileged kids who might not have had the necessary grades or particularly admirable lifestyles into his program. Talk to him long enough, and he could almost convince you that he was doing it to help kids who didn't have any other chance for a decent life. Talk to his critics, and they'd whisper that Tarkanian's primary goal was merely to win. Either way, nobody was more criticized or scrutinized through the years.

In 1998, after years of haggling in court, the NCAA finally paid Tarkanian $2.5 million in settlement of a suit filed by the coach, with mutual release of all claims relating to the pending actions of the suit, no admission of liability by any party, and dismissal of the actions cited in the suit. In basketball parlance, Tarkanian appeared to finally win in overtime.

If Newell's teams were UCLA's main adversaries early in Wooden's career, Tark's Long Beach State clubs proved major rivals during the Bruins' glory years. Some of the toughest games Wooden and his teams had to survive were not in the NCAA Finals but earlier in the tournament when they had to beat the 49ers merely to make it out of the West Regionals. By the time Tarkanian moved to UNLV and established his own mini-dynasty, Wooden no longer was coaching, and UCLA officials had no interest in scheduling the Rebels.

Newell said he first faced Wooden when he was coaching at San Francisco and Michigan State. "I remember we played UCLA in two games at USF," Newell says. "He upset us in the first game, but then in the second game we beat them. When I was at Michigan State, we beat a No. 1-rated Kansas State team, then the next night, UCLA beat us on our floor. I knew before we even played that he was a good coach. He'd come out from the Midwest, and I'd heard about him. I knew him as a great player, too, of course. But out in the West, we didn't get a lot of information back then. It was a different time. Other than USC, no one got much attention in our end of the country.

"I'd heard Wooden liked his teams to run, and he proved that early. He gave us an introduction to another style of basketball, another tempo at which the game was played. Before he arrived, those of us out here were real steeped in the basic mechanics of the game. We didn't want our team to shoot the ball until someone was in rebounding position. In a sense, we kept a rein on our shooters. He introduced the style where his teams would shoot first and worry about rebounding later. That style of transition basketball was practically unknown out here. He brought a freedom offensively that we'd never experienced before."

Tarkanian's introduction to Wooden came when he was still coaching in junior college. Before he ever made it to the Division I level, before he was ever labeled "Tark the Shark," he was a coaching legend in the California junior college ranks, first at Riverside City College, then Pasadena City College.

"When we were coaching in Pasadena, we had a reputation of having the best zone defense in the country," Tarkanian says. "Well, one day I get this phone call. It's from Jerry Norman [Wooden's assistant coach at UCLA]. He tells me Coach Wooden wants me to show him the basic concepts of our 1-2-2 zone. Well, can you imagine a JC coach getting a call like that? Shoot, that was better than having sex."

In the early years, Newell and Wooden weren't great friends. "I never knew John really well," Newell says. "We actually played totally different styles of basketball. He played run-and-gun. We were more of a half-court team. But he and I had some similar concepts. Both of us believed strongly in conditioning. One time we played each other at Cal, and we went thirty-eight minutes without a timeout. That's how well conditioned both of our teams were. Can you imagine that today, going thirty-eight minutes without even one timeout? It will never happen."

The contrast in the personalities of these two men was as fascinating as the differences in their teams. Wooden's clubs were flashier, but Newell's teams, rooted in defense, were even more fundamental and basic. "He beat me as many times as I beat him over the years," says Newell, who dominated the rivalry early. "But I soon noticed that Wooden's teams and his defense were getting better and better. I think his assistant, Jerry Norman, had something to do with that. He was a really good assistant."

Newell already was out of coaching for four years when Wooden won his first national title. But his old rival was always an interested observer. "I saw a real change in John when he won that first championship," Newell says. "I think, at first, he wasn't real comfortable out here. In Indiana, people are a lot closer than they are out here. California people were different than John. After he won, I think he began to feel more confident that what he was doing was right. Inside, he always knew he was a good coach, but I think he began to feel more secure. He became much more at ease, more like he is now.

"Before, he saw himself more as an outsider. He wasn't outgoing at all. He didn't fraternize with other coaches at the beginning. He wasn't very warm. You know how coaches are. We like to tell jokes, go out and have a belt or two with friends. He never did. John never drank.

"I remember one time at the Final Four, [Fordy] Anderson and I were just coming back to the hotel early in the morning, when John and Nell, who was always with him, were just getting up and walking into the lobby. It was pretty funny. But that's the way John was. He was not one of the guys. He kept himself separate."

Coaching-wise, what fascinated Newell the most about Wooden was his ability to adjust. "I don't think people realize how flexible he was," Newell says. "John won his first championship with two great guards [Walt Hazzard and Gail Goodrich]. He won his second with one great guard [Goodrich]. He never had a great center, but then Kareem comes along, and he's all-world for three years and they win three more. Then Kareem graduates. He has no top center and no great guards, but he manages to win with two forwards [Sidney Wicks and Curtis Rowe]. Then, he gets [Bill] Walton and wins again. Finally, in his last year, he has no really great, experienced players, and he still wins. That's what I call flexibility."

Tarkanian was more taken by another aspect of Wooden's coaching. "What impressed me so much was how simple he was in his coaching," he says. "He exploited you however you tried to guard him. When he had Alcindor and Walton, he played them on the block and made you defend them. If you tried to front them, his guards would throw that lob pass and kill you. If you tried to guard them from behind, [Keith] Wilkes or somebody would flash in for an easy hoop, or [Lynn] Shackelford would stand outside and hit those jumpers.

"Then, when he didn't have the big guy, he ran the high-post offense. Nobody could run it like he did," Tarkanian says. "Whatever he did, they executed perfectly. He puts that zone press in, and everybody then tried it. But he ran it perfectly. He never made any huge adjustments on the bench. It was all done in practice. He did simple things, like have his rebounders all have their arms up. He did that before anyone had thought of it. Wooden didn't outsmart you; he out-executed you. He also knew who his best players were, and he let them play."

Newell and Tarkanian both noticed the same thing in Wooden's UCLA teams once they were rolling along and winning championships at an unprecedented pace. There was a certain attitude they exuded. It was a combination of cockiness and confidence, and if it irked some opponents, it also helped embellish the aura for which they were becoming famous.

"Psychologically, UCLA always went on the floor thinking it was going to win," Newell says. "I think a lot of that goes back to their conditioning. When games get tight at the end, conditioning is a big factor. It was the same with my teams at Cal. When kids pay a price for conditioning, they don't forget it. It builds a sort of mental toughness, almost an arrogant manner. UCLA was like that. They'd come out before games and they wouldn't have the usual lay-up drill. They'd look over at the Straw Hat Band [at Cal] and they'd kind of have this arrogant, confident air about them. It was all part of the psyche they'd use to win a game."

Tarkanian never bought the conditioning theory. "All Wooden's players talked about how they were in better shape than anybody. Well, Kenny Booker [who played at UCLA] played with a lot of my guys, and he said our practices were a lot harder than theirs. But Wooden had guys believing they were in better shape than everybody. You know, he never practiced on Saturday or Sunday. I never gave my kids more than one day off. He told me he never practiced on the weekend, and I started giving my kids more time off. I honestly believe Wooden made his kids think they were in better shape. His practices lasted two hours, maybe two hours and twenty minutes. Mine went three, three and a half hours. I always figured he was just better organized. He got more done in less time than the rest of us."

For Newell, who wasn't impressed with Wooden's defense in his early years at UCLA, the biggest change in the Bruins' coach came at that end of the floor. "I think when he first came out here, defense was not a high priority for him," Newell says. "He wanted to outscore the other team. But as his career went on, the most apparent and real attribute was, to me, his pressing defense, especially with that first championship team. Back in Indiana in those days, nobody played the press. They still had the center jump after every basket when John was there.

"So he came out here, and Ralph Miller at Oregon State [another coach Wooden regarded highly] had good success against him with the press. We always played a press against him, too. We used to use it at USF and Michigan State, as well. When John decided to adopt it, he did a heckuva job. He went full court with it, and I was impressed, because we didn't have the speed or quickness to do it.

"I remember a holiday tournament in L.A. when UCLA played a great Michigan team, and John tightened that press and took Cazzie Russell,

Michigan's best player, away. John had [Keith] Erickson as his safety in the press, and he was really an athlete, really phenomenal for his size. The thing about Wooden's press is that they played it, then they'd watch you try to adjust, and they'd counter your adjustment. John showed me a lot of ingenuity."

Soon enough, Wooden would also show him a long line of great players. "It's funny," Newell says, "but when I was GM of the Rockets, I saw Walton play in high school in San Diego. We had three-man summer teams back then, and Walton played on one of those teams. I was actually hoping he'd go to Cal, because his father went to Cal. Anyway, I was attending the Holiday Tournament in New York, and I was talking to this basketball guy. We were discussing high school players, and he was telling me he'd just seen the greatest high school player he'd ever watched. His name was Tom McMillen. Well, I told the guy if McMillen played in San Diego, he'd only be the second greatest. The guy just laughed. I told him I'd bet him that Walton not only will become college Player of the Year before McMillen, but he'll be drafted higher in the NBA. I was proved right, of course. McMillen was a good player, but there were a lot of McMillens out there. There was only one Walton."

Both Newell and Tarkanian still marvel at Wooden's overall achievements. "I don't think there is anybody who can dispute what he did," Newell says. "He won with record consistency. And I can tell you from personal experience, it's hard to win a national championship, and it is even harder to repeat. The fact he won ten out of twelve is remarkable, and you can't forget that he did it with all different kind of teams."

Tarkanian agrees with almost all the coaches in the sport that we'll never see a streak like Wooden's again. "Nobody could ever win that much," Tarkanian says. "If you had a collection of college all-stars every year, you'd still have to be not only great but lucky to win anything close to that. This guy won thirty-eight games in a row in the NCAA Tournament. To me, that's the most amazing stat ever, in any era. If you let someone pick the five best players every year, you can't do that. I hear people say he had great players. Yeah, he did, but a lot of guys would have taken those great players and screwed them up. He won with all different kinds of teams. How incredible is it that his press worked the way it did when the biggest guy on his team was six foot five?"

Through the years, Wooden's championship teams had many close calls, several of them in the NCAA Tournament. Newell's assessment is that their confidence always carried them through. "They knew they were going to win, and they almost always did," he says.

Tarkanian has a different theory, one that is truly unique. "I honestly believe the Good Lord stepped in and rewarded this man who lived up to all the principles of his religion," Tarkanian says. "He was a great coach, regardless of anything you want to say. But God pulled out some of those close games. He had to, there were so many. Nobody can win seven in a row like he did and ten out of twelve national titles without some divine intervention."

Tarkanian isn't kidding. He truly believes this. "I'll never forget Freddie Boyd of Oregon State kicking a ball off his foot to lose a game against UCLA," Tarkanian says. "Here's the best guard in the country, and that happens to him? I'm telling you, some of the most amazing things that ever happened on a court happened in games with UCLA when Wooden was coaching."

One of those, of course, involved Tarkanian's Long Beach State team. The year was 1971, and the occasion was the West Regional Finals in Salt Lake City, Utah. Tark's 49ers were led by Ed Ratleff, a velvety smooth, NBA-bound guard/forward who might have been the best player in the country that year.

"That was the craziest game I've ever been involved in," Tarkanian says. "We outplayed them so much. Our zone had them baffled. We were up by eleven or something midway through the second half, and suddenly J. D. Morgan [UCLA's athletic director] comes down near the floor and starts yelling at Art White, one of the officials, complaining about our players. Before you know it, White fouls out Ratleff. As far as I was concerned, White should have got the MVP award for that regional. That was the only game Ratleff fouled out of in his whole career.

"Anyway, we'd had a four-point lead when Ratleff fouled out. Inside of thirty seconds, the game is tied, with not much time left. So, I spread the court and hold the ball. Wooden doesn't do anything. He's letting us stall. We take a minute and a half off the clock, and we get a shot blocked by [Larry] Farmer that goes out of bounds. So, we wait another minute, take another shot, and Wicks blocks it. Now we have the ball again, and I'm thinking we're going to get the last shot. I wanted George Trapp to take the last shot.

"I had a kid on that team named Dwight Taylor, and all year I didn't let him shoot because he had this crooked-elbow style that just didn't work. He couldn't shoot. So now Dwight has the ball and drives into the corner, and [Henry] Bibby lets him shoot. What possessed him to shoot I'll never know. Believe me, if I'd had a gun, I would have shot him before letting him shoot the ball in that spot. But he shot, missed it, and they get the rebound. They come down the court, and Taylor fouls Wicks, who gets two free throws, and they win, 57–55."

"So," Tarkanian is asked, "are you saying the officials favored Wooden?"

Tark smiles. "No," he says, "I'm only saying the Good Lord helped him. Look, he was this guy who, after winning the national championship, would get off the plane and first thing he'd do was start hugging his grandchildren. Then he'd take them and the rest of his family out for a milkshake. Me, I'd go get a bottle of wine and celebrate with friends. But he never did. I'm telling you, the guy lived an amazing life. But to win that many times in a lifetime is a miracle. To win as many titles in a row as he did, he had to have God looking after him."

If Wooden competed fiercely against both Newell and Tarkanian when he was coaching, their relationship has changed dramatically in the ensuing years. "John and I are now good friends," says Newell, who lives in Rancho Santa Fe, just outside San Diego, and is still active and amazingly involved for someone his age. "I was the first recipient of the Humanitarian Award, in Boise, Idaho, one year. It's called the John and Nell Wooden Award, and he recommended me for the honor. We've been on the same basketball panels lots of times, and we enjoy being around each other and talking about the game and old times."

Tarkanian, now seventy-four, has been startled to discover it was Wooden who recommended him for jobs, including the one at Indiana University before Knight accepted the head-coaching position there. "He's always been so nice to me," Tarkanian says. "He'd come to Vegas to speak, and my son, Danny, would pick him up at the airport. The thing about him is that, even in his nineties, he's still so sharp. You know, I've heard him speak at clinics, and you compare him to someone like Bob Boyd, and you put them both at a blackboard, and people come away thinking Bob is very sharp at Xs and Os. Next to someone like that, Wooden would come off very basic. If you went to a clinic to hear his secret formula, he was not going to give you that. I think there really wasn't a secret. He just taught very basic fundamental basketball. I'll tell you what, though. Whatever it is he did, it sure worked."

Perfecting the Art of Ref Baiting

The surprise isn't so much that John Wooden would bait referees. The surprise is that he would admit it.

"Oh, yes, I'd try to work them," Wooden says. "I'd say things like 'Don't be a homer,' or 'Call them the same at both ends.'"

Jim Tunney, the celebrated former NFL official, refereed basketball games when Wooden was coaching at UCLA. "John would get on us plenty," Tunney says. "I remember during the Alcindor years, he'd yell, 'They're killing Lewis in there, they're killing him.' He'd tell us to call them the same for both teams, things like that. But I do have to say I never heard him utter a cuss word. Not once. That wasn't always the case with some of his assistants, however."

Surprisingly, Wooden admits he wasn't above heckling opposing players. "I'd do that to try to get them thinking about you, hoping it would get them off their game," he says.

Wooden's style was different than most college basketball coaches, who, back then and even now, storm off their chairs and stand and scream until their faces often turn as bright as their school colors. Wooden was more subtle. He rarely left his chair. He'd sit there with his program rolled up and bark at officials or opposing players from a seated position.

"My feeling always was that if you got up, you were taking away from the confidence of your players," he says. "I wanted them to know that I'd already done my job, now it's time for you to do yours."

Still, it was often funny to watch referees or players from other teams do double takes when they realized it was Wooden, of all people, who was getting on them from the UCLA bench.

"In forty years of teaching, I received two technicals," Wooden says, "and one of those I didn't deserve. If someone said what that [official] thought was said, it wasn't by me."

It doesn't take Wooden long to remember the most anger he's felt on a basketball court. "It was in our very last game with Kentucky [in the NCAA Finals in San Diego in 1975]," he says. "They called a technical on Dave Meyers, and there was no question in my mind that it was a bad call. They called a charge on him that wasn't, and David didn't say a word. He just threw up his arm, and they called a technical.

"What ripped me off is that the day before, the officials met with the coaches and tournament officials. They warned us to stay on the bench and for the players to stay controlled. Yet Joe Hall [the Kentucky coach] spent the whole game charging so far from his bench that I could have shaken hands with him. I didn't want the officials to give him a technical, but they should have if they were going to give Meyers one."

The fact that Wooden would bait officials and opposing players didn't fit with the "St. John" image so many people claim he tried to portray. I can remember one USC player, in particular, calling a reporter over in the locker room and saying, "You wouldn't believe what Wooden was yelling at me out there."

If anything, it only proves that even someone as accomplished as Wooden is human. You can't be the great coach that he was without also being a great competitor. As much as he tried to maintain a certain presence by remaining seated during games, his competitiveness occasionally got the best of him, and he could, at times, complain and bark and rail at officials with the best of them.

The Loyal Assistant

Of all the people who have observed John Wooden through the years, perhaps none qualifies as an expert on the coach more than Gary Cunningham, who played for him, served as his freshman coach and his assistant coach for a ten seasons, became and still is one of his closest friends, and, maybe inevitably, succeeded him after the brief tenure of Gene Bartow.

Cunningham has viewed him from all sides, beginning from the time he joined the team as a skinny kid who could shoot the light outs in the early 1960s until now, when, as the distinguished athletic director at UC Santa Barbara, he continues a warm, lasting, lifetime relationship with the man.

A three-year starter at UCLA, Cunningham was co-captain of the 1962 team—the one with Walt Hazzard as a sophomore guard that pushed a heavily favored University of Cincinnati team to the final seconds before losing, 72–70, in the NCAA semifinals in Wooden's first appearance in the Final Four. One of the best pure shooters of the Wooden Era, Cunningham made twenty-eight of twenty-eight free throws in his sophomore year in league play. After a short but successful run as UCLA head basketball coach in 1977-79, achieving a 50–8 record and two conference championships, Cunningham decided his future might be best served in another form of intercollegiate athletics. He became athletic director at Western Oregon State College, the University of Wyoming, and then at Fresno State, before accepting the AD job at UC Santa Barbara in 1995.

Considering this is someone who can now be described as an expert on college sports, it is interesting to hear Cunningham discuss Wooden, not only as his coach but also as his boss from 1965 to 1975.

"I can still remember meeting him for the first time," Cunningham says. "I thought he was a very nice man. When he first started recruiting me, I did not know very much about him as a coach. I was just a high school kid who was recruited by quite a few schools on the coast, and I had actually always been a USC fan all my life. I'd been very impressed with Cal, because Pete Newell was there, and they were winning and eventually would go on to win the national championship. There was no letter of intent at the time, but I actually committed to Cal."

Then Cunningham, who grew up in Inglewood, not far from where the Los Angeles Lakers would eventually play at the Forum, met Eddie Sheldrake, the former UCLA point guard on Wooden's first team in Westwood. "Boosters were allowed to help with recruiting back then," Cunningham says, "and Eddie worked on me all summer. I wasn't really impressed with the facilities at UCLA, but I thought I had more of a chance to play." So in August, with the fiery Sheldrake's help, Cunningham changed his mind and decided to go to UCLA.

"As a player, I thought Coach Wooden was an outstanding teacher, well-organized, a hard taskmaster, who never swore at you but could yell at you," Cunningham says. "He got your attention. Always teaching, always teaching. He wanted things done precisely the way he believed that they should be done. I didn't play for him my freshman year, because we had to play freshman basketball, and I played for Jerry Norman. But he used to come in and watch the practices, and there was great respect for him. In those days, the coach wasn't your buddy-buddy. I found out he was more my friend after I got finished playing than when I played. But that was the way things were in those times. You did things with the assistant coaches. Today, I think the head coaches are a lot more in tune with their athletes and what goes on day by day and week by week. I used to go in and talk to Coach, but a lot of my teammates were afraid to do that. They were afraid of him. I used to just drop in."

The 1960s were considerably different than the 1970s, when Bill Walton would challenge the coach at the drop of a clipboard. "I grew up in an era that when the coach said, 'Do this.' You never questioned anything," Cunningham says. "You did it, because you had the coach on this pedestal, where today a kid might come in and say, 'Coach, why are we doing that?' I would never do that. If the coach told me to run through the wall, I would run through the wall. That's the way it was in high school. That's the way it was in college. It's kind of like that saying, 'Rule one: The Captain is always right. Rule two: If you don't like it, refer to rule one.' So we just trusted the coach all the time."

After his college playing career was over, Cunningham was tired of school. He went on a goodwill tour to the Orient to play basketball, then wound up as a player and teacher for a team in Manilla, in the Philippines. When he returned home two years later, he completed his master's degree in physical education at UCLA, then taught at the school before starting on his doctorate at USC. But on one fateful day in the summer of 1965, he happened to be in the student union at UCLA eating breakfast when he heard a familiar voice.

"Can I join you?" John Wooden asked.

"Of course," said his former player, who had just signed a contract to teach at UCLA." "Coach looked at me and said, 'You know, I just lost my freshman basketball coach yesterday. How would you like to coach the freshman team?'"

Cunningham wasn't sure what to say. "I don't know, give me a day," he finally replied.

"I told him it would be fun, but I needed to talk to the department chairman and make sure it's okay with him," Cunningham says." So, that's what I did, and he said, 'Fine, as long as it doesn't affect your teaching.' That's how I got into coaching. I accepted the job, never thinking I would stay in it. I went to graduate school one year at UCLA, but I was able to go to UCLA to complete my doctorate degree and did. But I didn't get any units transferred. I started over. I was never going to stay in coaching. Never. But I got waylaid. I got into this coaching, and pretty soon they paid me more. I got my doctorate, and I stayed in coaching until 1975. I gave up teaching after two years, but I worked with Coach Wooden for ten years. I coached the freshmen for six years and assisted with the varsity. I did almost every job that you can do. In those days, they didn't have academic counselors. I was the academic counselor. I did recruiting. I did it all."

The Wooden his former player would experience as a boss didn't seem too much different than the man who used to coach him. "I didn't perceive a change," Cunningham says. But it was a different view working alongside him all the time. "I was in the inner circle," he says. "When you're in the inner circle, you get to go plan the practices, and you get to listen to some of his thoughts. I was able to express my thoughts on recruits, on players, and

COURTESY OF UCLA ATHLETIC DEPARTMENT

Wooden and Cunningham watch intently from the bench during another Bruins romp. Cunningham starred on Wooden's teams in the early 1960s and eventually was one of his successors at UCLA.

make other observations, whereas as a player, you don't get to do that. I didn't see a change in him then.

"But I think he did change over a period of time, in that he became more attuned. He didn't compromise his principles, but he became more attuned with young people and what they were going through. He was still a disciplinarian, but he opened his door more. He might tell you his door was always open. He would tell us that, but everybody in his playing days was fearful of going in there. I think that, later on, he had more communication off the court with players than he did probably when I was playing. So, I think he changed in that regard, but never, never on the court, and never his principles."

Cunningham's biggest embarrassment early on as a freshman coach was also one of his greatest successes. He was the coach of the Lew Alcindor frosh team that flattened UCLA's defending national champs in a freshman-varsity game that marked the debut of Pauley Pavilion.

"My reaction was immature," Cunningham says. "This was the dedication of a facility that he had dreamed about since coming in 1948 to UCLA. All those years of playing in places like B. O. Barn, and finally he had the facility he had dreamed of. Prior to the game, most of his former players came on the floor and formed a human tunnel. He walks through it, and they dedicate Pauley, and we're going to have the game. We win pretty easy, and afterwards, there was a big reception for all the former players. Here I am, the young buck coach, twenty-five years old, with a wealth of talent, but I got them to play together and do all these things, and there was the famous UCLA press that we broke. I devised a system to get through it, and it worked. I didn't know whether it would work, but it did. So we end up winning by fifteen points. We had four scholarship players [at least three of them high school All-Americans], and I had three other walk-on kids that were pretty good.

"Well, I didn't know how to handle it afterwards. I go in the locker room and won't come out and talk to the press. I was being immature. I was embarrassed. I beat the coach, and it was his night. I felt bad about it. At the reception, I told my wife I wanted to just stay over in the corner, and that's what we did. I don't think it affected Coach at all. I think he was consistent. It was the way I behaved that was immature."

The only problem Cunningham had as a freshman coach after that was keeping the scores semi-respectable. He had so much talent on his team in those years that in games versus junior colleges, which freshmen often played against, the baby Bruins used to win by scores of 151–49 and 149–51.

"Coach wanted me to play the scholarship players at least thirty minutes a game," Cunningham recalls. "Where I had a problem, when you're up by forty points and I've still got four scholarship players in there, you look like you're pouring it on. With the Kareem team, especially, what I would do after the game was shake the [opposing] coach's hand and apologize, telling him [my] coach makes me play these guys that long."

As an assistant, Cunningham saw the same type of practices he participated in as a player, only from the other side. "Practices were the same," he says. "Practices were demanding. He had lots of fire on the court until the last couple of years that he coached, because he had a health problem. He relied at that time much more on us, his assistants, than he had prior to that, even though we always had a role as an assistant, and I always felt that I could stop practice and say something without him jumping all over me. I don't believe that he changed much on the court. We didn't press as much at the end. Attacks caught up with pressing. We still pressed some, though, because there were certain byproducts that you got from it.

"I think one of the things he really did well—and may not even have realized it—was letting his assistants help plan practice. We could challenge him on something. If he thought the pivot ought to be this way, and, say, I thought it should be another way, if I could prove to him that it was better the other way, then he would do it the other way. It was like proving a physics experiment or something. But he let us have freedom during games. My role on the bench a lot of times was to make the press adjustments and so forth, and he let me kind of develop a whole coaching philosophy with big men. I think all of it proved that his system was sound and good, and he mentored all of us to be successful head coaches. And he trusted us. He trusted us with the team.

"During the timeouts," Cunningham says, "you'd only have a limited amount of time, and all three of us [the other assistant at the time was Denny Crum, the future Louisville coach] would be talking simultaneously. So we had to work out the system. He's the head coach. He talks first, and then he would say, 'Gary, do you have anything to add? Or Denny?' And that's the way it worked. [Wooden would later say that Cunningham and Crum, with distinctly different personalities, were the best complementary assistants he had.]

"I think all of us, by having that experience, whether we were coaches or didn't coach, are better off as people as a result of that—the freedom to express our opinion and so forth. I've taken that to what I do now. This is my twenty-eighth year as an administrator—and they're hard jobs. The one thing I do is give my administrators a lot of freedom to express themselves, and I instill a lot of trust in them to get their jobs done. All that comes from working with the coach."

Cunningham took some of that trust and ran with it. He challenged Wooden on his philosophy. He argued, almost always in vain, that the team needed to play some zone defense to go along with the coach's preferred man-to-man precepts. He also installed some new wrinkles in the offense, although he probably wasn't as argumentative as Crum, who was the more emotional of the two assistants.

"Coach did not want assistants that were yes men," Cunningham says. "This is something else I've put into my philosophy. I don't want my assistants to come in here, and if they don't agree with me, I don't want them to say, 'Yeah, that's right, that's right.' I want them to tell me why, and Coach's philosophy was, we get better if we don't agree on something. We're going to get a better solution than if we say, 'Gee, that's great.' Maybe it's not great, and then you have a problem."

The one overwhelming trademark of all those championship UCLA teams was their confidence. They played with a swagger that suggested they knew they could beat you. No matter how close games might get in the final minutes—and believe it or not, several of them grew tight through the years—you always had the impression the Bruins would be the ones to make the big shot or grab the pivotal rebound. Cunningham explained that didn't happen by accident.

"It's a hard thing to pinpoint," he says, "but it got to the point where our players believed that we weren't going to lose. And a lot of people wanted to take that last shot, or make that crucial play. I think that came over a period of time from winning and tradition, and other teams were somewhat intimidated by UCLA during those years. The freshmen would come in, and they would learn from the senior class. And then you'd have another group doing the same. Our teams went to battle feeling that we were going to win.

"Coach never talked about winning, though," Cunningham says. "Never can I ever remember him basing a talk or anything about winning or about losing. It was about giving your best. It was always, 'Give your best, play as a team,' and those kinds of principles. But leadership came from him in a quiet way, and there were leaders who emerged on the team. When I played for him, I wanted to take the last shot. I wanted it. And I think most of the players were like that. They just believed that they would find a way to get it done. But I think it was something that was established early on, and then it just perpetuated itself through his coaching and through his fundamentals and all the other things I've mentioned."

Much was made about the pressure that was attached to UCLA's winning streaks, to the eighty-eight in a row, as well as the string of forty-seven consecutive victories. But Cunningham says Wooden was never caught up in those numbers.

"He wasn't concerned about the streaks," he says. "The media was, more than the coaches, but it did affect the players. The players would read that stuff, and one of the things that we had to work on so much was to keep our players' feet on the ground. Rather than believing your headlines, you still had to go out and do the job on the court. It isn't going to be given to you. That was a hard challenge when you got the streaks going, you're winning your league, and the senior on your team has the pro element to worry about. In his mind, he's got to average twenty points a game in order to be a pro. Well, you didn't have to at UCLA. So, to convince them that, if the team wins and we have balance if the team wins, it will help his candidacy. I think that was proven out. I mean, there was at least one first-round draft choice almost every year."

Even after the streaks came to an end, like the time Notre Dame stopped the Bruins after eighty-eight wins in a row, no one seemed to adjust as easily as Wooden.

"He was fine after that," Cunningham says. "Yes, he wants to win, and he'd like to beat Notre Dame, but he was fine after that. Actually, I think that with the eighty-eight, he realized that things have to come to an end. I remember him saying to me that if it had to come to an end, he'd rather have it come to an end in a non-conference game than a conference game. It took a lot of pressure off us. I mean, when it got up there, the pressure was incredible. I think he was relieved."

The more he observed his boss, the more Cunningham realized that Wooden was different from most head coaches. He didn't socialize the same way. He didn't go out drinking with the guys. "I think, because he won so much, that there was jealousy in the coaching ranks towards him," Cunningham says. "I don't think Coach was hostile towards other coaches, but he wasn't a guy who was going to be buddy-buddy. That's just not him. He's not going to go out with the guys and do all that stuff. I think he had a lot of acquaintances in the coaching field, but he wasn't close to a lot of coaches.

"One guy he was close to—and they were total opposites—was Press Maravich at LSU. Coach used to go back to a basketball camp for kids in Buies Creek, North Carolina, and Press and Coach used to room together at Campbell College. They would participate in this big camp, and they became really good friends. They had some great times together. He had other good friends, but he didn't spend a lot of time playing golf with coaches and doing all that stuff. His life was his family and his job, and he was very accessible in the office to any coach, anybody who wanted to come in and talk to him. He's the same today. Anybody can call him up and go over and talk to him. In many respects—and this is a fine trait—he is too generous with his time for people."

Cunningham's tenure as an assistant encompassed the glory years at UCLA. Wooden's teams won ten national championships in twelve years, eight of them with the tall, blond, former player sitting beside him on the bench. The consistency was staggering, and Cunningham knew one of the reasons.

"Coach never relaxed. He never relaxed," Cunningham says. "He always had an incredible work ethic. He never got carried away with his achievements, but he never relaxed. I also think he had a good support staff. I'm not tooting my own horn, because there's Jerry Norman, there's Denny Crum, there's Frank Arnold. I think we were all a good fit for him, and I think we helped. Of course, he should get the credit, because he's the head coach, and it was his program, and he did the most for it. But he never got the big head. Even today, you look at a man who's won every award—almost every award there is in sports—won ten national championships, and he's still a very humble man."

With success, of course, came pressure. At times, it seemed like excruciating pressure. "It got very unrealistic with the fans, because fans could come up and say, 'You know, I'm going to skip the regionals this year and just go to the Finals,'" Cunningham says. "That's what bothered Coach a great deal—that people were taking winning for granted when it was hard to win. He actually got some letters the year we lost to North Carolina State, in 1974. We should have won the game. We had a big lead in the last few minutes of the game, but we didn't win. And they were a very good team. There were people who were writing the athletic director that this guy is over the hill—we need to get a new coach. That's how unrealistic the whole thing got. And then we came back the next year with a good team, but not as good a team as we had in 1974, a team with more freshmen playing key roles, and we won. It was his last year, and we won the whole thing."

Presumably, there were no letters of complaint after that season, except for the flood of reaction that must have ensued when people realized Wooden was leaving. Although Cunningham eventually moved on, leaving the coaching profession to become one of the more respected and influential athletic directors in the country, he still maintains his close ties to Wooden.

"I have a different relationship with him than most people," Cunningham says. "It's more like a father-son relationship, even though we're older people. I guess, of the Wooden family, I'm in the inner circle. I know the family and I know him very, very well. When we talk about things, we have some fun, because we can share them openly with trust. Ours is a more natural friendship. It goes back—we have many, many years of experience, of working together, playing. Sometimes I'll tell him something that we did as players that he didn't know, and he doesn't believe it, but it's true.

"He is really connected now with lots of his former players. It's amazing how many people who have played for him, who might have left and weren't that connected with him, who have come back. I mean, if I want to know where somebody is, I call him, because the players kind of check in with him a lot."

Like most of the people close to John Wooden, Cunningham was concerned in the weeks and months immediately following the death of the coach's wife, Nell, in 1985. "He didn't do well for a long time right after she passed away, because they were very close," Cunningham says. "I think what has sustained him has been his family, the support of his family. He loves his grandkids and great-grandkids. I also think he had the support of his former players,,who were there for him to get through that."

Cunningham was there for him. He will always be there for him. The relationship he has had with this legendary man is special to him, because he knows it is special to Wooden, as well.

"Yeah, it is," Cunningham says. "I'm sixty-four years old, and I'm still one of his boys. We're all his boys."

John Wooden on the Current State of the Game

John Wooden loves basketball. He just doesn't necessarily love the way it is being played today, at least by men. "I actually prefer watching the way the women play now," he says. "I think they play more in the style of which I enjoy."

The men, Wooden believes, play too wildly and out of control, as a group. "Each year, I see less of the unselfish team play I have always preferred," he says. The kids coming out of high school today are all about soaring dunks and putting on a show. Wooden hates that. "If I want a show, I'll watch the Globetrotters," he says. "I have always been against showmanship. I don't like it. I don't like to see players celebrating, either. When I was coaching, I wouldn't permit it."

The NBA, to Wooden, is even worse. "Do they even know what traveling is, anymore?" he asks. "If they do, they never call it. And they allow palming the ball all the time. There is no question the skill and athleticism is greater now than it's ever been, but there is too much one-on-one and too little team concept. It is much the same way in college. Occasionally, you still see a player who plays the right way, like John Stockton used to for Gonzaga and then Utah. But too often, someone like Stockton is the exception."

Wooden even hates the new style of long, baggy shorts players wear, calling them "pantaloons" or "bloomers." "I don't like them very much," he says.

He often brings up the players he sees now on breakaways. When he was coaching, his kids always went up for a simple lay-in under such circumstances. Nowadays, kids have to dribble between their legs, go up, do a "360" in the air, and then slam down a rim-shattering dunk.

"What would you have done if one of your players had tried that?" he is often asked. His answer is always the same:

"I would have had him out of there before his feet hit the floor."

The Controversial
Assistant

The Jerry Norman people see now bears little resemblance to the one they remember from UCLA's glory days. The young, fiery assistant coach who could challenge his boss, John Wooden, as quickly as he could challenge a referee has been replaced by an older, calmer, gray-haired businessman who has quietly become a multimillionaire far from the madding crowd at loud basketball arenas.

"I've been lucky," Norman says, noting that his JNJN Investment Company has done extremely well, including running "a couple of thousand apartments" in Tennessee, many of which Norman owns. The money and the security for his family have been rewarding, but there have to be times in Norman's life when he wonders what might have been.

Norman was not just another assistant coach at UCLA. He was the most famous No. 2 man in college basketball. He was the one who turned the Bruins' recruiting around. He was the one who pushed the idea of the zone press that brought Wooden and the Bruins their first national championship, and he also was the one who helped devise the diamond-and-one defense that allowed UCLA to avenge its famous loss to Houston and Elvin Hayes. He was tan, with good looks that led many to remark he could have doubled for golf superstar Arnold Palmer.

In today's world, with ESPN, Fox, and the Internet providing such intense coverage, Norman would have been the hottest commodity on the market. The offers from big-time schools would have come flooding in. It would only have been a matter of time before he was a head coach making a million dollars a year at a major university, instead of a frustrated assistant who would eventually decide there was just not enough money or enough new challenges to make him stay in basketball.

"I don't have any qualms," Norman says now. "Coaching is a very addictive profession. It's like smoking. Either you stop, or you don't stop. I just left and never looked back."

Many UCLA alums and boosters still do, though. They still smile when his name is mentioned. They still wonder what might have happened if he'd hung on for another seven years, until Wooden retired. They still envision him taking over and the dynasty carrying on long after the Wizard departed. UCLA basketball was at its zenith when Norman was assisting Wooden, with J. D. Morgan as athletic director and Franklin Murphy as university chancellor. These four men formed an alliance of power and strength that perhaps never again will be matched in college basketball.

In many ways, Norman was the assistant who nudged Wooden into greatness. But it is also a measure of the game's most legendary coach that he would actively seek out this former player he knew would be anything but a sycophant.

"I've never wanted a yes man," Wooden says. "I always preferred someone who would stand up to me. A rebel, you might say."

Norman certainly fit that mold. A starting forward on Wooden's teams from 1950 to 1952, even though he stood only six feet two, Norman became better known for his temper than his skills. "He was obstinate and profane," Wooden says.

Norman's pal and former teammate Eddie Sheldrake still remembers the time the coach kicked Jerry out of practice and told him never to come back. He came back, of course, apologized to the team, and eventually endeared himself to Wooden as a fierce competitor, although it did take some convincing from Sheldrake.

"I was coaching the freshman team at Harvard High School in the San Fernando Valley, then went into the Navy and served during the Korean War for three and a half years," Norman says. "When I got out of the Navy, I coached at West Covina High School, where Cat Wooden, the coach's brother, was principal." Norman had been contacted while still in the Navy by his old coach, who wondered if he'd be interested in an assistant's job eventually. After a year at West Covina, Norman joined the UCLA faculty as a physical education instructor who coached the freshman team. "I remember I taught 'The Theory of Coaching Basketball,' and Pete Dalis [UCLA's future athletic director] was in my class," Norman says.

In the fall of 1959, Norman became a full-time assistant, and much of the tone of Wooden's program began to change. It wasn't that the Bruins hadn't been successful earlier. They had. But winning in the conference and competing nationally were two different things.

UCLA's image on the bench changed, too. Wooden always made it a habit to stay seated during games. He would roll up his program and shout at officials, but he always gave a more dignified impression while he was doing so. Norman did not. Norman would leap off the bench and rail at the refs.

"He could say some really ugly things," says Jim Tunney, a now-retired NFL official who was working college basketball games back then. "Norman would really go after you. There were more than a few times I'd have to tell Wooden, 'John, you'd better get this guy to back off.' He would, of course, but it wasn't always easy."

Norman brought that same heated, competitive nature to UCLA's recruiting. "When I first started there, our recruiting budget was $500," he says. Norman and Sheldrake, who had become a prominent alum and booster, took over the school's annual freshman-varsity game and made $3,000 a year—all of which went into recruiting. "Back then, Cal and Pete Newell were the dominant team; they were winning the national championship," Norman says. "We weren't even competitive. The bottom line is that UCLA didn't have any players. We thought we'd better start getting some."

It wasn't long before they did. They landed Ron Lawson and Johnny Green and Gary Cunningham, all of whom would be strong contributors. But the big catch was Walt Hazzard. "He was originally going to Kansas," says Norman, "but in those days a school like that couldn't have too many black players. So, he became interested in UCLA. Willie Naulls helped in the recruiting, too."

As a sophomore, after a stop at Santa Monica City College to improve his grades, Hazzard took the Bruins to their first Final Four, coming within a two-point semifinal loss to Cincinnati of making it into the NCAA Finals. But then they lost Cunningham, Green, and Pete Blackman to graduation, and although the Bruins returned to the NCAA Tournament the following season, they were blown out by Arizona State in the first round. It was that loss to the Sun Devils that triggered what eventually would become the Golden Era at UCLA.

"We looked at our roster, and we realized we didn't have any size," Norman says. "That's when I went to Wooden and said that we needed to force teams to run against us. We needed to force up the tempo. The only way to do that was to play a zone press."

Wooden admits he wasn't thrilled with the idea at first. He'd used a zone press in high school, but he felt that college guards, with more experience and skill, wouldn't have much trouble breaking it. Norman, who often clashed with his boss over strategy and tactics, usually lost most of these battles. This time he won. This time he convinced Wooden. "He was willing to try it," Norman says. "He knew we had to do something."

What they did was shake the very foundation of college basketball. UCLA's zone press became the most talked-about defense in the sport. "When we went to that first Final Four," Norman says, "other coaches who were there at the convention they have every year, they would watch us in practice, then come over afterward and ask, 'Wow. How did you guys get here?' Well, we were small, sure. But we were also a great defensive team. With the press, at first we wanted to keep it simple. We used a 2-2-1, and we wanted to make sure we were doubling the closest guy to the ball. That's what we stressed to the two middle guys in our press. You've got to go to the guy closest to the ball."

Whatever they stressed, it obviously worked. "We never could have dreamed it would work as good as it did," Norman says. "Opposing coaches thought what we were trying to do was steal the ball, but we weren't. We were trying to force tempo. We had the perfect personnel for it, too. Walt [Hazzard] was a great, great player in the open court. And Gail [Goodrich], he was the most instinctive player ever. Keith [Erickson], of course, was tremendous as the safety guy at the other end. I think if we hadn't used the press that year, we would have lost six or seven games. We certainly wouldn't have beat Duke in the Finals, not with our six-foot-five center [Fred Slaughter] and their two six-foot-ten guys. What the press did was, it really minimized size. It kept the other team's big guys from the basket."

It also turned Wooden from a coach who had been celebrated for the fast-break style of offense he introduced to the West Coast into something of a defensive master. "Jerry Norman was a fiery assistant who got a lot of technicals," Wooden says. "But he was also a very fine assistant, very smart. Jerry was insistent I stick with the press, or I might not have."

Newell, Wooden's old nemesis from Cal, looks back now and marvels at how much UCLA's coach improved his defense, beginning with the press. "Of course," Newell often adds, "he had a great assistant in Jerry Norman."

All this coincided with J. D. Morgan's ascension to the athletic director's office in 1963. "People outside of the program didn't like him," says Norman, "but if you worked for J. D., you liked him. No question he was the most influential athletic director in history. He had a very good business head on his shoulders.

"Not long after he got the job, J. D. made a deal with us," Norman says, referring to himself and Sheldrake. "He wanted the school to take over the frosh-soph game we made so much money off. In return, he said we could have as much money as we needed to boost recruiting."

That's when UCLA began to go out of town on a regular basis, going after the Alcindors and the Lucius Allens. "With Lew [Alcindor], I got close to his parents," Norman says. "I called him, and he told me he was going to announce he was coming to UCLA, but he said, 'I don't have my parents' permission.' That's when Coach and I visited New York.

Jerry Norman played for Wooden at UCLA, then became his assistant, helping to mold the Bruins' first national championship team. It was Norman who prodded Wooden into using the fabled zone press.

Lew's dad was a plainclothesman for the MTA, and he worked the late shift. The night we got there, he didn't get home until late. I don't know how long we stayed that night, but I know it was very early in the morning when we left."

When Alcindor did sign and flew West, UCLA's program soared with him. The Bruins won their third national championship in three years during his sophomore season, then captured another his junior year to make it four out of five.

In 1968, it was Norman's diamond-and-one defense, with Wooden's blessing, that smothered Houston and Elvin Hayes in the storied rematch of their Astrodome game at the L.A. Sports Arena. "I think it was one of the best games I ever saw UCLA play while I was there," Norman says. "Certainly, the best first half. Lynn Shackelford was the player who had to chase Hayes around the court, and he did an unbelievable job. The funny thing is, there were weaknesses in that diamond-and-one, but Houston never figured out what they were."

Then, with both his career and UCLA's dynasty at their peak, Norman unloaded a bombshell after that 1968 season: He was leaving to go into private business. "I was originally leaving the year before," he says, "but J. D. asked me to stay another year. 'Why not try the new job at the stock brokerage in the mornings and keep coaching in the afternoon, to make sure it's the right move for you?' he said. So I did. But by the next January, I decided I wanted to leave. I had a growing family, and I needed to make more money. When I left, Wooden was making $17,500. I was making $14,000. I wasn't leaving because I was upset or mad. It was just time. I felt like I had given the job everything I had."

Still, the news kick-started gossip everywhere UCLA fans gathered. Norman was only thirty-eight at the time. Why wouldn't he hang on and become Wooden's natural successor? The word was that he was earning twice as much money selling stocks as he was selling young, new players on the press. But why would he leave coaching altogether? the fans wondered. There had to be other schools out there that would be interested in John Wooden's top lieutenant.

"I would have loved to stay on the West Coast and coached at USC, Cal, or Stanford," Norman says. "But back in those days, there was no way USC was going to hire a UCLA guy, and the jobs at Cal and Stanford weren't open. I'd had some feelers from other schools, but I didn't want to live somewhere in Indiana. I wanted to stay in California. If I had decided to stay at UCLA, I would have been forty-five years old by the time Coach decided to retire in 1975. I had two girls at the time, and I realized coaching basketball was a 24–7 proposition. It was all encompassing, even in the off-season, when you had to recruit and go watch kids in the summer leagues. It was not a good family job. My wife was happy with the decision, but I think she would have gone along with whatever I decided."

Push him on the subject, and Norman says the challenge was gone. "We'd won four national titles, and it was a case of where do you go from there? What else was there to achieve? I guess I just needed some new personal challenge."

Neither Wooden nor Norman will discuss it at any length, but something else was at work, too. Even today, there is not the closeness between them that Wooden shares with almost all his other former assistants and players. "We had a great relationship when I was there, but he's gone his way and I've gone mine," Norman says, somewhat cryptically. And while Norman doesn't hesitate to compliment the man most describe as the greatest coach of all time, he doesn't gush over him, either.

"He's a very good organizer and a very good practice coach," Norman says. "He's very good at choosing a player's right position, and he has a very good relationship with his players. Overall, he's an excellent coach, a very smart guy. But I wouldn't call him a particularly imaginative coach. Our relationship was different than most. He liked to play devil's advocate. If I had a new idea, he wanted to see how much conviction I had."

As with any strong, vital assistant, there were the inevitable whispers that UCLA would slip when Norman left. But such was hardly the case. Wooden's teams would go on to win six more national championships, demonstrating that this was a coach whose ability to adjust was one of his greatest strengths.

"I think he changed in his last four or five years," Norman says. "I think his last team, the one without a real dominant player, might have been the best coaching job he did at UCLA."

The coolness that remains between the Hall of Fame coach and his most controversial assistant—Norman still attends UCLA games but rarely pauses to chat with Wooden—might involve how much credit each deserved and how it was parceled out at the time. There is no question that when Norman was there, along with Morgan and Chancellor Franklin Murphy, UCLA basketball was probably the strongest and most balanced it has been before or since. Norman's contributions were huge, although Wooden's ability to listen and experiment and even admit when he was wrong was every bit as important. But as exciting and flashy as the zone press was, Wooden would go on to win with two great forwards in Sidney Wicks and Curtis Rowe, with dominant big men playing down low, in Lew Alcindor and Bill Walton, and with one of his old-fashioned, high-post, man-to-man defending teams, as he did in his final season in 1975.

Norman might not fully realize it, but if Wooden was fortunate to have him, Norman was fortunate to have been linked to this coach and this program at the perfect time. Would he have been successful anywhere he had gone as an assistant or even a head coach? Absolutely. But would he have been this successful? Probably not. The list of outstanding Wooden assistants through the years includes Eddie Powell, Denny Crum, Frank Arnold, and Gary Cunningham, among others. Norman certainly belongs at, or near, the top of that group. Like Wooden always said, when it came to assistants, he didn't want a yes man.

When they look back through the history books at the greatest of all college basketball programs, Jerry Norman can rest assured that being a yes man is one thing of which he'll never be accused.

The Lakers and San Diego
Both Came Calling

Not surprisingly, when the most successful basketball coach of all time is working in your neighborhood, the pros definitely take notice. John Wooden turned down lucrative offers from both the NBA's Los Angeles Lakers and the old ABA's San Diego Conquistadors.

"I remember Fred Schaus [then the Lakers' GM] was a good friend of mine, and he finally convinced me to go see Jack Kent Cooke, who was the owner of the Lakers at the time," Wooden says. "Well, I did go, and Cooke handed me a contract that I couldn't believe. 'This kind of money is ridiculous. Nobody is worth that,' I told him."

The late Cooke was a very imposing figure, with an ego that couldn't have been housed in the then-state-of-the-art building he'd designed, modestly known as "The Fabulous Forum." He was incredulous that Wooden wouldn't take a contract that apparently would have made him one of the highest-, if not the highest-paid coach in professional sports.

"He raised his voice and said, 'Well, what do you want then?'" Wooden recalls. "I told him, 'I don't want to coach the Lakers.' He got angry at that point and shouted, 'Get out!'

"It was all very abrupt," the coach says. "I think it turned out right, though. I don't think I would have enjoyed working for Jack Kent Cooke."

Wooden's dealings in San Diego, with the Conquistadors back in the early 1970s, were much more tame.

"Leonard Bloom was the owner of the team," Wooden says, "and he offered me a very generous contract and then, as a signing bonus, he said I could pick out any condominium in La Jolla I wanted." The condos in question are worth in the millions today.

"I thanked him and told him I was flattered by the offer," Wooden says. "But my answer was no."

The Pastor

What are the odds that the pastor of Shepherd of the Hills Church in the Porter Ranch section of Southern California's San Fernando Valley, where John Wooden spent most of the last decade as a congregant, would be a life-long college basketball fan who grew up in the Midwest and followed UCLA's national success with great interest?

"That's actually the way it was for me," says Pastor Dudley Rutherford. "I grew up in Kansas, and as a teenager I was a huge fan of UCLA. I always dreamed of meeting Coach Wooden some day."

Years later, after Rutherford had moved to California and had his own congregation in the Valley, he was standing outside the church one day when he looked up and thought he was imagining things. There, seemingly out of nowhere, appeared an elderly gentleman who looked very much like John Wooden. As he drew closer, the pastor realized the man not only looked like Wooden, it *was* Wooden.

"I couldn't believe it," said Rutherford. "Here it had been my lifelong dream to meet this man, and I saw him walking toward my church. I said, 'Coach, what are you doing?' He told me he was looking for a new church to join. From that day on, we've been good friends. He asks me to pray at the John Wooden Award Banquet every year."

Wooden was forced into finding a new church when the one he used to regularly attend with Nellie was destroyed in Southern California's 1994 earthquake. "I had just by chance seen Dudley Rutherford on television giving an address, so I decided to drive down to his church and take a look," Wooden says. "The funny thing is, the day I went, my car broke down about a mile from there, and I had to call Nan to come and pick me up. I remember thinking maybe this was a message and someone was telling me this is not the church I want to attend. But then I went back and realized it was fine. I like Pastor Rutherford very much. He's a lot of fun. He even wanted me to sit on his bench when he was coaching a traveling team. I said, 'Oh no.' But we still got along fine."

One of Wooden's favorite stories, one he loves to tell, centers around a moment that occurred while he was attending this church. It had become a habit for him to bring guests to services. In one four-week stretch, he was joined by former players Mike Warren and Kenny Washington and their families, as well as current Portland coach Michael Holton and Lorenzo Romar, who is now the University of Washington coach. Wooden then showed up the following Sunday by himself, whereupon a fellow member of the church who usually sits directly in front of him turned and caught his attention.

"Excuse me, Coach, but do you mind if I ask you a question?" the gentleman said. "Of course not," said Wooden. "What is it?" The gentleman hesitated for a moment and then said, "Don't you have any white friends?" Wooden always laughs heartily when the story is finished.

Not surprisingly, Pastor Rutherford grew to know and appreciate the man more and more through the years. "One day I asked him about his father, because I knew how much he had been influenced by him," the pastor said. "He described his dad as 'the most gentle man in the world.' I just looked at him and said, 'Coach, that's you. You are describing yourself.' As you and I know, Coach Wooden is a mirror of his parents. Unfortunately, I never had a chance to meet the man, but I can tell you a lot about Coach's father just from being around Coach. It's funny, but when he introduces me now to other people, he says, 'He's the guy who got me not to wear a tie to church.' I think he always did as a youngster. I think he was taught that you should always dress like that to go to church. I guess I convinced him that a tie isn't really necessary."

Rutherford says Wooden came to his house of worship for nine years, but the coach finally had to switch churches again recently because of a family situation. "He did not miss a week of church, unless he was out of town," says the pastor. "I have to tell you, it was a little intimidating at times looking out and seeing him sitting there. He is known as a great teacher, but here he was, at age ninety-three, and he was learning and sharing. Here is this master teacher, and he was still sitting there trying to learn as much as he can. To me, that speaks to this greatness.

"I think he is a man of principle and a man of faith. When his wife, Nellie, passed away, he grasped, as we all do, the awareness that we're all only here for a few short years. I felt that he was almost looking forward to the time when he would be moving on. I know he wants to be reunited with Nellie in the worst way. When you've been to the mountaintop in this life, the way he has, I think you long for what the next life might be like. I honestly feel he is prepared to go to heaven."

Wooden certainly doesn't fear death, but he also cherishes life, and the pastor, in turn, cherishes their friendship. "Sometimes I sit down and ask him a few basketball questions," Rutherford says. "I help coach a girls team, and once I took them all over to his condo. Naturally, he was great with the girls, sitting patiently and answering all their questions. He loves being around young people. You can see that. I've learned you have to be careful with him, though. He doesn't like you to use certain words. He has told me many times that I use the word *great* too often. Most of the time, I think, I use it to describe him. That's the way he is, though. He doesn't like it when people make too much of a fuss over him."

The pastor loves telling some of his favorite Wooden stories. "I was sitting with him at a UCLA basketball game one day a few years ago," he says, "and I leaned over and asked, 'Could you coach these guys?' He shook his head no. I asked him why. He said, 'Too many earrings, too many tattoos.' And right then, right at that very moment, Baron Davis dribbled the ball around his back, then went between his legs, and bounced the ball off the backboard to Jelani McCoy, who slammed it down. Wooden looked over and said, 'And too much stuff like that.'"

Another time, the pastor was anxious to have Wooden meet his wife. "She knows nothing about basketball," Rutherford says. "I mean absolutely nothing. She couldn't tell you what a zone defense was if her life depended on it. She's just not into basketball. Still, I had been trying to tell her how great a man Coach is. Finally, one day, she was at church and Coach was there, and I was able to get them together and I introduced her. I leaned over and whispered in Coach's ear, 'She's my better three-quarters.' He says, 'You need to say that so she can hear you.' Right then my wife turns around and asks, 'What did you say?' So I told her what Coach Wooden had said. She turned to him, smiled, and said, 'You really are a good coach.'

"Another time, we were sitting at a UCLA game, and there was this little kid behind us. He had to be about seven or eight years old. He was bored, so he was looking up at the rafters at Pauley [Pavilion] and trying to count the national championship banners. He would go one-two-three, then he'd lose his spot. He'd start over and go one-two-three, and he finally got up to seven, but he kept losing the count. Coach was totally oblivious to this. So, I finally leaned over to Coach and said, 'If you get into heaven by winning national championships, you're looking pretty good right now.' But the thing about him is, he knows you don't get to heaven by winning national championships. Ultimately, he realizes success is not what brings a person happiness. It's not the things you do. It is all about faith and family, and clearly those are the two pillars of his life."

The pastor has come to understand that Wooden's former players are part of his family. "I'm amazed how much respect the guys who played for him still have for this man," he says. "In many cases, these are young men who fought him and battled him on issues. Like Bill Walton, of course. He was the wild child of UCLA basketball, and Coach had to use tough love in his case and in many others. But that's what he was about, coaching and guiding and correcting all in the context of love.

"Obviously, he is a man of great patience. I've sat with him at basketball games where people form these huge lines right by where his seat is. And he sits there and graciously signs autographs, never turning anyone down, never saying no to anybody, no matter how long the line is. It is a remarkable thing to watch. You think of yourself trying to do something like that, and eventually you feel you might get angry or lose your temper. He never does. It's just amazing."

The pastor is not ashamed to admit that there are times when he seeks Wooden out for assistance. "I go to him for advice sometimes," he says. It is the same with many of the coach's former players and coaches. They, too, seek him out, knowing that there is no one else who is so wise and yet so gentle to talk to, no one else who will listen and understand and offer what words he can to help.

When told that the title of the book I was writing would be *John Wooden: An American Treasure*, Pastor Rutherford chuckles softly and says, "That's good, that's very good. That's exactly what he is. To me, it's almost as if he is on hallowed ground. Look around, there is no one in our generation like that. I put only a few people in the world on his level. Mother Teresa, Bob Hope, Coach Wooden. I think they all belong together. The sad part is that our generation is not producing people like that. Our generation is all about me-me-me and the pursuit of the almighty dollar.

"People who give of themselves, who always put other people first, there is no one like that around today," he says. "This generation is all about how big a house you have and how nice a car you drive. That's not Coach. That's not what his heart is about.

"John Wooden is about love and caring, about faith and family. He has as much impact today as he had when he was winning all those national championships. He is a remarkable man, and your title is correct. He really is an American treasure."

Coach Wooden's All-Time Team

If you know John Wooden, you realize he doesn't like to give too many opinions on players, for fear of bruising other players' feelings. He would never, for instance, pick an All-Time UCLA Team, because he cares about all his players and wouldn't want anyone to think he is partial to one over the others.

But after considerable prodding, I was able to get him to pick his All-Time Non-UCLA Team. Here they are, the finest basketball players Wooden has ever seen, excluding the Alcindors and Waltons, etc. from the equation.

Guard:	**Oscar Robertson**
Guard:	**Michael Jordan**
Center:	**Bill Russell**
Forward:	**Larry Bird**
Forward:	**Elgin Baylor**

"Robertson had everything you could want in a basketball player," Wooden says. "He was a fine defensive player, he was tough inside and outside, and he had great vision. It's not by chance that he was the all-time assists leader when he retired. I saw Oscar play for the first time when he was a high school senior. I thought then that he was the only high school player I ever saw who could move directly into the pros and immediately be a star.

"I saw [Michael] Jordan first at the McDonald's High School All-American Game. There was no question about his ability. He stood out, even then."

At center, the old Russell vs. Wilt Chamberlain debate is a no-brainer for Wooden.

"I don't know if I've ever seen a defensive player with better timing than Russell," he says. "He was not that tall, but he was sinewy. He was never hurt, and he was very selfless. Wilt was a physically tremendous specimen. He was probably as powerful as anybody who ever played the game and a tremendous athlete. A much better athlete than Shaquille [O'Neal]. Wilt ran the quarter-mile in under fifty seconds. But I didn't like the way he played all that well. He took fallaway shots, and when he did that, he was never on the board. I preferred the way Russell played."

At forward, Wooden first mentions Baylor. "Elgin was the first one I ever saw where the expression 'hang time' came out," Wooden says. "He had an amazing knack for hanging in the air. He also had great hands and was a remarkable rebounder for his size. He could shoot, too. He was a great player."

At the other forward, Wooden again favors a player with all-around skills. "Bird did everything," he says. "Julius Erving, he was amazing, just amazing, when he first came along. Then again, he was not that great of a defensive player. Bird was so instinctive. He was a tremendous shooter and was one of the great passers ever to play the game."

If you're wondering where Magic Johnson is, you're not alone. Wooden says Magic "handled the ball too much" for his taste. If forced to choose a third guard, he would prefer Jerry West, not Magic.

The Broadcaster

I t was one of those happy coincidences life sometimes can throw at you like a crazy bounce pass. That UCLA basketball and Dick Enberg would arrive at the same point with their futures both about to skyrocket to another level proved to be a wonderful bonus for sports fans in Southern California.

Before Enberg embarked on his stellar career in broadcasting, he was a professor and assistant baseball coach at Cal State Northridge. This pleasant, articulate gentleman, who has a doctorate in health education and safety, broke into the business announcing boxing, of all things, at grungy Olympic Auditorium in downtown Los Angeles.

"I had left Cal State Northridge to come to KTLA-TV in L.A. to do sports news but then quickly began broadcasting boxing at the Olympic," Enberg says. "It was right after the Ali–Liston controversy and all, and I thought, *Oh my God, I get my first shot at play-by-play and I land with a dying sport*. But it turned out fine."

It turned out more than fine. It quickly became clear that Enberg was smooth, intelligent, hardworking, likeable, and unfailingly enthusiastic. Bob Speck, then sports director at the station, decided Enberg was the perfect person to announce UCLA basketball, a product he sensed was about to take off in sports-crazed Los Angeles.

"I started in 1966, Lew Alcindor's sophomore year," Enberg says. "I did the away games live and the home games tape delayed, coming on after the eleven o'clock news. When they first told me, I thought there was no way in the world the tape-delayed part would work. Well, I couldn't have been more wrong."

The lure of Alcindor and a young, talent-laden college basketball team unlike any the city—or the country—had ever seen proved to be a huge hit in the ratings. "The tape-delayed games became like a cult thing," Enberg says. "Even people who were at Pauley for the games would go home and watch the replays. They became immensely popular. On Friday nights, they were beating Johnny Carson in the ratings, and that was a big victory for KTLA."

It wasn't long before Enberg put his own unique touch on the broadcasts, even if it did happen as something of an accident. "It was in early January of 1970, and it was a rainy night, with Oregon coming into Pauley for the conference opener. The Bruins went on one of their typical early tears and were leading, 12–4 or something, when Oregon began holding onto the ball and refusing to shoot. John Wooden told his defense to stay back, and so the action literally stopped.

"So here I am, trying to broadcast the game on my own, with no action to call," he says. "I recited a bunch of stats, gave background on as many players as possible. I was telling the viewers not to forget next week's telecast. Then I looked up, and there were still thirteen minutes to play in the half, and nothing was happening. I guess the teacher in me learned to be honest in the classroom. I said, 'Folks, you can see nothing is happening on the court. And there is this song I can't get out of my head.' It was when the movie *Butch Cassidy and the Sundance Kid* was out, and B. J. Thomas had a huge hit song from the movie called 'Raindrops Keep Falling on My Head.' So I started humming the song on the air. I can't carry a tune in a bucket, but there was nothing else to do, so I kept humming it.

"The next night, before a game with Oregon State, about ten different UCLA kids came up to me with lyrics for the song. So, at one point during that broadcast, I said, 'For all you music lovers out there, it seems kind of appropriate because UCLA's opponents must feel like raindrops keep falling, because losses keep falling on their heads.' Then, casually, near the end of the broadcast, I said if and when the Bruins win the conference title, I'll go down at midcourt and sing the lyrics of the song. At 1:30 in the morning, you figure who cares?

"Well, that became like Red Auerbach's victory cigar at UCLA. Whenever the game would be decided, the bandleader would strike up the band and they'd play the song, and all the kids in the stands would turn up and shout and point at me: 'You will sing—You will sing—'

"When UCLA finally clinched the conference championship against Cal, I kind of lingered in the booth a while shuffling papers, hoping no one would remember. But all 12,000 in the building were waiting for me to go out there and make a fool of myself. So, I went down to center court and I sang. I never did get in key, but when I started to sing, all the kids in the students section suddenly opened up

Dick Enberg first attracted national attention when he broadcast UCLA basketball games on KTLA during John Wooden's peak years in Los Angeles. He and Wooden have remained close friends.

umbrellas they'd brought to the game. I thought, *Wow, this relationship we have is really something special.*

"The next week, in the student newspaper, *The Daily Bruin*, they ran a headline that said 'Enberg for Governor.' I wrote a letter to the editor and said I must respectfully decline. You know, to this day, I still have people shouting out to me at airports, 'Hey, Enberg, when are you going to sing?'"

Soon enough, Enberg would become completely entranced by Wooden's basketball melody. "It was as if you were describing a Bruin ballet," he says. "You almost always knew the scenario. It was just a matter of how it played out. My job was to develop some kind of story line. Wooden was very cooperative. He allowed me to come to practice, to watch and listen. It wasn't the kind of relationship a broadcaster and a coach would have today.

"I didn't always travel with the team, but for Pac-10 games, I usually traveled with them between cities. I remember once, we were going from Seattle to Spokane by bus, and the team manager came up to me and said, 'The coach would like you to sit with him.' It was the first time he'd ever made that offer.

251

I figured this would be great. He was going to give me so much material. I couldn't believe it.

"Well, I sit down, and the first thing he asks me is, 'Do you like poetry?' I said I did. So he asks if I like Edna St. Vincent Millay, and he starts quoting her poems. Then we talked about other poets, and the conversation drifted to other subjects. Before I realized it, the two-hour trip was over without either of us ever mentioning the word *basketball*. To me, it was a real insight into the man. It made me realize how intelligent and well-rounded he was."

Enberg, the former professor, became more like a student, examining the fascinating nuances that made Wooden such an exceptional coach. "He spoke in generalities about basketball," Enberg says. "You suspect that's the way he spoke to his players. He didn't talk about winning and losing. If the team won by thirty-five points and he didn't feel the kids played their best, he'd still chew them out. Or, if they won by only a couple of points and played great, he'd tell them that. He did it in such a mature way. He exuded confidence. You could see it in his carriage, in the way he walked onto the floor before a game.

"You talk about presence," he says. "He had that folded program and the way he addressed his players before tipoff. You sensed immediately this was a guy in command of the game. He had sort of a quiet charisma. Some college coaches have more than others. I often likened Dean Smith to Wooden. I think Smith saw him and watched the way he worked and even developed some of his mannerisms.

"Don't let anyone tell you Wooden wasn't a competitor, though. It's just that he was so subtle about it. In his own way, he was rough with officials. He kept that program close to his face so others couldn't hear. But he'd get on officials all the time. And if, as a broadcaster, you delved into some controversy he didn't want to address, he'd let you know it. What you'd get was sort of a registered silence that told you, 'We're not going down that road anymore.' Before a game, you could sense his intensity. He had a way of letting you know things had changed. It was a time not to be social. It was a time to lead the team to be the best it could be."

Enberg had the good fortune of broadcasting many of Wooden's landmark moments at UCLA in his nine years behind the microphone for the Bruins. "Of all the games I've done in any sport, I don't think any had the impact of that Houston game in the Astrodome in 1968," Enberg says. "It was the first time a non-playoff game was telecast in prime time. It had a huge national audience, with Alcindor playing against Elvin Hayes, and the biggest live crowd ever to watch college basketball, some 52,000 or 53,000 people. Lew

[Alcindor] was hurt, and UCLA didn't win, of course, but that game meant so much to the sport. It also set up the most eagerly awaited rematch anyone could remember, when the two teams played again in the NCAA semifinals in L.A. In that game, the Bruins played the greatest half of basketball I've ever seen and beat Houston easily. I remember interviewing Wooden after that game, and there was some international crisis going on at the time. He said, 'Well, in light of what is happening elsewhere, this game wasn't that important.' He said it was a learning experience and that the team would move on.

"A few years later, I also did the game at Notre Dame that snapped UCLA's eighty-eight-game winning streak, and the next week there was a rematch at Pauley Pavilion, and again, the Bruins killed them. That Notre Dame rematch was the highest-rated TV show ever in the eleven o'clock time slot. There is no question that the exposure I received on those games, along with Wooden's patience, helped catapult me to the network."

Enberg made a name for himself not only by broadcasting the UCLA games but by moving over to do the play-by-play of Los Angeles Rams games. He was named California Sportscaster of the Year four times before accepting a position with NBC, where he spent the next twenty-five years, beginning as a play-by-play announcer for college basketball. He eventually worked thirty-six seasons broadcasting the NFL and has done the Super Bowl eight times, the Rose Bowl nine times, Wimbledon twenty times, the U.S. Open Golf Tournament five times—and that is just a brief part of his résumé. He currently works many of the world's top sports events for CBS.

Enberg has won thirteen Emmy Awards, nine Sportscaster of the Year awards, the Ronald Reagan Media Award, and the Victor Award as the top sportscaster of the past twenty-five years. He is the only person to win an Emmy as a sportscaster (four times), a writer (five times), and a producer (once).

In 1998, he became only the fourth sportscaster to be honored with a star on the Hollywood Walk of Fame. A few of his other honors include the 1984 Eclipse Award (thoroughbred racing), the 1995 National Basketball Hall of Fame's Curt Gowdy Award, and the 1999 Pro Football Hall of Fame's Pete Rozelle Award.

Some three decades after broadcasting his last John Wooden-coached game, the man who has worked almost every major sporting event in the world, the consummate professional who is likely to be remembered as much for his remarkable versatility as he is for his famous "Oh my!" signature line, still shakes his head in admiration over a coach who hasn't worked a game in more than twenty-nine years. "For starters, he's the greatest basketball coach in my fifty years of observation," Enberg says of Wooden. "It's easy to point to his ten national championships, the eighty-eight victories in a row. But to me, the one record that will never be broken is thirty-eight [wins] in a row in the NCAA Tournament. It's like DiMaggio or Ripken. It is almost too mind-boggling to consider.

"If you were giving a gold medal for total human quality, he'd get it. Even now, I have so much admiration for him. You can tell, talking to him, that he wants the game to be better. He is not afraid to say he'd rather watch women's basketball than men's basketball today. Those kids he coached, I don't know if they realize how fortunate they were. He's still teaching us all how to live.

"I think we all overuse the word *great*," Enberg says. "But other than my father, he is the greatest person I've ever met. To have rubbed shoulders with his greatness for ten years was truly extraordinary. Even now, when you're with him, you know you're not just close to greatness, you're close to *goodness*. To spend time with him is like a religious experience. When you think about the relationship he had with black athletes at a time when civil rights was a major issue in this country, you remember something Al Maguire once said: 'I don't see color. I only see character.'

"I think the same could be said of Wooden. John is a churchgoer, yet he never tries to impose that on anyone else. In a way, that's what he's all about. He'll give you an example, a chance to learn. Then it is up to you to make the decisions. John Wooden, I think, is about as perfect as God makes them."

Although he hasn't regularly broadcast UCLA games for twenty-nine years, Enberg has maintained a relationship with Wooden. "Whenever I call, he always picks up the phone during the message part he has," Enberg says. "I want to call him more often to see how he is, but I realize he has a lot of friends who are closer than me. I do think he likes me, though. He's said nice things about me in the past. I couldn't be more honored by that relationship."

When Wooden coached his last basketball game at UCLA in 1975, Enberg, who wasn't working the nationally televised event, was vacationing in Palm Springs, California. "I remember watching that game against Kentucky, and I remember bawling like a baby when UCLA won and Wooden walked off the floor smiling. It was then I realized I cared too much. It was time to move on."

THE MEDAL OF FREEDOM

John Wooden has won just about every award and honor available for his coaching and playing prowess. But the one he was presented in July 2003, the Presidential Medal of Freedom, has to rank as the greatest of the bunch. It is the highest award a United States civilian can receive.

Quietly, without the coach knowing it, several of his friends had been campaigning on his behalf for some time. Andy Hill, the former disgruntled UCLA player and ex-president of CBS Productions chronicled earlier in these pages, reached a few political and personal contacts with direct access to the White House. Andre McCarter, who was one of the stars on Wooden's final team in 1975, collected letters and sent them to the White House for three years.

None of them seemed to be having much effect until Wooden received a FedEx package in the mail, ripped it open and found a letter from President Bush. When asked what it was, the coach's eyes filled with tears. "I'm just not worthy," he said. The reaction of everyone who knew him was: If he's not worthy, then who is? Of course John Wooden was worthy.

The date of the actual award ceremony was July 23, and the coach's son and daughter and their spouses were invited, along with Hill, who has become very close with Wooden, and Hill's wife. Since Hill and I both have our admiration for Wooden in common, and have both worked on books about him, we have become regular correspondents. This is the way Hill described that day and those memorable moments in the East Room of the White House for me in an e-mail:

> The Medal of Freedom recipients started to file into the room with their Marine escorts. Then, without any visible or audible signal, the room fell into complete and total silence. It was eerie, and it only served to up the voltage. After about a minute of silence, the Marine Band struck up the first chords of "Hail to the Chief." Everyone I spoke to agreed that the hair stood up on the backs of their neck as the president and first lady entered the East Room. At that moment, it didn't matter if you were a Republican or a Democrat, we all rose to our feet in respect. We were a room full of Americans there to honor some incredibly accomplished people.
>
> As President Bush started to make his remarks, I took a look at Coach Wooden sitting just a few feet behind the president. I've seen his face after victorious national championship games, but I am sure I never saw him look this happy before. As Mr. Bush briefly summarized the accomplishments of the

honorees that included Julia Child, Roberto Clemente, Van Cliburn, Jacques Barzun, Charlton Heston, Vaclav Havel, Edward Teller, R. David Thomas, Byron "Whizzer" White, James Q. Wilson, and Coach Wooden, the enormity of the award was underscored. These people had influenced our lives in so many profound ways and enriched our nation and our world.

Coach was the last person to get an award, and President Bush could see that he needed some extra help getting out of his seat. The president graciously went over to assist him. As Coach stood side by side with the leader of the free world, we all welled up with emotion. He has received every award the sports world can confer, but this moment transcended sports and placed Coach in the context of national hero that he so richly deserves. When the remarks about Coach concluded with a statement of how proud Nellie would have been to see Coach honored, I don't mind saying that I spilled a few tears. So did Coach.

Later, after the festivities were over, Hill wrote:

When we finally reconnected with the rest of our party, Coach was sitting comfortably greeting friends and strangers alike. The Medal of Freedom hanging from his neck, he was positively glowing, sitting close by a fireplace that had a huge portrait of Abraham Lincoln hanging on the wall above it.

In describing the day to me later, Hill said he never remembered seeing Wooden as moved by something as he was by receiving this honor. "On the plane ride back," Hill said, "Coach never took the medal off all the way home."

A couple of months after the ceremony, at his ninety-third birthday party, Wooden received a gift from his daughter, Nan Muehlhausen. It was three pictures in a large frame of President Bush; his wife, Laura; Nan; and Wooden's son, Jim. Also included was this letter on White House stationery, dated Aug. 1, 2003, which said:

Dear John,

Thank you for the signed copy of your book, "Wooden." Laura and I appreciate your thoughtful gesture.

I was honored to present you with the 2003 Medal of Freedom last week.

Best regards.

Sincerely,

George W. Bush

The Sportswriter

It is a funny thing about this profession. Sometimes, you have to be an old sportswriter before you begin to understand how blessed you were as a young sportswriter. That certainly is true in my case, considering that, at the ripe old age of twenty-six, I looked up one day and found the greatest coach in the history of his sport, if not any sport, smiling and greeting me at one of his afternoon practices at UCLA.

"Why don't you pull up a chair and sit here with me?" said John Wooden, as the squeaky cacophony of basketball shoes cutting on the floor of Pauley Pavilion echoed in the background. It sounded like a good idea to me. The regular seats didn't provide a particularly great view, and as long as I happened to be the only beat writer attending that day, it seemed nice of UCLA's coach to invite me down.

As I watched this grandfatherly gentleman in shorts, his stark white legs contrasting with his Bruin-blue warm-up jacket, lecture his players and drill them on fundamental after fundamental, Wooden would come over, chat amiably, and answer any questions I had. Afterward, driving home, I remember thinking it had been a useful session and that he'd given me enough for a decent story. But I really didn't think about it any deeper than that.

Thirty-six years later, I can't believe how naïve I was. How could I not have realized, on those rare days when I innocently sat there with him, that it was something I would want to tell my grandkids about some day? Hanging out with John Wooden at basketball practice? Come on. That must have been like sitting next to Hemingway as he started a novel, or standing next to Sinatra as he rehearsed an album. It was a rare entrée into the style and mind of a man who was the best ever at his profession. The only regret I have is that I didn't know enough then to inhale it all, to remember every priceless thing I heard and saw.

Growing up in Southern California in the 1950s as a young man who loved sports, I was familiar enough with John Wooden's name. Especially since I was a UCLA fan as a pre-teen and teenager and loved watching Wooden's fast-breaking teams compete for the old Pacific Coast Conference championship on television. A few years later, friends invited me along to one of the Bruins' freshman-varsity scrimmages, when a junior college transfer named Walt Hazzard and a skinny first-year player named Gail Goodrich proceeded to put on the kind of show I'd never seen before at the collegiate level. Maybe that's why, even though I attended USC's School of Journalism and was co-sports editor of the *Daily Trojan*, my favorite basketball team of that era was Wooden's 1964 group that won his first national championship.

Sitting with my buddies at the L.A. Sports Arena during the Christmas holidays of 1963, watching Hazzard and Goodrich and Keith Erickson carve up No. 1-rated Michigan, I could barely contain myself. My friends, all fellow USC students, couldn't believe it. "Those are our crosstown rivals you're cheering for," I was reminded more than once. I couldn't help it. This was the most exciting college basketball team I'd seen, or have seen since, and besides, I was never one of those guys who hated everything blue and gold. It's a good thing, too, I guess, considering I eventually married a UCLA graduate.

To someone on the West Coast, where basketball remained far down on the interest meter in those days, that Wooden team was a revelation, with its suffocating full-court zone press, its quickness and athleticism, its ability to run off blurring 12–0 and 14–2 spurts, and the fact that the tallest player was a six-foot-five center who was built more like a linebacker. As a writer just learning the nuances of sports, I'd become fascinated with coaches, with the Red Auerbachs and the Weeb Ewbanks and the Pete Newells of that era. But most of all, I'd become enthralled with Wooden and the way he put his UCLA teams together, first with Hazzard and Goodrich, and then, of course, with Lew Alcindor.

The marvel of it all was that I would be covering that Alcindor team a few years later. And suddenly, instead of a fan, I had to become a professional who could write objectively. UCLA won so much, there was little to be critical about. But still, observing this coach and the quality of players he was now bringing in was pretty amazing stuff. As mentioned in an earlier chapter, I happened to be elected president of the Southern California Basketball Writers Association during Alcindor's senior year. At one of our weekly meetings, attended by coaches from every school in the area, I decided to make a plea for my fellow writers.

Wooden's rule during the Alcindor Era was that reporters were not allowed in the post-game dressing room. He decided what athletes he would allow to be interviewed, after the school's sports information director took an informal poll of writers late in games. That whole idea seemed wrong, especially since this was the No. 1 team in America. Everyone wanted to read about these guys, and how could we get to know them if we rarely had a chance to hear them speak? I thought I had calmly made a strong argument, but when I was done, Wooden rose from his seat. He was not "pleased," as he so often liked to say. He was almost livid.

For one of the few times any of us could remember, he raised his voice, criticizing me personally and defending his stance. When he was finished, there was a long, uncomfortable silence, and I quietly adjourned the meeting. The irony was, later that day, I was scheduled to be the guest on Wooden's weekly half-hour television show at KTLA's studio. I came home after the luncheon and informed my wife, Marsha, that she had to come with me to the studio. Actually, I pleaded with her to come. I didn't know what would happen seeing Wooden for the first time after our confrontation at the luncheon.

After a few nervous hours of waiting, we drove to Hollywood. I remember my hand was practically shaking as we opened the door to the studio. Wooden spotted us immediately. He walked over, and, as I held my breath, he smiled warmly. "I just wanted to say I'm sorry about what happened at the luncheon today," he said. I don't know what my reply was, but I think it was mumbled. "You and the writers have a right to express your opinion, and I respect that," he said. "I think I got a little carried away. Let's just forget it and try to enjoy ourselves on the show."

Later that day, and for years afterward, I marveled at John Wooden apologizing to a young, inexperienced kid who probably had picked the wrong time to stick up for his profession. Looking back now, I realize it was my first inside glimpse at what this man is really about.

Interestingly, during the Alcindor Era and later in the early Bill Walton years, you got the sense from watching Wooden was that he was thankful to have all that talent but he wasn't completely happy. He never liked expectations, and with perhaps the two greatest college centers of all time, the projections practically went through the roof at Pauley. In one of his more revealing moments,

I remember Wooden quietly confiding to a couple of writers: "You know, sometimes I feel like we're playing more not to lose than we are to win."

UCLA basketball became the bulls-eye at which every other program in America took aim. Wooden and the Bruins had no off nights. Not when every team they played made it a major event and considered it a moral victory even to stay in the game against them. Another memorable quote from the coach: "There are times when it isn't necessarily bad to lose a game, especially a non-conference game. A loss can sometimes be good for your team."

A few years later, as a columnist for a San Diego newspaper, I remembered that latter piece of advice, and after Wooden's UCLA team had run off a record-breaking eighty-eight victories in a row, I startled more than a few people by predicting, in print, that their streak would come to an end against Notre Dame in a game at South Bend. My reasoning was simple. I knew the pressure that had been building over the streak and understood Wooden hated everything that went with it. Notre Dame, rated No. 2 in the country, was always tough at home, and with a loud, ear-splitting crowd in the kind of non-conference game Wooden wasn't desperate about, I sensed this could be the time. The final score was 71–70, so it wasn't as if I couldn't have been wrong with a different bounce here or there. But the next day, when I read that Wooden had said he hated to lose but it could prove to be good for the team, I smiled. If I closed my eyes, I could almost hear him saying that same thing to a couple of us a few years earlier.

As fate would have it, the 1975 Final Four was scheduled for San Diego, and I couldn't have been happier. Working 120 miles from Los Angeles, I hadn't been able to attend many UCLA games, and I fully expected the Bruins to make it to my new town for another shot at a national championship. What I didn't expect was for it to develop into one of the more emotional, newsworthy weekends in years.

The Bruins' semifinal game against Louisville was thrilling enough, with Terry Howard, one of Denny Crum's best shooters, a kid who hadn't missed a free throw all season, standing at the line for a one-and-one with twenty seconds left in overtime and his team leading by a point. If he hits the two shots, UCLA and Wooden go home. Lots of people I know now say that some strange, outside force wouldn't allow that first free throw to go in. I don't know about that. I do know, however, that the whole weekend almost seemed preordained. It was as if Wooden couldn't possibly lose, especially after his shocking announcement following the pulsating victory over Louisville. He was retiring, he said. Monday night's title game against Kentucky would be his last as UCLA coach. And all of us just sat there stunned for a few minutes before racing to interview the players.

There are very few times in my thirty-nine years of sports writing where I've actively rooted while covering an event. But I confess I was guilty during this one. I desperately wanted Wooden to win his final game. Quietly, with only a little body language giving me away to my San Diego colleague sitting next to me, Nick Canepa, I rooted like

FROM THE AUTHOR'S COLLECTION

Author Steve Bisheff and wife Marsha join the coach at the tenth John R. Wooden Classic, in December 2003.

heck for UCLA to beat Kentucky. As it turned out, I needn't have worried. That Wooden team played textbook basketball, capping maybe his finest single-season coaching job yet with a convincing victory. Considering what it meant and how it played out, not to mention the historical significance, it still ranks as one of the more memorable sporting events I've ever covered.

Happily, not long after moving to the *Orange County Register* in 1982, I was able to renew my relationship with Wooden, especially once the John R. Wooden Classic became an annual event at the Arrowhead Pond in Anaheim. That gave me the perfect excuse to drop in on him at least twice a year, even if the traffic-strewn, 60-mile drive from Irvine to Encino could be intimidating. Of all the places I've shared time with him, nothing rivals the unforgettable hours spent in his condo, where, relaxed and talkative, he can sit for hours and tell stories and read poetry and wax philosophical. One moment he will recite a litany of old Abe Lemons stories and one-liners and laugh until tears almost appear in his eyes. The next moment he'll show you a project his great-granddaughter has made for him and tell you how proud he is of it. He will discuss Abe Lincoln, or Mother Teresa, or, if you want, Tim Duncan, or even Alex Rodriguez. In between the unrelenting phone calls he receives, you learn that he contributes to and works for more charities, especially those involving children, than anyone will ever know.

But as busy as he is, he truly seems to enjoy having company, which is why I've brought my wife and friends and assorted guests with me at times. After the Anaheim Angels won the World Series in 2002, I arranged to meet Mike

Scioscia, the Angels' manager, and take him to see Wooden, who'd become enamored with the Angels for their selfless, team-oriented style. After they'd spent more than two hours together, I walked out with Scioscia. "Man, that was something," he said. "John Wooden transcends sports. Going to his home, it's like a pilgrimage, you know?"

Everyone who has been there says the same thing. There is a sort of aura that surrounds you in that tiny space. It is a feeling you don't get anywhere this side of your neighborhood church or synagogue. Not to over-dramatize it, but there is a sense of warmth and kindliness, of grace and dignity, associated with John Wooden that you simply don't find in many people. Then there are his principles, the ones that he sticks to like a strong, old piece of adhesive.

He joined the Navy as a youngster during World War II, even though, as a teacher, he wouldn't have been drafted. He was homesick for Indiana and desperately wanted to leave UCLA after two years, but he stayed because the contract he had signed was for three years. He deserved a huge increase in salary but refused to approach university officials about it, hoping they would come to him. Even now, a couple of his grandchildren and great-grandchildren could have gained entrance to UCLA if he'd just spoken up in their behalf, but he refused, believing people should earn their rewards on their own, a rigid stance that has angered some in his own family.

It is that strength and his gentleness, the same traits he speaks of in his late father, that make him so unique. Somehow, just his appearance can make even the most divergent audiences grow quiet and rapt with attention. You see it with kids at a clinic, where they squat down in front of him, wide-eyed and interested, even when they don't realize how famous he is. You see it with people meeting him for the first time at banquets or speaking engagements. You see it with former players who haven't been in his presence for decades. Spending time with him and sensing his inherent goodness makes you feel better about the world. It makes you feel better about people. It makes you feel better about yourself.

The more you are around John Wooden, the more you realize that's the one thing that separates him from his peers as much as his glittering stack of honors and trophies. It seems impossible in this era of soaring egos and wild hyperbole. It sounds incongruous in an age of greed and overindulgence. It remains unexplainable at a time when winning is all that is supposed to matter. But somehow, to an older, somewhat wiser sportswriter friend, it remains the most humbling fact of all.

Twenty-nine years after walking away from the game, the greatest coach in the history of sports has proved to be an even greater man.

Index